# THEOLOGY OF THE
# ENGLISH REFORMERS

# THEOLOGY OF THE
# ENGLISH REFORMERS

—

*Philip Edgcumbe Hughes*

HODDER AND STOUGHTON

DEDICATED TO
MY FRIENDS AND FELLOW-PILGRIMS

"The victory is kept by that same means as it is obtained."
*John Jewel*

All quotations are from the Parker Society Edition of the writings of the English Reformers (the volumes of which were published between the years 1841 and 1854), with a few exceptions where the references are adequately given

Printed in Great Britain for Hodder and Stoughton Limited, St. Paul's House, Warwick Lane, London, E.C.4, by The Aberdeen University Press

# CONTENTS

# FOREWORD

The numerous volumes of the Parker Society edition of the writings of the English Reformers have long since been out of print and are now difficult to obtain. The renewed appreciation of the significance for our day of these churchmen and their writings is being shown in various ways, not least in the fact that some of their more important works are now beginning to be reprinted. There is, however, a real need for a single book which will supply a compendious statement of their theological position. This I have endeavoured to provide in the present volume. My purpose has been to allow the Reformers to speak for themselves, rather than to impose my own interpretations and applications of their teaching on the reader. Hence the preponderance of quotation in the pages that follow. Obviously, this has meant the exercise of restraint in selecting which passages were to be included and which to be omitted (for it would not have been difficult to provide a book many times larger than this one); and it has also meant that many excellent passages have been excluded. But I have felt it would be advantageous to restrict myself to the provision of a chrestomathy of the doctrine of the Reformers on certain main themes which are of constant importance for the Christian Church.

It is necessary to point out that, in a volume of this nature, it has not been possible to give any adequate indication of the copiousness of the evidence which the Reformers adduced in vindication of their theological position from Scripture and the early fathers, thus demonstrating, in answer to their opponents, that, so far from being promoters of novelties and innovations, let alone errors, theirs was a just claim to be in harmony and continuity with the faith of the original Church—indeed, that they were deliberately seeking to return to the fountainhead of the New Testament and to recall the Church of their day to its true evangelical and apostolic heritage.

Perhaps I ought to mention that the slight modifications of the Reformers' language by way of modernization or simplification which, with the contemporary reader in mind, I have occasionally introduced affect only minor terms and phrases, without distorting the strength, the sense, or the substance of what they wrote. For example, I have altered the pronoun "which" to "who" where it stands for a person, and an infrequent double negative has been simplified (thus "Christ never made no such article of our faith" becomes "Christ never made any such article of our faith"). Such small adjustments are in fact not foreign to the idiom of the Reformers and do not detract from the authentic flavour and vigour of their sixteenth-century English, which, of course, I have been concerned to preserve.

I acknowledge gratefully my indebtedness to the Oxford Evangelical Research Trust who encouraged the preparation of this volume by the giving of a generous financial grant. I express my gratitude also to the Gordon Divinity School in Massachusetts, at whose invitation the chapters of this book were delivered, in their first draft, as the McElwain Lectures for 1962. It is my hope that the reading of these chapters will help many to "discover" the English Reformers for themselves and to experience the pleasure of sitting at their feet.

P. E. H.

# I

# HOLY SCRIPTURE

This book, which is the Word of God, the most precious jewel, the most holy relic that remaineth upon earth.

*Thomas Cranmer*

The Scripture is that wherewith God draweth us unto Him. The Scriptures sprang out of God, and flow unto Christ, and were given to lead us to Christ. Thou must therefore go along by the Scripture as by a line, until thou come at Christ, which is the way's end and resting-place.

*William Tyndale*

# I

# HOLY SCRIPTURE

In England, as in other countries, the Reformation of the sixteenth century was in its essence a spiritual movement which, in its internal as well as its external development, flowed from the rediscovery of the Gospel of divine grace to which the pages of Holy Scripture bear testimony. This is exemplified in the experience of Thomas Bilney, "Little Bilney" as he came affectionately to be known, the Cambridge scholar who, on the publication of the second edition of Erasmus' *Novum Testamentum* in 1519, eagerly procured a copy—not, however, that he might study it as the Word of God, but rather be charmed with the elegance of the great Dutch humanist's Latin: "Being allured rather by the Latin than by the Word of God (for at that time I knew not what it meant), I bought it even by the providence of God," he himself confessed.[1] None the less, the outcome of this simple purchase was that he met God in a manner which was to revolutionize his own life and, through his subsequent witness, the lives of many others who were seeking reality. Bilney, indeed, had been an earnest man; but he was a stranger to the light of the Gospel. Punctilious in the performance of his offices as a priest of the Church, he yet lacked the inward peace and assurance of the man who knows that all is well between himself and God. Confessions and absolutions, penances, vigils, almsgivings and other deeds of charity failed utterly to give him that peace of heart for which he longed. But it is promised to those that hunger and thirst after righteousness that they shall be filled (Mt. 5:6); and God's moment came when Bilney took up and opened his newly purchased volume: "At the first reading, as I well remember," he recounts, "I chanced upon this sentence of St. Paul (O most sweet and comfortable sentence to my soul!), 'It is a true saying and worthy of all men to be embraced, that Christ Jesus came into the world to save sinners, of whom I am the chief' (I Tim. 1:15)."[2] Here, at last and at once, was the end of all his searching: God, through the sending of His Son into the

---

[1] Foxe, *Acts and Monuments*, Vol. IV, London, 1841, p. 633.
[2] Foxe, *loc. cit.*

world, had done all that was needful for man's salvation, with the consequence that he who desires that peace which passes all understanding must rest in Christ, and in His finished work of redemption, not upon the illusory merit of any works which he himself may hope to perform. Now Thomas Bilney laid firm hold of the great evangelical truth that all is of divine grace, and that man's part is by unrestrained faith to cast himself upon the mercy of God freely offered in Christ Jesus.

Thus was Bilney set free by discovering the central message of the New Testament. The transformation by this means of his life and of the lives of others led to the reformation of the Church. The New Testament now ceased to be for him the preserve of pedants and pundits who had the ability to read Greek and Latin. In one dynamic moment it became the vibrant Word of the Living God—the authentic message of God's saving act in Jesus Christ. It is this unique and authoritative Word of the Gospel that sinful man (and that means *every* man) desperately needs. Consequently, he who has experienced it must communicate it. He is under obligation. He is Christ's ambassador. He cannot keep silence. Foxe tells us[1] that Bilney was now filled with "an incredible desire" to bring this glorious message to others, so that they too might share in the joy and freedom which he had found in Christ. The Holy Spirit was moving upon the face of England. It was in this way that the English Reformation had its first dawning, and it was in this same way that it continued to the fulness of its noon.

As he witnessed to his new-found light Bilney gradually gathered around him that famous group of scholars who used to meet with him in Cambridge at the White Horse Inn for the purpose of searching out the truths of God's Word, which were at the same time the principles of the Reformation. God placed His hand on one man after another and trained them by His Word and Spirit to overcome by the blood of the Lamb and by the word of their testimony, and not to love their lives unto the death (Rev. 12:11). That "little Bilney's" zeal was coupled with ingenuity and courage is shown by the method which he employed to bring the message of the Gospel to Hugh Latimer, who in those early days was an eloquent opponent of the "new learning". Bilney won over Latimer by requesting him, as a priest, to hear his confession, and

[1] Vol. IV, p 620.

then, kneeling before him in his study, he confessed—the Gospel! But let Latimer himself tell the story (in the course of a sermon preached in 1552, more than twenty years after Bilney had suffered martyrdom for publicly preaching the Good News): "Master Bilney, or rather Saint Bilney, that suffered death for God's Word sake, the same Bilney was the instrument whereby God called me to knowledge; for I may thank him, next to God, for that knowledge that I have in the Word of God. For I was as obstinate a papist as any was in England, insomuch that when I should be made Bachelor of Divinity, my whole oration went against Philip Melanchthon and against his opinions. Bilney heard me at that time, and perceived that I was zealous without knowledge; and he came to me afterward in my study, and desired me, for God's sake, to hear his confession. I did so; and, to say the truth, by his confession I learnt more than before in many years. So from that time forward I began to smell the Word of God, and forsook the school-doctors and such fooleries."[1] Hugh Latimer, thus won for Christ by "little Bilney", became the great preacher of the English Reformation, until, in 1555, he too suffered death by burning at the stake.

THE BIBLE IN ENGLISH

But it was not enough that certain scholars, who had a knowledge of the languages of the ancient world, should be able to read the Bible for themselves in Hebrew and Greek and Latin. If the work of the Reformation was to be carried forward it was essential that the ordinary people should have the Bible in their own tongue, so that they could by daily study become familiar with its teaching and so learn to distinguish between truth and error. This was a necessity of which the Reformers soon became conscious, and God did not fail to raise up His man for the tremendous task of translating the Bible into the English tongue. This man was William Tyndale, a scholar who had studied at both Oxford and Cambridge, and who in all likelihood had come within the orbit of Bilney's circle while at the latter university. Accepting appointment as tutor in the household of Sir John Walsh at Little Sodbury in the West Country, he soon became appalled at the ignorance and crudeness of his fellow ecclesiastics and distressed at their wanton neglect of the flocks over which they had been set as pastors. His

[1] Latimer: *Works*, Vol. I, pp. 334 f.

own probity of life and zeal in preaching the Gospel did not make him popular with such men, and it was to one of his clerical critics that he made the famous remark: "If God spare my life, ere many years pass I will cause a boy that driveth the plough shall know more of the Scriptures than thou dost."[1]

Unable, however, to obtain any encouragement from the leaders of the Church for this project of translating the Bible into English, Tyndale came to realize that if the task which God had set before him was to be achieved it would have to be achieved elsewhere than in England. And so he crossed the Channel and devoted the remaining twelve years of his life to the work of translation, an exile and a fugitive, constantly hunted by the enemies of the Gospel, and finally betrayed, imprisoned, and, in 1536, martyred in Belgium. The extent of the harvest of his faithfulness is something beyond calculation. He rendered the Scriptures into the purest English of all time, and through his obedience a whole nation has been blessed and enriched. "Some man will ask, peradventure, why I take the labour to make this work, inasmuch as they will burn it, seeing they burnt the Gospel," he wrote in 1527, in the Preface to his *Parable of the Wicked Mammon.* "I answer, In burning the New Testament they did none other thing than that I looked for; no more shall they do, if they burn me also, if it be God's will it shall be so. Nevertheless, in translating the New Testament I did my duty, and so do I now, and will do as much more as God hath ordained me to do."[2]

Sixteen years after Tyndale's death, Latimer was able to preach in the following words: "Truly we are much bound to God that he Hath set out this His will in our natural mother tongue, in English, I say, so that now you may not only hear it, but also read

---

[1] Foxe, Vol. IV, p. 117. Cf. the words of Erasmus published at about this time in the third edition of his *Novum Testamentum* (1522) and translated into English in 1529: "The Scripture of Christ should be translated into all tongues that it may be read diligently of the private and secular men and women. . . . I would to God the ploughman would sing a text of the Scripture at his ploughbeam, and that the weaver at his loom with this would drive away the tediousness of time. I would the wayfaring man with this pastime would expel the weariness of his journey. And to be short I would that all the communication of the Christian should be of the Scripture." Had Tyndale read this a little while before he uttered his famous saying, so that the thought was running subconsciously in his mind?    [2] Tyndale: *Works*, Vol. I, pp. 43 f.

it yourselves; which thing is a great comfort to every Christian heart. For now you can no more be deceived, as you have been in times past, when we did bear you in hand that popery was the Word of God: which falsehood we could not have brought to pass if the Word of God, the Bible, had been abroad in the common tongue: for then you might have perceived yourselves our falsehood and blindness. This I speak to that end, to move you to thankfulness towards Him who so lovingly provideth all things necessary to our salvation."[1] Again, on another occasion, he says with reference to Paul's description of the Word of God as the sword of the Spirit (Eph. 6:17): "Now, I pray you, how could the lay people have that sword, how could they fight with the devil, when all things were in Latin, so that they could not understand it? Therefore, how needful it is for every man to have God's Word, it appeareth here; for only with the Word of God we must fight against the devil, which devil intendeth daily to do us mischief. How could the unlearned fight against him when all things were in Latin, so that they might not come to the understanding of God's Word? Therefore let us give God most hearty thanks that we have God's Word, and let us thankfully use the same; for only with God's Word shall we avoid and chase the devil, and with nothing else. Our Saviour when he was tempted, what were His weapons? Wherewith fought He? Nothing else but with God's Word. When the devil tempted Him, He ever said, *Scriptum est*, 'It is written' . . . So likewise we must have God's Word to fight with the devil and to withstand his temptations and assaults."[2]

Within two or three years after his martyrdom William Tyndale's last prayer, "Lord, open the King of England's eyes", was answered, when, through the instrumentality of the Archbishop of Canterbury, Thomas Cranmer, English Bibles were set up in the parish churches, for any to read for their edification and comfort, and a royal proclamation made it permissible at last for private persons to buy Bibles and keep them in their homes.[3]

In his Preface to the Great Bible of 1539 Cranmer wrote as follows: "Here may all manner of persons, men, women, young, old, learned, unlearned, rich, poor, priests, laymen, lords, ladies, officers, tenants, and mean men, virgins, wives, widows, lawyers,

---

[1] Latimer: *Works*, Vol. I, pp. 369 f.   [2] Latimer: *Ibid.*, pp. 505 f.
[3] Strype: *Memorials of Archbishop Cranmer*, Vol. III (Oxford, 1954), pp. 385 f.

merchants, artificers, husbandmen, and all manner of persons of what estate or condition soever they be, may in this book learn all things that they ought to believe, what they ought to do, and what they should not do, as well concerning Almighty God, as also concerning themselves and all others. Briefly, to the reading of the Scripture none can be enemy, but that either be so sick that they love not to hear of any medicine, or else that be so ignorant that they know not Scripture to be the most healthful medicine . . . Wherefore I would advise you all that come to the reading or hearing of this book, which is the Word of God, the most precious jewel, the most holy relic that remaineth upon earth, that you bring with you the fear of God, and that you do it with all due reverence, and use your knowledge thereof not to vainglory of frivolous disputation, but to the honour of God, increase of virtue, and edification both of yourselves and of others."[1]

Writing in Elizabeth's reign, William Whitaker, Regius Professor of Divinity in the University of Cambridge, whose *Disputation on Holy Scripture* is the most extensive work on the subject of the Bible from the pen of an English author of the period, uses six arguments "to prove that the Scriptures are to be set forth before all Christians in their vernacular tongues, so as that every individual may be enabled to read them."

Firstly, he argues that "God hath commanded all to read the Scriptures: therefore all are bound to read the Scriptures", citing as evidence Dt. 31:11f., 17:19f., 6:6–9, Jer. 36:6f., Jn. 5:39, 20:31, and Rom. 15:4.

Secondly: "The people should not be deprived of those arms by which they are to be protected against Satan. Now the Scriptures are such arms: therefore the Scriptures should not be take away from the people; for taken away they are if the people be prevented from reading them." He invokes (as we have seen Latimer did) the example of Christ Himself (Mt. 4:4ff.) and Paul's description of the Word of God as the sword of the Spirit (Eph. 6:17). "If Christ defended Himself against Satan with the Scriptures," reasons Whitaker, "how much more needful are the Scriptures to us against the same enemy! And it was for this end that Christ used the weapons of Scripture against Satan, that He might afford us an example; for He could have repelled Satan with a single word. We therefore ought to resist Satan in the same manner. It is folly to

[1] Strype: *Op. cit.*, Appendix volume, pp. 689 f.

suppose that Satan can be driven away by bare ceremonies, exorcisms, gesticulations, and outward fopperies. We must fight with arguments drawn from Scripture and the examples of the holy fathers: the Scriptures are the only arms which can prevail, or ought to be used against him. Those, therefore, who take the Holy Scriptures away from the people leave them exposed naked to Satan, and hurl them into most certain destruction."

Thirdly: "The Scriptures are to be read publicly in such a manner as that the people may be able to derive some advantage from them. But they cannot be useful to the people in an unknown tongue: therefore they should be translated into a language known to the people." In support he cites I Cor. 14:6f., where the Apostle emphasizes the importance of worshipping God with the understanding in public gatherings.

Fourthly: "The Lord commands and requires that the people should be instructed, full of wisdom and knowledge, and perfectly acquainted with the mysteries of salvation . . . Therefore the people ought to read the Scriptures, since without the reading of the Scriptures they cannot acquire such knowledge. Now they cannot read them unless they be translated: therefore the Scriptures ought to be translated." In this connection the following passages are cited: Dt. 4:6, Col. 3:16, 1:9, 2:2, II Cor. 8:7, Num. 2:29, I Cor. 14:5, Phil. 1:9, and II Pet. 1:5. Turning to the fathers, he points out that they urge that "a knowledge of and acquaintance with the Scriptures is necessary for all Christians". Thus Jerome, commenting on Col. 3:16, says that "the laity ought to have not only a sufficient but an abundant knowledge of the Scriptures, and also to instruct each other"; and Chrysostom, with reference to the same text, observes that "the Apostle requires the people to know the Word of God, *not simply, but in great abundance*".

Fifthly: "Christ taught the people in their mother tongue; so also the apostles and disciples of Christ, as well when upon the day of Pentecost they published the Gospel in a known tongue, as afterwards when, scattered over the whole world, they taught all nations in their own native languages. Hence we draw our conclusion thus: The holy doctrine of the Gospel is not contaminated when preached or taught in the vernacular tongue; therefore, not when it is written or read in the vernacular tongue."

The sixth and final argument relates to the use and practice of the ancient church: It is "evident from history and the books of the holy fathers that the Scriptures were translated into all languages and that the people were always admonished by their pastors to read them with diligence and assiduity. Hence we draw our conclusion thus: Formerly the Scriptures were extant in vernacular languages and were also read by the people. Therefore the same is lawful at the present day." Among the substantiating evidence from the writings of the fathers Chrysostom's assertion that "the one great cause of all evils is ignorance of Scripture" is cited.[1] It will be appreciated that persistent Roman Catholic opposition made it desirable for the Reformed theologians to justify their action in giving the Bible to the people in their own language. In particular, Whitaker's *magnum opus* was a defence of the Reformed doctrine of Scripture against the assaults of the famous Jesuit scholar, Cardinal Bellarmine.

Bound up with all this is the question of the necessity of the Scriptures. They are necessary, declares Whitaker, because they contain "that necessary doctrine without which we cannot be saved". They are necessary, further, because they "preserve the doctrine and religion of God from being corrupted or destroyed or forgotten". That is, they serve to guarantee *certainty* of doctrine: "for those things which are taught orally have not the same firmness and certainty as those which are written and consigned in books." Again, the Scriptures are necessary to us, negatively, "lest we should fall into error", and, positively, "for the obtaining of faith and eternal life, since it was for that purpose they were written".[2] Similarly, Bishop Jewel writes of their necessity in his *Treatise of the Holy Scriptures*: "If we seek to know the sacraments of the church, what are they; if we would be instructed in the sacrament of baptism or in the sacrament of the body and blood of Christ; if we would learn to know our Creator, and to put the difference between the Creator and a creature; if we desire to know what this present life is and what is that life which is to come; if we would believe in God, and call upon the name of God, and do worship unto God; if we would be settled in perfect zeal and true knowledge; if we would have an upright conscience towards God; if we would know which is the true church of God: it is very needful that we hear the Word of God. There is no other word that teacheth us unto salvation."[3]

[1] Whitaker: *Disputation on Holy Scripture*, pp. 235 ff.
[2] Whitaker: *Op. cit.*, pp. 521 f.    [3] Jewel: *Works*, Vol. IV, p. 1179.

## THE AUTHORITY OF SCRIPTURE

Holy Scripture was, indeed, the formal principle of the Reformation. It was consistently applied in every sphere of private and social life as the supreme standard of faith, worship, and conduct. This is evident not only everywhere in the writings of the Reformers and in the Book of Common Prayer, but also in the Thirty-Nine Articles of Religion of the Church of England, in which the comprehensive character of the scriptural principle is amply illustrated. Thus, "Holy Scripture containeth all things necessary to salvation; so that whatsoever is not read therein, nor may be proved thereby, is not to be required of any man, that it should be believed as an article of the faith, or be thought requisite or necessary to salvation" (Article VI). The three creeds "ought thoroughly to be received; for they may be proved by most certain warrants of Holy Scripture" (Article VIII). We must, says Article XVII, "receive God's promises in such wise as they be generally set forth to us in Holy Scripture, and in our doings that will of God is to be followed, which we have expressly declared unto us in the Word of God". Those persons are to be regarded as accursed who presume to say that men may be saved by adherence to some law or sect or the light of nature; for, Article XVIII reminds us, "Holy Scripture doth set out unto us only the Name of Jesus Christ whereby men must be saved."

Nor may the Church be exalted to a position or vested with an authority above Holy Scripture. The visible Church of Christ is, according to Article XIX, "a congregation of faithful men", the distinguishing marks of which are the preaching of "the pure Word of God" and the due ministration of the sacraments "according to Christ's ordinance". Article XX grants that the Church has "power to decree rites or ceremonies and authority in controversies of faith", but with the explicit qualification that "it is not lawful for the Church to ordain anything that is contrary to God's Word written", nor so to "expound one place of Scripture that it be repugnant to another"; and concludes that "although the Church be a witness and keeper of Holy Writ, yet, as it ought not to decree any thing against the same, so besides the same ought it not to enforce any thing to be believed for necessity of salvation". The authority of general councils is similarly circumscribed, for Article XXI affirms that, "forasmuch as they be an assembly of men, whereof all be not governed with the Spirit and Word of God, they may err, and sometimes have erred, even in things pertaining unto God". Consequently, "things ordained by them as necessary to salvation have neither strength nor authority, unless it may be declared that they be taken out of Holy Scripture".

Amongst things falsely decreed by the Church, Article XXII specifically mentions "the Romish doctrine concerning purgatory, pardons, worshipping and adoration as well of images as of relics, and also invocation of saints", as "a fond thing vainly invented, and grounded upon no warranty of Scripture, but rather repugnant to the Word of God". "To have public prayer in the church, or to minister the sacraments, in a tongue not understanded of the people" is deplored, in Article XXIV, as "plainly repugnant to the Word of God and the custom of the primitive Church". Again, Article XXVIII dismisses transubstantiation, "or the change of the substance of the bread and wine in the supper of the Lord", on the ground that it "cannot be proved by Holy Writ, but is repugnant to the plain words of Scripture, overthroweth the nature of a sacrament, and hath given occasion to many superstitions". Article XXX denounces the denial of the cup to the laity precisely because it is "by Christ's ordinance and commandment" that both parts of the Lord's sacrament ought to be ministered to all Christian men alike. Clerical celibacy is "not commanded by God's law", asserts Article XXXII. There is no necessity of uniformity of traditions and ceremonies in the Church, but rather according to circumstances, they may differ from time to time and from place to place, provided that "nothing be ordained against God's Word" (Article XXXIV).

Scripture, in fact, is the very foundation of the Reformed faith. Whatever is found in Holy Scripture, affirms Archbishop Cranmer, "must be taken for a most sure ground and an infallible truth; and whatsoever cannot be grounded upon the same, touching our faith, is man's device, changeable and uncertain".[1] And, with reference to "the scholastical writers", from whom he quotes, he emphasizes: "I make no foundation at all upon them, but my very foundation is only upon God's Word, which foundation is so sure that it will never fail."[2] "No service we do to God can please Him," admonishes Archbishop Sandys, "but such as Himself in His Word hath prescribed: He will be served as He hath

---

[1] Cranmer: *Works*, Vol. I, p. 24.          [2] Cranmer: *Ibid.*, p. 255.

commanded in His law, and not as thou hast devised with thyself."
The purpose of the precise instructions concerning the structure
of the tabernacle was "to teach us that in the spiritual tabernacle, in
matters of religion, pertaining to the service and worship of God,
all things should be done according to the rule of His own will,
which is set down in His written Word".[1] This is an important
mark of difference between the Reformed faith and the religion of
Rome which is founded upon other principles besides Scripture,
such as tradition and papacy. "We disagree in the very foundation," explains Sandys. ". . . The foundation of our religion is the
written Word, the Scriptures of God, the undoubted records of
the Holy Ghost. We require no credit to be given to any part or
parcel of our doctrine, further than the same may be clearly and
manifestly proved by the plain words of the law of God, which
remaineth in writing, to be seen, read, and examined of all men.
This we do, first, because we know that God hath caused His
whole law to be written: secondly, because we see that it hath been
the practice of all the defenders of the truth since the beginnings to
rely their faith only upon the Scripture and written Word;
thirdly, because it is evident and plain that we cannot receive any
other foundation of heavenly truth without the overthrow of
Christian faith."[2]

This conviction that the Bible is the supreme authority in all
that affects the Church and its members was the consequence of
the unhesitating belief of the Reformers that God, and none other,
was its primary author, coupled with their own transforming
experience of the truth and power of its message. Their attitude
is well expressed by James Pilkington (who prior to Mary's
accession was Regius Professor of Divinity in the University of
Cambridge and under Elizabeth became Bishop of Durham) who
writes as follows in his *Exposition upon Nehemiah*: "Scripture
cometh not first from man, but from God; and therefore God is
to be taken for the author of it, and not man. The gospel saith.
'It is not you that speak, but the Spirit of your Father that speaketh
in you'.[3] And St. Peter saith, 'Prophecy came not in old time by the
will of man, but holy men of God spake as they were moved by the
Holy Ghost'.[4] Augustine saith well, 'The Scripture is a letter sent
from God the Creator unto man His creature'. Therefore, when

---

[1] Sandys: *Works*, pp. 221 f.       [2] Sandys: *Ibid.*, p. 12.
[3] Mt. 10: 20       [4] II Pet. 1: 21.

thou readest this book [Nehemiah] or other parts of the Scripture, do it as gladly and reverently, yea, and much more too, than thou wouldest use and read the prince's or thy friends' letters, seeing it is a letter sent to thee from thy God for thy salvation. God then is the chiefest author of this book, as He is of the rest of the Scripture, and Nehemiah the pen or writer of all these mysteries."[1]

Similarly, Hugh Latimer proclaims: "The excellency of this Word is so great, and of so high dignity, that there is no earthly thing to be compared unto it. The author thereof is so great, that is, God Himself, eternal, almighty, everlasting. The Scripture, because of Him, is also great, eternal, most mighty and holy."[2] And Thomas Cranmer exhorts: "Let us stay, quiet, and certify our consciences with the most infallible certainty, truth, and perpetual assurance of them [the Scriptures]. Let us pray to God, the only author of these heavenly studies, that we may speak, think, believe, live, and depart hence according to the wholesome doctrine and verities of them"[3]—as indeed this great archbishop faithfully did in both his ministry and his martyrdom. "Scripture hath for its author God Himself, from whom it first proceeded and came forth," writes William Whitaker. "Therefore the authority of Scripture may be proved from the Author Himself, since the authority of God Himself shines forth in it."[4]

In his *Piteous Lamentation of the Miserable Estate of the Church of in England*, written following the accession of Mary to the throne, Nicholas Ridley mourns that "where of late the Word of God was truly preached, was read and heard in every town, in every church, in every village, yea, and almost every honest man's house, alas, now it is exiled and banished out of the whole realm"; and he proceeds to an extended eulogy of Holy Scripture: 'the eternal Word of God, that abideth for ever, and the undefiled law of the Lord, which turneth the soul from all wickedness and giveth wisdom unto the innocent babes; I mean that milk which is without all guile, as Peter doth call it, that good Word of God, that Word of truth, which must be graven within the heart, and then is able to save men's souls; that wholesome seed, not mortal but immortal, of the eternal and everliving God, whereby the man

---

[1] Pilkington: *Works*, pp. 286 f.     [2] Latimer: *Works*, Vol. I, p. 85.
[3] "A Faithful Exhortation to the Reading and Knowledge of Holy Scripture", *ad fin.*, in the first book of *Homilies*, p. 9. London, 1899.
[4] Whitaker: *Disputation on Holy Scripture*, p. 289.

is born anew and made the child of God; that seed of God, whereby the man of God, so being born, cannot sin, as John saith (he meaneth, so long as that seed doth abide in him); that Holy Scripture which hath not been devised by the wit of man, but taught from heaven by the inspiration of the Holy Ghost; . . . this holy and wholesome true Word, that teacheth us truly our bounden duty towards our Lord God in every point, what His blessed will and pleasure is, what His infinite great goodness and mercy is, what He hath done for us, how He hath given His only dear beloved to death for our salvation, and by Him hath sent us the revelation of His blessed will and pleasure; what His eternal Word willeth us both to believe and also to do, and hath for the same purpose inspired the holy Apostles with the Holy Ghost, and sent them abroad into all the world, and also made them, and other disciples of Christ, inspired by the same Spirit, to write and leave behind them the same things that they taught, which as they did proceed of the Spirit of truth, so by the confession of all them that ever were endued with the Spirit of God, were sufficient to the obtaining of eternal salvation."[1]

Consonant with the conviction that God is the author of Holy Scripture is the description of the Bible as *the Word of God*. "The Scriptures", says John Jewel, "are 'the Word of God'. What title can there be of greater value? What may be said of them to make them of greater authority, than to say, 'The Lord hath spoken them'? that 'they came not by the will of men, but holy men of God spake as they were moved by the Holy Ghost'? . . . The word of the Gospel is not as the word of an earthly prince. It is of more majesty than the word of an angel . . . For it is the Word of the living and almighty God, the God of hosts, who hath done whatsoever pleased him, both in heaven and in earth. By this Word He maketh His will known . . . This Word the angels and blessed spirits used, when they came down from heaven, to speak unto the people; when they came to the blessed virgin and to Joseph and to others: they spake as it is written in the prophets and in the Scriptures of God: they thought not their own authority sufficient but they took credit to their saying, and authority to their message, out of the Word of God . . . Whatsoever truth is brought unto us contrary to the Word of God, it is not truth, but falsehood and error: whatsoever honour done unto God disagreeth from the

---

[1] Ridley: *Works*, p. 56.

honour required by His Word, it is not honour unto God, but blasphemy . . . Tyrants and pharisees and heretics and the enemies of the cross of Christ have an end; but the Word of God hath no end. No force shall be able to decay it. The gates of hell shall not prevail against it. Cities shall fall: kingdoms shall come to nothing; empires shall fade away as the smoke; but the truth of the Lord shall continue for ever. Burn it, it will rise again; kill it, it will live again; cut it down by the root, it will spring again . . . The Word of the Lord is the bush, out of which issueth a flame of fire. The Scriptures of God are the mount, from which the Lord of hosts doth show Himself. In them God speaketh to us; in them we hear the words of everlasting life."[1]

In 1554, while suffering the imprisonment that preceded their martyrdom, John Bradford and certain others composed a declaration of the doctrine and faith which they professed—"to seal up the same, we are ready, through God's help and grace, to give our lives to the halter or stake"—of which the following article was given priority of position: "First, we confess and believe all the canonical books of the Old Testament, and all the books of the New Testament, to be the very true 'Word of God', and to be written by the inspiration of the Holy Ghost; and therefore to be heard accordingly, as the judge in all controversies and matters of religion."[2]

THE INTERNAL WITNESS OF THE HOLY SPIRIT

As the Word of God, the Scriptures are, of course, the Word of God *to man*. God's Word is not spoken, as it were, into the air: it is addressed specifically to man, and, more specifically still, to man who, because of his sin, is a fallen and lost creature. But the Reformers repeatedly emphasize the truth that it is only through the grace of the internal operation of the Holy Spirit in heart and mind that the message of Scripture can be understood and appropriated. The Divine Spirit is both the author of Scripture and the interpreter of His own Word. "The Scripture speaketh many things as the world speaketh," declares William Tyndale; "but they may not be worldly understood, but ghostly and spiritually: yea, the Spirit of God only understandeth them; and where He is not, there is not the understanding of Scripture, but unfruitful

---

[1] Jewel: *A Treatise of the Holy Scriptures*, in *Works*, Vol. IV, pp. 1163 f., 1188.        [2] Bradford: *Writings*, Vol. I, p. 370.

disputing and brawling about words. The Scripture saith, God seeth, God heareth, God smelleth, God walketh, God is with them, God is not with them, God is angry, God is pleased, God sendeth His Spirit, God taketh His Spirit away, and a thousand such like; and yet is none of them true after the worldly manner, and as the words sound." After citing I Cor. 2:11f. ("The natural man understandeth not the things of God, but the Spirit of God only; and we have received the Spirit which is of God, to understand the things which are given us of God") and Rom. 8:14 ("They that are led with the Spirit of God are the sons of God") and verse 9 ("He that hath not the Spirit of Christ is none of His"), Tyndale proceeds: "Now 'he that is of God heareth the Word of God', John 8. And who is of God but he that hath the Spirit of God? Furthermore, saith He, 'Ye hear it not because ye are not of God'; that is, ye have no lust in the Word of God, for ye understand it not; and that because His Spirit is not in you. Forasmuch then as the Scripture is nothing else but that which the Spirit of God hath spoken by the prophets and apostles, and cannot be understood but of the same Spirit, let every man pray to God to send him His Spirit".[1] The following admonition is given by Pilkington: "God inspired the apostles with all knowledge of the Scriptures suddenly, who were unlearned and never went to school; yet may not we think that we will be learned after the same sort without study and prayer: for then we tempt God, refusing such helps as He hath appointed for us to come to learning by. And though we study and pray never so much, yet we shall understand nothing until He give us His Holy Spirit, the schoolmaster of all truth, to lighten our minds and give understanding of His holy will."[2]

In enumerating the evidences which, as propounded by Calvin (*Institutes*, I, viii), bear testimony to the divine origin of the biblical writings—namely, the majesty of the doctrine which everywhere shines forth in the canonical books; the simplicity, purity, and divinity of the style; the authority belonging to the antiquity of the books themselves; the precise fulfilment of the prophecies in them; the truth of the miracles they recount; the futile attempts of the enemies of these books to destroy them; the testimonies of martyrs who have sealed the doctrine of Scripture by their confession and their blood; and indeed the very type of men who, far from being professional authors, God employed in the writing of

---

[1] Tyndale: *Works*, Vol. I, p. 88.    [2] Pilkington: *Works*, p. 329.

Scripture—William Whitaker takes care to emphasize what Calvin had emphasized before him, namely, that "these topics may prove that these books are divine, yet will never be sufficient to bring conviction to our souls so as to make us assent, unless the testimony of the Holy Spirit be added. When this is added, it fills our minds with a wonderful plentitude of assurance, confirms them, and causes us most gladly to embrace the Scriptures, giving force to the preceding arguments. Those previous arguments may indeed urge and constrain us; but this (I mean the internal testimony of the Holy Spirit) is the only argument which can persuade us." We shall be mistaken if we imagine that the authority of the Church, unbroken though its judgment may be, will be adequate to persuade us—although it "may perhaps suffice to keep men in some external obedience, may induce them to render an external consent, and to persevere in an external unity"; for "the Church can of itself by no means persuade us to assent to these oracles as divine". There can be but one conclusion: "In order, therefore, that we should be internally in our consciences persuaded of the authority of Scripture, it is needful that the testimony of the Holy Ghost should be added. And He, as He seals all the doctrines of faith and the whole teaching of salvation in our hearts, and confirms them in our consciences, so also does He give us a certain persuasion that these books, from which are drawn all the doctrines of faith and salvation, are sacred and canonical."[1]

He who has the Holy Spirit cannot fail to recognize the voice of God in Scripture. To quote Whitaker again: "As the brightest light appears in the sun, so the greatest splendour of divinity shines forth in the Word of God. The blind cannot perceive even the light of the sun; nor can they distinguish the splendour of the Scriptures whose minds are not divinely illuminated. But those who have the eyes of faith can behold this light. Besides, if we recognize men when they speak, why should we not also hear and recognize God speaking in His Word? . . . But they [the papists] object that we cannot recognize the voice of God, because we do not hear God speaking. This I deny. For those who have the Holy Spirit are *taught of God*: these can recognize the voice of God as much as any one can recognize a friend, with whom he hath long and familiarly lived, by his voice . . . If we do not understand, the reason is because we have not the Spirit, by whom our hearts

[1] Whitaker: *Op. cit.*, pp. 294 f.

should be enlightened. With respect to us, therefore, the authority of the Scripture depends upon, and is made clear by, the internal witness of the Holy Spirit; without which, though you were to hear a thousand times that this is the Word of God, yet you could never believe in such a manner as to acquiesce with an entire assent."[1]

In answer to the objection that Scripture is not the voice of God, but the Word of God; "that is, it does not proceed immediately from God, but is delivered mediately to us through others", Whitaker offers this comment: "We confess that God hath not spoken by Himself, but by others. Yet this does not diminish the authority of Scripture. For God inspired the prophets with what they said, and made use of their mouths, tongues, and hands: the Scripture, therefore, is even immediately the voice of God. The apostles and prophets were only the organs of God." This assertion he supports by citing Heb. 1:1 and II Pet. 1:21, which declare respectively that it was God who spoke to the fathers by the prophets and that holy men of God spoke as they were moved by the Holy Spirit.[2]

THE SENSE OF SCRIPTURE

An important point at issue at the time of the Reformation was the sense in which Scripture should be interpreted. It was the contention of the English Reformers that the only proper sense was that which the Holy Spirit intended, and this they defined as the *literal* sense (not to be confused with literalism: it is the equivalent of what we today would call the *natural* sense). Prior to the Reformation, in the medieval period, it had become customary for the schoolmen to distinguish four senses of Scripture: literal, tropological, anagogical, and allegorical. But Tyndale rightly pointed out that the last three of these could all be placed under the one head of allegory. "Tropological and anagogical are terms of their own feigning, and altogether unnecessary," he says. "For they are but allegories, both two of them; and this word allegory comprehendeth them both, and is enough. For tropological is but an allegory of manners; and anagogical an allegory of hope." But the allegorical is not an alternative sense to the literal. "The Scripture hath but one sense," he insists, "which is the literal sense. And that literal sense is the root and ground of all, and the

[1] Whitaker: *Op. cit.*, pp. 289 f.      [2] Whitaker: *Op. cit.*, p. 296.

anchor that never faileth, whereunto if thou cleave, thou canst never err or go out of the way. And if thou leave the literal sense, thou canst not but go out of the way. The Scripture indeed useth proverbs, similitudes, riddles, or allegories, as all other speeches do; but that which the proverb, similitude, riddle, or allegory signifieth is ever the literal sense, which thou must seek out diligently."[1]

Moreover, an excessive addiction to an allegorical interpretation of Scripture had been the cause of much harm in the Church, as Tyndale explains in a lively passage:"The greatest cause of which captivity and the decay of the faith, and this blindness wherein we now are, sprang first of allegories. For Origen and the doctors of his time drew all the Scripture unto allegories; whose example they that came after followed so long, till they at last forgot the order and process of the text, supposing that the Scripture served but to feign allegories upon; insomuch that twenty doctors expound one text twenty ways, as children make descant upon plain song. Then came our sophisters with their anagogical and chopological sense, and with an antitheme of half an inch, out of which some of them drew a thread of nine days long. Yea, thou shalt find enough that will preach Christ, and prove whatsoever point of the faith that thou wilt, as well out of a fable of Ovid or any other poet as out of St. John's gospel or Paul's epistles. Yea, they are come unto such blindness that they not only say the literal sense profiteth not, but also that it is hurtful, and noisome, and killeth the soul."[2]

The literal sense, further, is at the same time, the *spiritual* sense. Thus, for example, "the similitudes of the gospel are allegories, borrowed of worldly matters", but their purpose is "to express spiritual things". Accordingly, when Scripture speaks of Christ as a lamb, it does not mean "a lamb that beareth wool, but a meek and patient lamb, which is beaten for other men's faults". The plea that Scripture should be understood in a spiritual sense follows from the premise of the divine authorship of the Bible: "God is a Spirit, and all His words are spiritual. His literal sense is spiritual, and all His words are spiritual."[3]

Whitaker also expresses himself clearly to the same effect. After reminding his readers that Christ has enjoined us "to investigate the true sense of Scripture", and wisely observing that "the

---

[1] Tyndale: *Works*, Vol. I, pp. 303 f.
[2] Tyndale: *Ibid.*, pp. 307 f.　　　　[3] Tyndale: *Ibid.*, pp. 305, 309.

Scripture consists not in the bare words, but in the sense, interpretation, and meaning of the words", he goes on to write as follows about the manner of interpreting Holy Scripture: "It is surely foolish to say that there are as many senses of Scripture as the words themselves may be transferred and accommodated to bear. For although the words may be applied and accommodated tropologically, allegorically, anagogically, or any other way, yet there are not therefore various senses, various interpretations and explications of Scripture, but there is but one sense, and that the literal, which may be variously accommodated, and from which various things may be collected." Again, "there is but one true and genuine sense of Scripture, namely, the literal or grammatical, whether it arise from the words taken strictly, or from the words figuratively understood, or from both together." And again: "Since then that is the sense of Scripture, and the literal sense, which the Holy Spirit intends, however it may be gathered, certainly, if the Holy Spirit intended the tropologic, anagogic, or allegoric sense of any place, these senses are not different from the literal . . . Therefore, tropology, allegory, and anagoge, if they are real meanings, are literal ones. Now the reason why sound arguments are always derived from the literal sense is this, because it is certain that that which is derived from the words themselves is ever the sense of the Holy Spirit . . . We must not bring any private meanings, or private opinions, but only such as agree with the mind, intention, and dictate of the Holy Spirit. For since He is the author of the Scriptures, it is fit that we should follow Him in interpreting Scripture."[1]

This emphasis on the understanding of Scripture in its natural sense represented a real revolution in the use of the Bible, which for generations had been the preserve of intellectual charlatans and religious sophists who pretended to an esoteric exegesis which was as fanciful as it was illegitimate. The Reformation restored an approach to the Bible which evinced a proper respect for it not only as the Word of God but also as a revelation addressed to all men. This recovered seriousness was indicative of reverence coupled with sanity and sobriety in expounding the meaning of the text. It was like a fresh wind which blew away the intricate cobwebs that had been spun round the pages over the centuries and allowed the Word to live and breathe again and to speak for itself.

[1] Whitaker: *Op. cit.*, pp. 402, 405, 406, 408ff.

The Reformers were great students of the patristic literature. It was their learning in this field that enabled them to demonstrate, as they so indefatigably did, that the doctrines of the Reformation, so far from being new-fangled inventions, were the very doctrines which the early Church had proclaimed and upheld. The question naturally arose, then, as to how far credence was to be given to the church fathers and their writings. Let Bishop Jewel answer: "What can we say of the fathers, Augustine, Ambrose, Jerome, Cyprian, etc.? What shall we think of them, or what account may we make of them? They be interpreters of the Word of God. They were learned men, and learned fathers, the instruments of the mercy of God, and vessels full of grace. We despise them not, we read them, we reverence them, and give thanks unto God for them. They were witnesses unto the truth, they were worthy pillars and ornaments in the Church of God. Yet may they not be compared with the Word of God. We may not build upon them; we may not make them the foundation and warrant of our conscience; we may not put our trust in them. Our trust is in the name of the Lord." This judgment, as Jewel points out, is, moreover, the judgment of the fathers themselves concerning the worth of their own writings. He cites the declaration of Augustine, the most famous of all the fathers, as follows: "Neither weigh we the writings of all men, be they never so worthy and catholic, as we weigh the canonical Scriptures; but that, saving the reverence that is due unto them, we may mislike and refuse somewhat in their writings, if we find that they have thought otherwise than the truth may bear. Such am I in the writings of others, and such would I wish others to be in mine."[1] "Some things I believe," Jewel resumes, "and some things which they write I cannot believe. I weigh them not as the holy and canonical Scriptures. Cyprian was a doctor of the Church, yet he was deceived; Jerome was a doctor of the Church, yet he was deceived; Augustine was a doctor of the Church, yet he wrote a book of Retractations: he acknowledged that he was deceived." After adducing further evidence from the patristic authors, Jewel concludes: "I could show many the like speeches of the ancient fathers, wherein they reverence the Holy Scriptures;

[1] Augustine: *Epist.* CXLVIII, *Ad Fortunatianum.*

as to which only they give consent without gainsaying; which can neither deceive nor be deceived."[1]

"What is the cause," asks Tyndale, "that we damn some of Origen's works and allow some? How know we that some is heresy and some not? By the Scripture, I trow. How know we that St. Augustine (who is the best, or one of the best, that ever wrote upon the Scripture) wrote many things amiss at the beginning, as many other doctors do? Verily, by the Scriptures; as he himself well perceived afterward, when he looked more diligently upon them, and revoked many things again. He wrote of many things which he understood not when he was newly converted, ere he had thoroughly seen the Scriptures, and followed the opinions of Plato, and the common persuasions of man's wisdom that were then famous."[2] So, too, Thomas Becon, in whose writings there are copious quotations from the fathers, is careful to make it clear that the patristic literature is never to be placed on a level with Holy Scripture. The authority of the one is relative, depending on its consonance with scriptural teaching; whereas the authority of the other is absolute. Accordingly, we find him making the following disclaimer: "Neither do I recite the testimonies of the old fathers to confirm and make our matter the more strong, which already is established by the Holy Scriptures; neither need they the confirmation of any man's doctrine, which of themselves ought to be believed without hesitation or doubting of the faithful, inasmuch as they be the oracles and infallible speeches of God, in which all necessary truth for our salvation is comprehended, and without the authority whereof all that is ever taught or written be but mere fantasies and human inventions."[3]

In the second chapter of his *Confutation of Unwritten Verities* Cranmer gives an extensive catena of quotations from the writings of the ancient fathers in proof that they constantly acknowledged the supreme authority of Holy Scripture in the establishment of every doctrine of the faith.[4] "All contention which the old fathers had with heretics was for the Scriptures," he observes; ". . . but for things which are not contained in the Scriptures they never accused any man of heresy. If there were any word of God beside the Scripture, we could never be certain of God's Word; and if we be uncertain of God's Word, the devil might bring in among us a

---

[1] Jewel: *Works*, Vol. IV, pp. 1173 f.   [2] Tyndale: *Works*, Vol. I, p. 154.
[3] Becon: *Works*, Vol. I, p. 134.     [4] Cranmer: *Works*, Vol. I, pp. 22 ff.

2

new word, a new doctrine, a new faith, a new church, a new god, yea, himself to be god . . . If the Church and the Christian faith did not stay itself upon the Word of God certain, as upon a sure and strong foundation, no man could know whether he had a right faith, and whether he were in the true Church of Christ, or in the synagogue of Satan."[1] Cranmer brings this work to its conclusion with the following exhortation: "Stand thou fast, and stay thy faith, whereupon thou shalt build all thy works, upon the strong rock of God's Word, written and contained within the Old Testament and the New, which is able sufficiently to instruct thee in all things needful to thy salvation, and to the attainment of the kingdom of heaven."[2]

Let us listen to Hugh Latimer preaching, in characteristic style, before the king: "I will tell you what a bishop of this realm said once to me: he sent for me, and marvelled that I would not consent to such traditions as were then set out. And I answered him that I would be ruled by God's book, and rather than I would dissent one jot from it, I would be torn with wild horses. And I chanced in our communication to name the Lord's Supper. "Tush", saith the bishop, "what do ye call the Lord's Supper? What new term is that?" There stood by him a dubber, one Doctor Dubber: he dubbed him by and by, and said that this term was seldom read in the doctors. And I made answer that I would rather follow Paul in using his terms than them, though they had all the doctors on their side."[3] Yet, like Jewel and the other Reformers, Latimer was no despiser of the fathers: "These doctors," he said in another sermon, "we have great cause to thank God for them, but yet I would not have them always to be allowed. They have handled many points of our faith very godly; and we may have a great stay in them in many things; we might not well lack them: but yet I would not have men to be sworn to them, and so addict as to take hand over head whatsoever they say: it were a great inconvenience so to do."[4]

In affirming the supremacy of Scripture, the Reformers naturally subjected themselves and their own writings, no less than those of the fathers, to its authority. The Reformation did not burst, like Athene from the head of Zeus, fully grown and fully armed upon the world. Its leaders did not reach their conclusions and lay down

---

[1] Cranmer: *Works*, Vol. I, p. 52.          [2] Cranmer: *Ibid.*, p. 67.
[3] Latimer: *Works*, Vol. I, p. 121.          [4] Latimer: *Ibid.*, p. 218.

their system of doctrine in a moment, but only, as it were, by degrees as the intensive study of Scripture led them into the depths of the revealed truth of God and away from their former errors and superstitions. "Oh, Luther, when he came into the world first, and disputed against the Decretals, the Clementines, Alexandrines, Extravagantines, what ado had he!" exclaimed Latimer in yet another of his sermons before the king. "But ye will say, peradventure he was deceived in some things. I will not take upon me to defend him in all points. I will not stand to it that all he wrote was true: I think he would not so himself: for there is no man but he may err. He came to further and further knowledge: but surely he was a goodly instrument."[1]

The Reformers confidently and consistently affirmed that their doctrine of Holy Scripture was confirmed up to the hilt by the testimony of the ancient fathers of the Church. "The fathers most clearly favour our opinion," declares Whitaker. "However, I bring them forward not to confirm a thing in itself dubious and uncertain, but to shed light upon a truth already ascertained, and to shut the mouths of our adversaries, who loudly, in every question, claim the fathers as their own. I should never make an end, were I to seek to enumerate all who stand on our side in this matter. There is almost not one single father, hardly any author of any kind, who does not support our opinion in this controversy."[2] The support of the fathers is then demonstrated by copious citations from their writings; but the whole of Whitaker's large work is lavishly supplied with quotations from the patristic authors. None the less, as we have seen, the Reformers refused to attach to the witness of the fathers an authority that was binding or absolute. Scripture alone was the definitive criterion by which all else, including the fathers, must be judged. To quote Whitaker again: "Even though the fathers were opposed to us, and we could give no answer to the arguments drawn from them, this could inflict no real damage upon our cause, since our faith does not depend upon the fathers, but upon the Scriptures. Nevertheless, I am far from approving the opinion of those who think that the testimonies of the fathers should be rejected or despised . . . However, we must take heed that we do not, with the papists, ascribe too much to the fathers, but use our rights and liberty when we read them; examining all their sayings by the rule of Scripture, receiving them when they

[1] Latimer: *Ibid.*, p. 212.      [2] Whitaker: *Op. cit.*, pp. 669 f.

agree with it, but freely and with their good leave rejecting them whenever they exhibit marks of discrepancy."[1]

## SCRIPTURE AND THE CHURCH

If the authority of the fathers must be subject to that of Holy Scripture, so also must the authority of the Church. We have already seen what the Thirty-Nine Articles have to say in this connection. In particular, Scripture is not dependent on the pronouncements of the Church for its authentication, for it is authenticated to every believer by the internal testimony of the Holy Spirit. Indeed, as being written under the inspiration of the Holy Spirit, it is, in a word, self-authenticating. "We do not deny," says Whitaker, "that it appertains to the Church to approve, acknowledge, receive, promulge, commend the Scriptures to all its members; and we say that this testimony is true and should be received by all. We do not, therefore, as the papists falsely say of us, refuse the testimony of the Church, but embrace it. But we deny that we believe the Scriptures solely on account of this commendation of them by the Church. For we say that there is a more certain and illustrious testimony, whereby we are persuaded of the sacred character of these books, that is to say, the internal testimony of the Holy Spirit, without which the commendation of the Church would have with us no weight or moment. The papists, therefore, are unjust to us when they affirm that we reject and make no account of the authority of the Church. For we gladly receive the testimony of the Church, and admit its authority; but we affirm that there is a far different more certain, true, and august testimony than that of the Church. The sum of our opinion is, that the Scripture is αὐτόπιστος, that is, hath all its authority and credit from itself; is to be acknowledged, is to be received, not only because the Church hath so determined and commanded, but because it comes from God, not by the Church, but by the Holy Ghost. Now by the Church we understand not, as they do, the pastors, bishops, councils, pope; but the whole multitude of the faithful. For this whole multitude hath learned from the Holy Spirit that this Scripture is sacred, that these books are divine. This persuasion the Holy Spirit hath sealed in the minds of all the faithful."[2] And again: "Now that it is in itself the Word of God they do not deny, but they say that we cannot be certain of it without the help of the Church: they confess

---

[1] Whitaker: *Op. cit.*, p. 565.　　　　[2] Whitaker: *Ibid.*, pp. 279 f.

that the voice of God sounds in our ears; but they say that we cannot believe it, except upon account of the Church's approbation. But now, if it be the Word of God which we hear, it must needs have a divine authority of itself, and should be believed by itself and for itself."[1]

The Church, in fact, has not shown itself a consistent and unvarying witness when speaking on matters of doctrine. And very much more so today than in Whitaker's day and in the preceding centuries the Church speaks, in so far as it may be said to do so, with divided and even contradictory voices where the doctrine of Scripture is concerned. "Must the truth and authority of the canonical Scripture be made to hang upon the judgment of the Church, and that judgment itself a variable one?" asks Whitaker. ". . . Churches indeed may judge variously and inconstantly, as was plainly the case in the ancient churches: but the Scriptures of God are always the same, consistent with themselves, and admitting of no variety. . . . We believe their canonicity, not only on account of the testimony or authority of the Church, but upon the inducement of other and more certain arguments, as the witness of the Holy Spirit, and the majesty of that heavenly doctrine which shines forth in the books themselves and the whole manner of their teaching."[2] To sum up: "The testimony of the Holy Spirit, and not the public judgment of the Church, is the true and proper cause of that authentic authority which the Scripture hath with us."[3]

Whitaker defines four "distinguished offices" which the Church has to fulfil in respect of Scripture. Firstly, "the Church is the witness and guardian of the sacred writings, and discharges, in this respect, as it were the function of a notary. In guardians the greatest fidelity is required: but no one would say that records were believed merely on the notary's authority, but on account of their own trustworthiness. So the Church ought carefully to guard the Scriptures, and yet we do not repose credit in the Scriptures merely on account of the testimony and authority of the Church." Secondly, it is the duty of the Church "to distinguish and discern the true, sincere, and genuine Scriptures from the spurious, false, and supposititious." In this "it discharges the office of a champion; and for the performance of this function it hath the

---

[1] Whitaker: *Op. cit.*, p. 290.    [2] Whitaker: *Ibid.*, p. 309.
[3] Whitaker: *Ibid.*, p. 334.

Spirit of Christ to enable it to distinguish the true from the false.
. . . The goldsmith with his scales and touchstone can distinguish
gold from copper and other metals; wherein he does not make gold,
even in respect of us, but only indicates what is gold, so that we the
more easily trust it. . . . In like manner the Church acknowledges
the Scriptures and declares them to be divine: we, admonished
and stirred up by the Church, perceive the matter to be so indeed."
Thirdly, it is the Church's duty "to publish, set forth, preach, and
promulgate the Scriptures". In doing so "it discharges the function
of a herald, who ought to pronounce with a loud voice the decrees
and edicts of the king, to omit nothing, to add nothing of his own".
And fourthly, "the office of the Church is to expound and interpret
the Scriptures". In this "its function is that of an interpreter";
and "here it should introduce no fictions of its own, but explain the
Scriptures by the Scriptures".[1]

The Bible is, it follows, the very touchstone of truth, by which
the Church, the fathers, and all traditions must be tested and
judged. "The Scripture is the touchstone that trieth all doctrines,
and that by which we know the false from the true," asserts
Tyndale in his Prologue to the book of Genesis.[2] "That Word,"
he says in another of his writings (*The Practice of Prelates*), "is
the chiefest of the apostles, and pope, and Christ's vicar, and head
of the Church, and the head of the general council. And unto the
authority of that ought the children of God to hearken without
respect of person."[3] Even in the case of learned and godly-minded
men, we are to believe them, admonishes Cranmer, "no further than
they can show their doctrine and exhortation to be agreeable with
the true Word of God written. For that is the very touchstone
which must, yea, and also will, try all doctrine or learning, whatsoever it be, whether it be good or evil, true or false".[4] In his
*Apology of the Church of England* Bishop Jewel speaks to the same
effect: "We receive and embrace all the canonical Scriptures, both
of the Old and New Testament, giving thanks to our God, who
hath raised up unto us that light which we might ever have before
our eyes, lest, either by the subtlety of man or by the snares of the

---

[1] Whitaker: *Op. cit.*, pp. 283 f.

[2] Tyndale: *Works*, Vol. I, p. 398.

[3] Tyndale, *Works*, Vol. II, p. 333.

[4] Cranmer: *A Confutation of Unwritten Verities*, in *Works*, Vol. II,
p. 14.

devil, we should be carried away to errors and lies." And he epitomizes the Reformed doctrine that the Scriptures are "the heavenly voices, whereby God hath opened unto us his will; and that only in them man's heart can have settled rest; that in them be abundantly and fully comprehended all things, whatsoever be needful for our salvation, as Origen, Augustine, Chrysostom, and Cyril have taught; that they be the very might and strength of God to attain to salvation; that they be the foundations of the prophets and apostles, whereupon is built the Church of God; that they be the very sure and infallible rule, whereby may be tried whether the Church doth stagger, or err, and wherunto all ecclesiastical doctrine ought to be brought to account; and that against these Scriptures neither law, nor ordinance, nor any custom ought to be heard; no, though Paul his own self, or an angel from heaven, should come and teach the contrary".[1]

Again, when commenting on the apostolic exhortation, "Try all things", in I Thess. 5:21, Jewel says: "Thus are the people of God called to try the truth, to judge between good and ill, between light and darkness. God hath made them the promise of His Spirit and hath left unto them His Word. They of Berea, when they heard the preaching of Paul, searched the Scriptures daily, whether those things were so as he taught them, and many of them believed. So do you: give heed to instruction, and yet receive not all things without proof and trial that they are not contrary to the wholesome doctrine of the Word of God."[2] As for traditions, they are, observes Whitaker, "either consonant to Scripture, and then they should be received, and those who do not receive them are condemned in these words; or they are, as Basil expresses it, alien from Scripture, and then they should be rejected".[3]

In the *Conferences* between Bishops Ridley and Latimer during the time of their imprisonment prior to their martyrdom, Ridley writes as follows concerning the rule by which "controversies in weighty matters" in the Church should be determined: "Now, further, for determination of all controversies in Christ's religion, Christ Himself hath left unto the Church not only Moses and the prophets, whom He willed His Church in all doubts to go unto and ask counsel at, but also the gospels and the rest of the body of the

---

[1] Jewel: *Works*, Vol. III, p. 62. The concluding allusion is to Gal. 1:8.

[2] Jewel: *Works*, Vol. II, p. 881.     [3] Whitaker: *Op. cit.*, p. 625.

New Testament; in the which whatsoever is hard in Moses and the prophets, whatsoever is necessary to be known unto salvation, is revealed and opened. So that now we have no need to say, Who shall climb into heaven, or who shall go down into the depth, to tell what is needful to be done? (Rom. 10). Christ hath done both, and hath commended unto us the word of faith, which also is abundantly declared unto us in His Word written: so that hereafter, as we walk earnestly in this way, to the searching out of the truth, it is not to be doubted but through the certain benefit of Christ's Spirit, which He hath promised unto His, we may find it, and obtain everlasting life," (pp. 131f.).[1]

THE PRACTICAL PURPOSE OF SCRIPTURE

The Reformer's view of Scripture was essentially dynamic and practical, as befitted those who humbly took their place before the Bible as the Word of God addressed to man. They perceived that the Written Word was integrally bound up with the revelation to fallen man of God's redemptive purposes, which find their focal point in the person and work of His Son, our Saviour Jesus Christ, who is Himself the Living Word. Scripture is, indeed, the quintessence of the testimony of the Holy Spirit to Christ (*cf.* Jn. 5:39, 14:26, 15:26, 16:13f.). "The Scripture," declares William Tyndale in memorable words, "is that wherewith God draweth us unto Him. The Scriptures sprang out of God, and flow unto Christ, and were given to lead us to Christ. Thou must therefore go along by the Scripture as by a line, until thou come at Christ, which is the way's end and resting-place."[2] And Jewel speaks of the Holy Scriptures as "the bright sun of God, which bring light unto our ways, and comfort to all parts of our life, and salvation to our souls; in which is made known to us our estate, and the mercy of God in Christ our Redeemer witnessed."[3]

The Reformers were not mere academic theologians in retreat! They proved for themselves the vitality and faithfulness of God's Word in the midst of fierce testing and persecution. They found that the Bible was a book for all times and seasons, fully relevant to every circumstance of daily life and struggle, its pages replete with

[1] Ridley: *Works*, pp. 131 f. The biblical allusions are to Rom. 10: 6f. and Lk. 11: 13.

[2] Tyndale: *Works*, Vol. I, p. 317.

[3] Jewel: *Works*, Vol. IV, p. 1163.

lessons that apply to the particular needs of all men. Jewel offers
the following comment on the apostolic affirmation that all Scripture is not only inspired but also profitable (II Tim. 3:16): "Many
think the apostle's speech is hardly true of the whole Scripture,
that all and every part of the Scripture is profitable. Much is
spoken of genealogies and pedigrees, of lepers, of sacrificing goats
and oxen, etc. These seem to have little profit in them, but to be
vain and idle. If they show vain in thine eyes, yet hath not God
set them down in vain . . . There is no sentence, no clause, no
word, no syllable, no letter, but it is written for thy instruction:
there is not one jot but it is sealed and signed with the blood of the
Lamb. Our imaginations are idle, our thoughts are vain: there is no
idleness, no vanity in the Word of God. Those oxen and goats
which were sacrificed teach thee to kill and sacrifice the uncleanness and filthiness of thy heart; they teach thee that thou art
guilty of death, when thy life must be redeemed by the death of
some beast; they lead thee to believe the forgiveness of sins by a
more perfect sacrifice, because it was not possible that the blood
of bulls and goats should take away sins. That leprosy teacheth
thee to know the uncleanness and leprosy of thy soul. Those
genealogies and pedigrees lead us to the birth of our Saviour
Christ. So that the whole Word of God is pure and holy: no word,
no letter, no syllable, no point or prick thereof, but is written and
preserved for thy sake."[1] For this reason "it maketh the man of
God absolute, and perfect unto all good works, perfect in faith,
perfect in hope, perfect in the love of God and of his neighbour,
perfect in his life, and perfect in his death. So great, so large and
ample, and heavenly, is the profit which we do reap by the Word of
God."[2]

"All that is written in the Word of God," says Jewel again, "is
not written for angels or archangels or heavenly spirits, but for the
sons of men, for us, and for our instruction; that by them we may
receive strength and comfort in all adversities, and have hope of the
life to come. It is the Word of God: God openeth His mouth and
speaketh to us, to guide us into all truth, to make us full and ready
in all good works, that we may be perfect men in Christ Jesus; so
rooted and grounded in Him, that we be not tossed to and fro with
every tempest."[3] And Tyndale writes: "Scripture is a light, and

---

[1] Jewel: *Ibid.*, p. 1175.    [2] Jewel: *Ibid.*, p. 1177.
[3] Jewel: *Ibid.*, p. 1166.

2*

showeth us the true way, both what to do and what to hope for, and
a defence from all error, and a comfort in adversity that we despair
not, and feareth us in prosperity that we sin not . . . As thou
readest, therefore, think that every syllable pertaineth to thine own
self, and suck out the pith of Scripture, and arm thyself against all
assaults."[1]

HOW TO STUDY SCRIPTURE

What are the means whereby we may discover the true sense of
Scripture? This is a question which Whitaker helps us to answer.
Having shown that "the supreme authority for interpreting
Scripture" belongs "to the Holy Spirit speaking in the Scriptures, and not to fathers or councils or pope", he proposes that,
"since the Scripture hath no audible voice, we must use certain
means to investigate what is the sense and what the mind of the
Scriptures. If Christ were now Himself with us, if the apostles and
prophets were living amongst us, we might repair to them and
entreat them to disclose to us the meaning of what they had
written. But since they have departed and left us only their books,
we must consider what means we should use to discover the true
sense of Scripture." Whitaker enumerates eight such means.

Firstly, "prayer is necessary for reading the Scriptures so as to
understand them". Among the fathers whom he cites in this connection are Origen, who (in the 12th Homily on Exodus) "says
that we must not only apply study in order to learn the sacred
Word, but also supplicate God and entreat Him night and day, that
the Lamb of the tribe of Judah may come and, taking Himself the
sealed book, vouchsafe to open it",[2] and Jerome, who writes
(*Epist. ad Laetam*): "Let reading follow prayer, and prayer
reading." This, declares Whitaker, "should be always the first
means, and the foundation of the rest".

Secondly (and this applies in particular to those whose calling it
is to teach or minister the Word), "we ought to know the original
languages. We should consult the Hebrew text in the Old Testament, the Greek in the New: we should approach the very
fountain-heads of the Scriptures, and not stay beside the derived
streams of versions" (as the Church in general had stayed for
centuries by the Vulgate version prior to the Reformation).

[1] Tyndale: *Prologue to the Book of Genesis*, in *Works*, Vol. I, pp. 399f.
[2] The allusion is to Rev. 5:4ff.

"Indeed," adds Whitaker, "the ignorance of these languages, the Hebrew and the Greek, hath been the source of many errors; at least, those who are not acquainted with them are destitute of the best helps and assistances, and are involved in frequent and unavoidable mistakes."

Thirdly, "in dealing with the words we should consider which are proper and which figurative and modified. For when words are taken figuratively they should not be expounded strictly. 'It is', says Augustine, in his books of Christian Doctrine, 'a wretched bondage of the soul when signs are taken for things';[1] that is, when what is spoken figuratively is expounded as if spoken strictly."

Fourthly (and arising from the preceding), "we ought to consider the scope, end, matter, circumstances, . . . the antecedents and consequents of each passage; and by this means it will be no hard matter both to refute many errors and to arrive at a clear understanding of those things which seemed at first obscure".

Fifthly, "one place must be compared and collated with another, the obscurer places with the plainer or less obscure. For though in one place the words may be obscure, they will be plainer in another."

Sixthly, "in the comparison of places, we must observe that not only similar passages are to be compared with similar, but dissimilar passages also are to be compared together". For example, Jn. 6:53, "unless ye eat the flesh of the Son of man and drink His blood, ye have no life in you", may with advantage be compared with the sixth commandment, "Thou shalt do no murder"—"for if it be a crime, yea, an enormity, to slay a man, it is certainly a far deeper crime to eat and devour a man; hence Augustine concludes (*De Doct. Christ.*, III, xvi) that these words must be understood and explained figuratively, because otherwise they would command a flagitious crime".

Seventhly, "all our expositions should accord with the analogy of faith" (cf. Rom. 12:6, Greek). This analogy of faith, with which interpretation must tally to be sound, is the sum of those central doctrines of the Christian faith which we believe on the authority of the clear and constant teaching of Scripture, "such as the articles of faith in the Creed, the contents of the Lord's Prayer, the Decalogue, and the whole Catechism. Whatever exposition is repugnant to this analogy must be false."

[1] Augustine: *De Doctrina Christiana*, III, v.

Finally, "since the unlearned know not how to make a right use of these means, they ought to have recourse to other persons better skilled than themselves, to read the books of others, to consult the commentaries and expositions of learned interpreters, and to confer with others". This, however, must not be done without due discrimination: "care must be taken that we do not ascribe too much to them, or suppose that their interpretations are to be received because they are theirs, but because they are supported by the authority of Scripture, or by reason, so as to allow them no weight in opposition to Scripture. We may use their labours, advice, prudence, and knowledge; but we should use them always cautiously, modestly, and discreetly, and so as still to retain our own liberty."

"He that shall be content to make such a use of these means," concludes Whitaker, "and will lay aside his prejudices and party zeal, which many bring with them to every question, will be enabled to gain an understanding of the Scriptures, if not in all places, yet in most; if not immediately, yet ultimately."[1]

There are doubtless some today who are inclined to dismiss the Reformers as uncritical or "precritical" in their approach to Scripture. But the great leaders and moulders of the Reformation must not be summarily written off on this score. Let us not forget the sort of men they were and the great things they achieved on the basis of these scriptural principles that they held to be so vital. They were men of exceptional intelligence, candour, and scholarship, whose study of the Scriptures was marked by both depth and integrity. Above all, they were men of profound spirituality, whose lives—mind as well as heart—had been radically transformed by the Good News of Jesus Christ which they had found set before them on no other place than the Bible. When they spoke of the internal testimony of the Holy Spirit within the believer to the divine inspiration of Scripture, they were speaking of what they had themselves experienced, as well as of what the Bible taught about itself. Those sceptical souls who do not know this internal witness of the Spirit as a truth of their own experience should earnestly question within themselves whether they are in fact qualified to pronounce against the Reformed doctrine of Holy Scripture.

The sixteenth century was inevitably a period of sustained

[1] Whitaker: *Op. cit.*, pp. 466ff.

theological controversy. Fundamental issues were involved. In all conflict, however, which is conducted in a spirit of seriousness, there is (while no quarter is asked or given) room for respect for one's opponent. There is something appealing about the respect which Bellarmine, the famous Jesuit scholar, and Whitaker, the Cambridge professor—the two redoubtable antagonists in the sixteenth-century debate over the scope and authority of Holy Scripture—had for each other. Whitaker's biographer writes: "I have heard it confessed of English papists themselves, who have been in Italy with Bellarmine himself, that he procured the true portraiture and effigies of this *Whitaker* to be brought to him, which he kept in his study. For he privately admired this man for his singular learning and ingenuity; and being asked of some of his friends, Jesuits, why he would have the picture of that heretic in his presence, he would answer, *Quod quamvis haereticus erat et adversarius, erat tamen doctus adversarius:* that 'although he was a heretic and his adversary, yet he was a learned adversary'."[1] In the Epistle Dedicatory prefixed to his *magnum opus*, Whitaker for his part wrote of Bellarmine: "I deemed him to be a man unquestionably learned, possessed of a happy genius, a penetrating judgment, and multifarious reading—one, moreover, who was wont to deal more plainly and honestly than is the custom of other papists, to press his arguments more home, and to stick more closely to the question."[2]

So far from finding the Bible tedious or outmoded, the Reformers experienced the greatest delight in the constant study of it. It was for them a thrilling book. "Here is to be seen the triumph of God, the Lord of lords, and the King of kings; how He hath made the name of His Son triumph over principalities and powers, and over the whole world," says Bishop Jewel in praise of the Bible. "Here is a paradise full of delights: no tongue is able to speak them, they are so many; no heart is able to conceive them, they be so great. Here is a shop, wherein is set out the wisdom and knowledge, the power, the judgments, and mercies of God. Which way soever we look, we see the works of His hands; His works of creation, and preservation of all things; His works of severe justice upon the wicked, and of gracious redemption to the believer. If we desire pleasant music or excellent harmony, it speaketh unto

[1] Quoted in the Preface to Whitaker: *Op. cit.,* p. x.
[2] Whitaker: *Op. cit.,* p. 6.

us the words of the Father and the consent of the Son; the excellent reports of the prophets, apostles, angels, and saints of God, who have been all taught by the Holy Ghost. If we would learn, it is a school; it giveth understanding to the simple . . . So manifold and marvellous are the pleasures which are given us in the Word of God. God hath made them, and wrought them all for the sons of men."[1] The Reformers can still help us today to recapture this very spirit of joy and wonder and gratitude before God's gift of the Scriptures. Indeed, is it not the need of every generation, ours as well as theirs, to rediscover the Bible as the Word of God to fallen mankind?

[1] Jewel: *Works*, Vol. IV, p. 1182.

# II
# JUSTIFICATION

That we say, faith only justifieth, ought to offend no man. For if this be true, that Christ only redeemed us, Christ only bore our sins, made satisfaction for them, and purchased us the favour of God; then must it needs be true that the trust only in Christ's deserving and in the promises of God the Father, made to us for Christ's sake, doth alone quiet the conscience and certify it that the sins are forgiven.

*William Tyndale*

# II

## JUSTIFICATION

"We are accounted righteous before God, only for the merit of our Lord and Saviour Jesus Christ by faith, and not for our own works or deservings: wherefore that we are justified by faith only is a most wholesome doctrine." So says the eleventh of the Thirty-Nine Articles. This wholesome doctrine is the cutting edge of the sword of the Spirit which is the Word of God. It is the heartbeat of the New Covenant. The rediscovery of the Bible as the dynamic Word of God revolved round the experience of the truth of this evangelical doctrine to which its pages bear testimony. The crucial cry of the Reformation, as it is also the radical problem of man in his fallenness, was: "How can a man be justified with God?" (Job 25:4). In view of its cardinal significance, not least in those days of renewal, it is not surprising that Luther should have called justification by faith the article of a standing or falling Church. It was, however, a doctrine which needed very careful definition and explanation if it was not to be misapplied and misrepresented. This the Reformers were soon to learn. It is not faith as such and by itself that justifies. Indeed, there can be no such thing as bare faith; for faith must have an object. And the object of Christian faith is Christ. The Reformed doctrine of justification *by faith alone* does not mean by faith in isolation. It means that, where man's salvation is concerned, there is, negatively, no room at all for any notion of human merit, and, positively, there is only room for the merit of Christ.

In the first place, then, it must be emphasized that the Reformed doctrine of justification by faith is entirely Christ-centred, and not in any way man-centred. Faith that is not directed upon Christ as man's Saviour and the Bearer of his sins is neither saving faith nor Christian faith. "Catch thou hold of our Saviour," preaches Hugh Latimer, "believe in Him, be assured in thy heart that He with His suffering took away all thy sins . . . When we believe in Him it is like as if we had no sins. For He changeth with us: He taketh our sins and wickedness from us, and giveth unto us His holiness, righteousness, justice, fulfilling of the law, and so, consequently, everlasting life: so that we be like as if we had done no sin at all;

for his righteousness standeth us in so good stead, as though we of our own selves had fulfilled the law to the uttermost . . . Like as when I owe a man a hundred pounds: the day is expired, he will have his money; I have it not, and for lack of it I am laid in prison. In such distress cometh a good friend and saith, 'Sir, be of good cheer, I will pay thy debts'; and forthwith payeth the whole sum, and setteth me at liberty. Such a friend is our Saviour. He hath paid our debts, and set us at liberty; else we should have been damned world without end in everlasting prison and darkness. Therefore, though our sins condemn us, yet when we allege Christ and believe in Him our sins shall not hurt us."[1]

"The love that God hath to Christ is infinite," writes William Tyndale in his work on *The Parable of the Wicked Mammon*; "and Christ did and suffered all things not for Himself, to obtain favour or aught else; for He had ever the full favour of God, and was ever Lord over all things; but to reconcile us to God, and to make us heirs with Him of His Father's kingdom. And God hath promised that whosoever calleth on His name shall never be confounded or ashamed.[2] . . . Who is righteous but he that trusteth in Christ's blood, be he never so weak? Christ is our righteousness; and in Him ought we to teach all men to trust, and to expound unto all men the testament that God hath made to us sinners in Christ's blood."[3]

### BY FAITH ALONE

"The sum and whole cause of the writing of this epistle," says Tyndale again, in his *Prologue to the Epistle to the Romans*, "is to prove that a man is justified by faith only; which proposition whoso denieth, to him is not only this epistle and all that Paul writeth, but also the whole Scripture, so locked up, that he shall never understand it to his soul's health . . . And by justifying, understand no other thing than to be reconciled to God, and to be restored unto His favour, and to have thy sins forgiven thee. And when I say, God justifieth us, understand thereby that God for

[1] Latimer: *Works*, Vol. I, pp. 329f.    [2] Rom. 10:11f.
[3] Tyndale: *Works*, Vol. I, p. 95. This work was first published in 1528. A second edition appeared in 1536 with the expanded title: "A Treatise of Justification by Faith only, otherwise called the Parable of the Wicked Mammon." This indicates more precisely the scope of this work, to which we shall have occasion to make further reference during the course of this chapter.

Christ's sake, merits, and deservings only, receiveth us unto His mercy, favour, and grace, and forgiveth us our sins. And when I say, Christ justifieth us, understand thereby that Christ only hath redeemed us, bought, and delivered us out of the wrath of God and damnation, and hath with His works only purchased us the mercy, the favour, and grace of God, and the forgiveness of our sins. And when I say that faith justifieth, understand thereby that faith and trust in the truth of God and in the mercy promised us for Christ's sake, and for His deserving and works only, doth quiet the conscience and certify her that our sins be forgiven, and we in the favour of God. Furthermore, set before thine eyes Christ's works and thine own works. Christ's works only justify thee and make satisfaction for thy sin, and not thine own works . . . For the promise of mercy is made thee for Christ's work's sake, and not for thine own work's sake . . . Finally, that we say, faith only justifieth, ought to offend no man. For if this be true, that Christ only redeemed us, Christ only bare our sins, made satisfaction for them, and purchased us the favour of God; then must it needs be true that the trust only in Christ's deserving and in the promises of God the Father, made to us for Christ's sake, doth alone quiet the conscience and certify it that the sins are forgiven."[1] This deserves to be taken as the classic definition of the Reformed doctrine of justification. It is this teaching which pervades, or undergirds, all the preaching and writing of the Reformation.

Archbishop Cranmer writes no less classically of this great doctrine when, referring likewise to the Epistle to the Romans, he points out that there are three things "which must concur and go together in our justification: upon God's part, His great mercy and grace; upon Christ's part, justice, that is, the satisfaction of God's justice, or price of our redemption, by the offering of His body and shedding of His blood, with fulfilling of the law perfectly and thoroughly; and upon our part, true and lively faith in the merits of Jesus Christ, which (faith) yet is not ours, but by God's working in us. So that in our justification is not only God's mercy and grace, but also His justice, which the apostle calleth the justice of God; and it consisteth in paying our ransom, and fulfilling of the law: and so the grace of God doth not exclude the justice of God in our justification, but only excludeth the justice of man, that is to say, the justice of our works, as to be merits of deserving our

---

[1] Tyndale: *Works*, Vol. I, pp. 508f.

justification. And therefore St. Paul declareth here nothing upon
the behalf of man concerning his justification, but only a true and
lively faith; which nevertheless is the gift of God, and not man's
only work without God." [1]

After calling attention to the fact that this apostolic doctrine is
maintained in the writings of "the old and ancient authors, both
Greeks and Latins", Cranmer goes on to explain further that
"this proposition, that we be justified by faith only, freely, and
without works, is spoken for to take away clearly all merit of our
works, as being insufficient to deserve our justification at God's
hands, and thereby most plainly to express the weakness of man
and the goodness of God, the great infirmity of ourselves and the
might and power of God, the imperfectness of our own works and
the most abundant grace of our Saviour Christ; and thereby
wholly to ascribe the merit and deserving of our justification unto
Christ only and His most precious blood-shedding. This faith
the Holy Scripture teacheth; this is the strong rock and foundation
of Christian religion; this doctrine all old and ancient authors of
Christ's Church do approve; this doctrine advanceth and setteth
forth the true glory of Christ, and suppresseth the vain-glory of
man; this whosoever denieth is not to be reputed for a true
Christian man, nor for a setter-forth of Christ's glory, but for an
adversary of Christ and His Gospel, and for a setter-forth of men's
vain-glory . . . Justification is not the office of man, but of God:
for man cannot justify himself by his own works, neither in part
nor in the whole; for that were the greatest arrogancy and presumption of man that antichrist could erect against God, to affirm
that a man might by his own works take away and purge his own
sins, and so justify himself. But justification is the office of God
only, and it is not a thing which we render unto Him, but which
we receive of Him; not which we give to Him, but which we take
of Him, by His free mercy, and by the only merits of His most
dearly beloved Son, our only Redeemer, Saviour, and Justifier,
Jesus Christ. So that the true understanding of this doctrine, we
be justified freely by faith without works, or that we be justified
by faith in Christ only, is not that this our own act to believe in
Christ, or this our faith in Christ, which is within us, doth justify
us, and merit our justification unto us (for that were to count ourselves to be justified by some act or virtue that is within ourselves):

---

[1] Cranmer: *Homily on Salvation*, in *Works*, Vol. II, p. 129.

but the true understanding and meaning thereof is, that although
we hear God's Word, and believe it; although we have faith, hope,
charity, repentance, dread, and fear of God within us, and do
never so many good works thereunto; yet we must renounce the
merit of all our said virtues, of faith, hope, charity, and all our
other virtues and good deeds, which we either have done, shall do,
or can do, as things that be far too weak and insufficient and imperfect to deserve remission of our sins and our justification; and
therefore we must trust only in God's mercy, and in that sacrifice
which our High Priest and Saviour Jesus Christ, the Son of God,
once offered for us upon the cross, to obtain thereby God's grace
and remission, as well of our original sin in baptism as of all actual
sin committed by us after our baptism . . . So that our faith in
Christ (as it were) saith unto us thus: 'It is not I that take away
your sins, but it is Christ only; and to Him only I send you for
that purpose, renouncing therein all your good virtues, words,
thoughts, and works, and only putting your trust in Christ.' "[1]

BY GRACE ALONE

The Reformed doctrine of justification *by faith alone* cannot be
understood apart from the Reformed doctrine of justification *by
grace alone*. They are the two sides of the same coin. Together they
set forth that ascription of all the glory for what we are and do to
God—*soli Deo gloria*—which is the hallmark of the Reformation.
The importance of this emphasis cannot be overstated, because it is
characteristic of fallen man to ascribe glory to himself instead of
to God, to whom alone it belongs. Self-glory is vain-glory: it is
an expression of the sinful desire of the creature to be as God.
The twin doctrine of *sola fide* and *sola gratia* is, therefore, essential
for every age; but it was, in a historical sense, especially necessary
when the Reformation came, because for centuries it had been to
all intents and purposes submerged and stifled under an unevangelical accumulation of doctrines of merits by works, penances,
and payments, whereby men were led to hope that they might
perhaps win some acceptance with God. This inevitably meant
that man's justification before God, inasmuch as it was mixed up
with what man did, became a matter of uncertainty. The rediscovery of the Gospel of free grace set forth in Holy Scripture,
however, involved also the rediscovery of the believer's eternal

[1] Cranmer: *Works*, Vol. II, pp. 131 f.

security in Christ. Salvation in which man has even the smallest
hand is thereby invested with a degree of doubt. But salvation which
from beginning to end is entirely the work of God is invested with
complete assurance: as God's work, it cannot fail or be frustrated.

Within this setting of the total inability of man and the total
ability of God in the work of salvation we are able to reach a
proper comprehension of Article X: Of Free Will, which states:
"The condition of man after the fall of Adam is such that he cannot
turn and prepare himself, by his own natural strength and good
works, to faith and calling upon God: wherefore we have no power
to do good works pleasant and acceptable to God without the grace
of God by Christ preventing us, that we may have a good will, and
working with us, when we have that good will." And the same thing
must be said of Article XII: of Works before Justification, according
to which "works done before the grace of Christ and the inspiration
of His Spirit are not pleasant to God, forasmuch as they spring not
of faith in Jesus Christ; neither do they make men meet to receive
grace, or (as the School-authors say) deserve grace of congruity:
yea rather, for that they are not done as God hath willed and commanded them to be done, we doubt not but they have the nature
of sin". These Articles have been misunderstood when they have
been torn from their framework of justification and then misapplied
to a theological background for which they were never intended.
The Reformers had no wish to deny that in human society there are
standards of moral behaviour by comparison with which actions
may be described as either good or bad. What they were intent on
denying was that fallen man, none of whose actions are performed
to the glory of God, could in any way contribute to his own or
anyone else's salvation.

In his *Sermon on Repentance* John Bradford urges his hearers
with the following exhortation: "Dearly beloved, therefore abhor
this abomination, even to think that there is any other satisfaction
to God-ward for sin than Christ's blood only. Blasphemy it is, and
that horrible, to think otherwise. 'The blood of Christ purifieth',
saith St. John, 'from all sin'.[1] And therefore He is called 'the Lamb
slain from the beginning of the world',[2] because there was never
sin forgiven of God, nor shall be, from the beginning unto the end
of the world, but only through Christ's death."[3] And so also with
regard to the origin of the faith by which a man is justified:

[1] I Jn. 1:7.        [2] Rev. 13:8.        [3] Bradford: *Works*, Vol. I, pp. 48f.

"Faith is so far from the reach of man's free will that to reason it is plain foolishness. Therefore thou must first go to God, whose gift it is; thou must, I say, get thee to the Father of Mercy, whose work it is; that, as He hath brought thee down by contrition and humbled thee, so He would give thee faith, raise thee up, and exalt thee."[1]

Similarly, Tyndale admonishes us that "the true faith springeth not of man's fantasy, neither is it in any man's power to obtain it; but it is altogether the pure gift of God poured into us freely, without all manner doing of us, without deserving and merits, yea, and without seeking for of us; and is (as saith Paul in the second to the Ephesians)[2] even God's gift and grace, purchased through Christ. Therefore is it mighty in operation, full of virtue, and ever working; which also reneweth a man, and begetteth him afresh, altereth him, changeth him, and turneth him altogether into a new nature and conversation; so that a man feeleth his heart altogether altered and changed, and far otherwise disposed than before; and hath power to love that which before he could not but hate; and delighteth in that which before he abhorred; and hateth that which before he could not but love. And it setteth the soul at liberty, and maketh her free to follow the will of God." Nor is this faith something in isolation; for the Giver is present with the gift: "The Spirit of God accompanieth faith, and bringeth with her light, wherewith a man beholdeth himself in the law of God, and seeth his miserable bondage and captivity, and humbleth himself, and abhorreth himself . . . God worketh with His Word, and in His Word: and when His Word is preached faith rooteth herself in the hearts of the elect; and as faith entereth, and the Word of God is believed, the power of God looseth the heart from the captivity and bondage under sin, and knitteth and coupleth him to God and to the will of God."[3]

Again, he describes the priority of God's grace in the following words: "God chooseth us first and loveth us first, and openeth our eyes to see His exceeding abundant love to us in Christ; and then love we again, and accept His will above all things, and serve Him in that office whereunto He hath chosen us."[4] And in his *Prologue to the Book of Leviticus* he declares that "all that repent and believe in Christ are saved from everlasting death, of pure grace, without,

---

[1] Bradford: *Works*, Vol. I, p. 65.   [2] Eph. 2:8.
[3] Tyndale: *Works*, Vol. I, pp. 53f.   [4] Tyndale: *Ibid.*, p. 87.

and before, their good works; and not to sin again, but to fight against sin, and henceforth to sin no more". Tyndale, with the other Reformers, had learnt, from Scripture and also from experience, that " all the deeds in the world, save the blood of Christ, can purchase no forgiveness of sins".[1] So, too, in his *Homily of Salvation*, Cranmer insists that "our justification doth come freely by the mere mercy of God, and of so great and free mercy that, whereas all the world was not able of themselves to pay any part towards their ransom, it pleased our heavenly Father, of His infinite mercy, without any of our desert or deserving, to prepare for us the most precious jewels of Christ's body and blood, whereby our ransom might be fully paid, the law fulfilled, and His justice fully satisfied."[2]

We hear Hugh Latimer hammering home the same truth when preaching on the clause in the Lord's Prayer, "Forgive us our trespasses, as we forgive them that trespass against us": "Do I now, in forgiving my neighbour his sins which he hath done against me, do I, I say, deserve or merit at God's hand forgiveness of my own sins? No, no; God forbid! for if this should be so, then farewell Christ: it taketh Him clean away, it diminisheth His honour, and it is very treason wrought against Christ. This hath been in times past taught openly in the pulpits and in the schools; but it was very treason against Christ: for in Him only, and in nothing else, neither in heaven nor in earth, is our remission; unto Him only pertaineth this honour. For remission of sins, wherein consisteth everlasting life, is such a treasure, that passeth all men's doings: it must not be our merits that shall serve, but His. He is our comfort: it is the majesty of Christ, and His blood-shedding, that cleanseth us from our sins . . . So you see, as touching our salvation, we must not go to working to think to get everlasting life with our own doings. No, this were to deny Christ. Salvation, and remission of sins, is His gift, His own and free gift."[3]

The necessity of faith is not a necessity of human initiative, but a necessity of response to the divine initiative. Faith, as Latimer graphically says, is the hand wherewith we receive Christ's benefits.[4] But its consequence is even more than a receiving: it is a

[1] Tyndale: *Works*, Vol. I, p. 427.
[2] Cranmer: *Works*, Vol. II, p. 130.  [3] Latimer: *Works*, Vol. I, pp. 419f.
[4] Latimer: *Ibid.*, p. 418; cf. p. 454: "Faith is the hand wherewith we take everlasting life."

union. And it is this oneness with and in Christ that is the guarantee of our eternal security: the believer's destiny is none other than the destiny of Christ Himself. "Christ is thine, and all His deeds are thy deeds," says Tyndale. "Christ is in thee, and thou in Him, knit together inseparably. Neither canst thou be damned, except Christ be damned with thee; neither can Christ be saved, except thou be saved with Him." It is, moreover, God the Holy Spirit who seals this assurance to the believing heart: "Whosoever repenteth, believeth the Gospel, and putteth his trust in Christ's merits, the same is heir with Christ of eternal life; for assurance whereof the Spirit of God is poured into his heart as an earnest."[1]

There is, however, a faith which is not unto salvation. The Reformers, indeed, frequently point out that there are two kinds of faith—a right faith and a wrong faith, a dead faith and a lively faith. Tyndale addresses his readers as follows: "I pray thee how many thousands are there of them that say, 'I believe that Christ was born of a virgin, that He died, that He rose again', and so forth, and thou canst not bring them in belief that they have any sin at all! . . . For though they believe that Christ died, yet believe they not that He died for their sins, and that His death is a sufficient satisfaction for their sins; and that God, for His sake, will be a father unto them, and give them power to resist sin."[2] And Cranmer admonishes: "That faith which bringeth forth (without repentance) either evil works, or no good works, is not a right, pure, and lively faith, but a dead, devilish, counterfeit, and feigned faith, as St. Paul and St. James call it. For even the devils know and believe that Christ was born of a virgin, that He fasted forty days and forty nights without meat and drink, that He wrought all kinds of miracles, declaring Himself very God. They believe also that Christ for our sakes suffered most painful death, to redeem us from eternal death, and that He rose again from death the third day. They believe that He ascended into heaven, and that He sitteth on the right hand of the Father, and at the last end of this world shall come again, and judge both the quick and the dead. These articles of our faith the devils believe, and so they believe all things that be written in the New and Old Testament to be true: and yet for all this faith they be but devils, remaining

---

[1] Tyndale: *Works*, Vol. I., pp. 79, 113.
[2] Tyndale: *Ibid.*, pp. 121ff.

still in their damnable estate, lacking the very true Christian faith.
For the right and true Christian faith is not only to believe that
Holy Scripture and all the foresaid articles of our faith are true, but
also to have a sure trust and confidence in God's merciful promises, to be saved from everlasting damnation by Christ: whereof
doth follow a loving heart to obey His commandments."[1]

FAITH AND WORKS

Although the Reformers strenuously denied that by his works or
dispositions man could contribute anything at all to his justification
yet it is very far from being the truth that they had no place in their
system of Christianity for good works (as was commonly and
maliciously charged by their enemies). On the contrary, they gave
particular prominence to the importance of good works. They
excluded them only as a means to justification: good works do not
and cannot precede justification; but they must follow it, as light
and warmth follow the rising of the sun. Justification is not the
reward of good works; but good works are the proof of justification. "How," asks Cranmer, "can a man have this true faith, this
sure trust and confidence in God, that by the merits of Christ his
sins be remitted, and he reconciled to the favour of God, and to be
partaker of the kingdom of heaven by Christ, when he liveth ungodly and denieth Christ in his deeds? Surely no such ungodly
man can have this faith and trust in God . . . Therefore, to conclude, considering the infinite benefits of God, shewed and ex-
hibited unto us mercifully without our deserts . . .: these great and
merciful benefits of God, if they be well considered, do neither
minister unto us occasion to be idle, and to live without doing any
good works, nor yet stir us to do evil things; but contrariwise, if
we be not desperate persons and our hearts harder than stones,
they move us to render ourselves unto God wholly, with all our
will, hearts, might, and power, to serve Him in all good deeds,
obeying His commandments during our lives, to seek in all things
His glory and honour, not our sensual pleasures and vain-glory;
evermore dreading willingly to offend such a merciful God and
loving Redeemer, in word, thought, or deed. And the said benefits
of God, deeply considered, do move us for His sake also to be ever
ready to give ourselves to our neighbours, and, as much as lieth
in us, to study with all our endeavour to do good to every man.

[1] Cranmer: *Works*, Vol. II, p. 133.

These be the fruits of the true faith, to do good, as much as lieth
in us, to every man, and, above all things, and in all things, to
advance the glory of God, of whom only we have our sanctification, justification, salvation, and redemption."[1]

In his *Homily of Faith* Cranmer explains how "a true faith cannot be kept secret", but "will break out and show itself by good
works". He marshals evidence to demonstrate that "all Holy
Scripture agreeably beareth witness that a true and lively faith in
Christ doth bring forth good works", with the consequence that
"every man must examine himself diligently, to know whether
he have the same true lively faith in his heart unfeignedly, or not;
which he shall know by the fruits thereof". "Deceive not yourselves therefore," he exhorts, "thinking that you have faith in God,
or that you love God, or do trust in Him, or do fear Him, when
you live in sin; for then your ungodly and sinful life declareth the
contrary, whatsoever ye say or think. It pertaineth to a Christian
man to have this true Christian faith, and to try himself whether
he hath it or no, and to know what belongeth to it, and how it doth
work in him . . . Christ Himself speaketh of this matter, and saith:
'The tree is known by the fruit'.[2] Therefore let us do good works,
and thereby declare our faith to be the lively Christian faith. Let us
by such virtues as ought to spring out of faith show our election
to be sure and stable, as St. Peter teacheth: 'Endeavour yourselves
to make your calling and election certain by good works.'[3] . . . So
shall we show indeed that we have the very lively Christian faith,
and may so both certify our conscience the better that we be in the
right faith, and also by these means confirm other men. If these
fruits do not follow, we do but mock with God, deceive ourselves,
and also other men. Well may we bear the name of Christian men,
but we do lack the true faith that doth belong thereunto. For
true faith doth ever bring forth good works, as St. James saith:
'Show me thy faith by thy deeds.' Thy deeds and works must be an
open testimonial of thy faith: otherwise thy faith, being without
good works, is but the devil's faith, the faith of the wicked, a
fantasy of faith, and not a true Christian faith . . . Therefore, as
you profess the name of Christ, good Christian people, let no such
fantasy and imagination of faith at any time beguile you; but be
sure of your faith: try it by your living."[4]

[1] Cranmer: *Ibid.*, pp. 133f.    [2] Lk. 6:43f.
[3] II Pet. 1:10.    [4] Cranmer: *Ibid.*, pp. 136ff.; cf. Jas. 2: 14ff.

Similarly, Thomas Becon affirms, in the Preface to his *Commonplaces of the Holy Scripture*, that "works are the fruits of faith, and good testimonies unto our conscience that our faith is true and unfeigned; but helpers unto our justification or salvation they are not . . . As the sun cannot be without light nor the fire without heat, no more can the true and Christian faith be without good works, whensoever occasion is offered either for the glory of God or for the profit of our neighbour. If such faith ceaseth to work, then it is not an evangelical but an historical faith".[1]

The good works that follow and testify to a right faith are no more meritorious, however, than are works performed apart from true faith. They are, indeed, acceptable and pleasing to God, and they are required of Him; but they are performed by reason of the inward operation of the Holy Spirit in the regenerate life, and all the glory belongs to God who thus enables man to perform what He commands. "We are sure," says Tyndale, "that God hath created and made us new in Christ, and put His Spirit in us, that we should live a new life, which is the life of good works . . . The life of a Christian man is inward between him and God, and properly is the consent of the Spirit to the will of God and to the honour of God. And God's honour is the final end of all good works."[2] Again: "Every Christian man ought to have Christ always before his eyes as an example to counterfeit and follow, and to do to his neighbour as Christ hath done to him . . . Moreover, though thou show mercy unto thy neighbour, yet if thou do it not with such burning love as Christ did unto thee, so must thou acknowledge thy sin and desire mercy in Christ. A Christian man hath nought to rejoice in, as concerning his deeds. His rejoicing is that Christ died for him, and that he is washed in Christ's blood."[3]

It is true that the New Testament speaks in terms of rewards for those who prove themselves good and faithful servants of their heavenly Master. But even so all the merit is Christ's, and the faithful servant works not for the sake and for the love of the reward (in so far as he does, he is unfaithful and governed by self-interest), but for the sake and for the love of Christ. His work is freely rendered, and without all self-seeking. "When the Gospel is preached unto us," says Tyndale again, "we believe the mercy of

[1] Becon: *Works*, Vol. II, p. 291.     [2] Tyndale: *Works*, Vol. I, p. 90.
[3] Tyndale: *Ibid.*, pp. 96f.

God; and in believing we receive the Spirit of God, who is the earnest of eternal life, and we are in eternal life already, and feel already in our hearts the sweetness thereof, and are overcome with the kindness of God and Christ; and therefore love the will of God, and of love are ready to work freely; and not to obtain that which is given us freely, and whereof we are heirs already . . . So let thine eye be single, and look unto good living only, and take no thought for the reward, but be content: forasmuch as thou knowest and art sure that the reward, and all things contained in Christ's promises, follow good living naturally; and thy good works do but testify only and certify thee that the Spirit of God is in thee, whom thou has received for an earnest of God's truth, and that thou art heir of all the promises of God, and that all good things are thine already, purchased by Christ's blood, and laid up in store against that day when every man shall receive according to his deeds,[1] that is, according as his deeds declare and testify what he is and was. For they that look unto the reward are slow, false, subtle, and crafty workers, and love the reward more than the work; yea, hate the labour; yea, hate God who commandeth the labour; and are weary both of the commandment and also of the commander; and work with tediousness. But he that worketh of pure love, without seeking of reward, worketh truly."[2]

"Your reward shall be great in heaven," quotes Latimer when preaching on the Beatitudes. "*Merces*, 'reward': this word soundeth as though we should merit somewhat by our own works," he exclaims: "for reward and merit are correspondent, one followeth the other; when I have merited, then I ought to have my reward. But we shall not think so: for ye must understand that all our works are imperfect; we cannot do them so perfectly as the law requireth, because of our flesh, which ever hindereth us. Wherefore is the kingdom of God called then a reward? Because it is merited by Christ: for as touching our salvation and eternal life, it must be merited, but not by our own works, but only by the merits of our Saviour Christ. Therefore believe in Him, trust in Him; it is He that merited heaven for us."[3] Tyndale sums the matter up admirably when he writes (in his *Prologue to the Book of Numbers*): "All that I do and suffer is but the way to the reward, and not the deserving thereof"; and again: "Christ is Lord over all, and whatsoever

---

[1] Cf. II Cor. 5:10, Rev. 22:12.    [2] Tyndale: *Ibid.*, pp. 65f.
[3] Latimer: *Works*, Vol. I, p. 488.

any man will have of God, he must have it freely given him for Christ's sake. Now to have heaven for mine own deserving is mine own praise, and not Christ's. For I cannot have it by favour and grace in Christ and by mine own merits also; for free giving and deserving cannot stand together."[1]

WORKS AND MERIT

The controversy over works and merit in the sixteenth century was, it must be remembered, a controversy concerned with the question of man's justification. It revolved around the doctrine of salvation. The doctrine of the common grace of God, whereby a measure of social morality and civic justice is preserved in the world at large, including unregenerate society, was not debated because it was not the point at issue. (The Reformers were not unfamiliar with the doctrine of common grace, as is shown, for example, by the assertion of Bradford that "the wicked have not God's Spirit of sanctification and regeneration to sanctify and regenerate them, though they have it concerning other gifts".)[2] The strictures of Articles XII, XIII, and XIV are not intended to deny the degrees of goodness in the social and civic realms, but to deny that good works are ever meritorious in such a way as to deserve the justification of sinful man before God. Thus Article XII, which relates to those works that are performed subsequently to salvation, declares: "Albeit that good works, which are the fruits of faith, and follow after justification, cannot put away our sins, and endure the severity of God's judgment; yet are they pleasing and acceptable to God in Christ, and do spring out necessarily from a true and lively faith, insomuch that by them a lively faith may be as evidently known as a tree discerned by the fruit." The scope of Article XIII is defined by its title, "Of Works before Justification": "Works done before the grace of Christ and the inspiration of His Spirit," it says, "are not pleasant to God, forasmuch as they spring not of faith in Jesus Christ, neither do they make men meet to receive grace, or (as the School authors say) deserve grace of congruity: yea, rather, for that they are not done as God hath willed and commanded them to be done, we doubt not but they have the nature of sin." And Article XIV addresses itself to the assumption that there is a possibility of doing more than God requires, with

[1] Tyndale: *Works*, Vol. I, pp. 434, 436.
[2] Bradford: *Works*, Vol. I, p. 303.

the corollary of the establishment of a bank of surplus merit which may be drawn upon, at a charge, by those whose works fall short in performance. "Voluntary works," it reads, "besides, over, and above God's commandments, which they call works of supererogation, cannot be taught without arrogancy and impiety: for by them men do declare that they do not only render unto God as much as they are bound to do, but that they do more for His sake than of bounden duty is required: whereas Christ saith plainly, 'When ye have done all that are commanded to you, say, we are unprofitable servants.' "[1]

Pilkington explains that "although God do work all things Himself, and as He hath appointed so they fall out, yet He worketh them not without us: we must not be idle, we must show our diligence and due obedience to our God, that He hath made us, and commanded us to exercise ourselves in these things; and yet, when we have done all we can, all the praise must be given to Him, and we must say, 'We be unprofitable servants'. We be as an axe in the carpenter's hand," he continues, "where the axe may not claim the praise of well-doing from his master that worketh with it: and though the axe be a dead instrument without life or feeling, and man hath life, wit, and reason given him to do things withal; yet is man as unable to work his own salvation without the free mercy and special grace of God as the axe is unable to build the house without the direction and ruling of the carpenter."[2] And Bradford preaches as follows: "As concerning satisfaction by their *opera indebita*, 'undue works', that is, by such works as they need not to do but of their own voluntariness and wilfulness (wilfulness indeed!), who seeth not monstrous abomination, blasphemy, and even open fighting against God? For if satisfaction can be done by man, then Christ dies in vain for him that so satisfieth: and so reigneth He in vain; so is He a bishop and a priest in vain. God's law requireth love to God with all our heart, soul, power, might, and strength; so that there is nothing can be done to God-ward which is not contained in this commandment; nothing can be done over and above this. Again Christ requireth that to man-ward 'we should love one one another as He loved us': and trow we that we can do any good thing to our neighbour-ward which is not herein comprised? . . . Dearly beloved, therefore, abhor this abomination, even to think that there is any other satisfaction to God-ward for sin than

[1] Lk. 17:10.  [2] Pilkington: *Works*, p. 445.

Christ's blood only. Blasphemy it is, and that horrible, to think otherwise. 'The blood of Christ purifieth', saith St. John, 'from all sin'.[1] And therefore He is called 'the Lamb slain from the beginning of the world';[2] because there was never sin forgiven of God, nor shall be, from the beginning unto the end of the world, but only through Christ's death."[3]

The conception of works of supererogation implied a two-level doctrine of Christian morality. Such supererogatory works belonged not to the sphere of the ordinary man and woman but to the small super-Christian minority who, by voluntarily living as solitary hermits or in monastic communities, by voluntarily submitting themselves to the rule of poverty, chastity, and obedience, and by voluntarily afflicting their bodies with painful indignities, were regarded as having achieved a holiness beyond what was required of them. But with ordinary-level Christianity the situation was very different. It was not long after the apostolic period when, with a view to the improvement of church discipline, and coupled with a particular application of passages like Heb. 6:4f. and 10:26f., the doctrine was developed that at baptism all sins were washed away by the blood of Christ, but that this blood did not avail for sins committed after baptism, with the result that such sins could be expiated only by the endurance of such penalties and penances as the Church might impose on the offender. This led to the phase in church history when it became a common practice for persons to postpone their baptism, if possible, until the hour of death, in the hope that in this way they might be assured of passing into the next world free from sin. Such, indeed, was the spiritual insecurity and uncertainty engendered by this teaching that it led further to the doctrine of purgatory, according to which, no penances, however many and severe, being regarded as sufficient to purge away all the defilements of post-baptismal sin, the Christian man would ordinarily have to pass through a prolonged period of purgation by flames before he was fit to enter into the heavenly state. For ordinary-level Christians accordingly—and that meant the great mass of church members—the Christian way after baptism became one of self-effort and self-suffering, without that assured confidence in the redeeming work and suffering of Christ in which the New Testament encourages us to trust. And for Christianity at both levels life became a preoccupation with

[1] Jn. 1:7.　　　[2] Rev. 13:8.　　　[3] Bradford: *Works*, Vol. I, pp. 47ff.

the inescapable problem of one's own justification and acceptance before God.

The rediscovery of the Gospel which brought in the Reformation inevitably meant the exposure of the unevangelical nature of all such teaching. Hence the statement of Article XVI, entitled "Of Sin after Baptism": "Not every deadly sin willingly committed after baptism is sin against the Holy Ghost, and unpardonable. Wherefore the grant of repentance is not to be denied to such as fall into sin after baptism. After we have received the Holy Ghost we may depart from grace given and fall into sin, and by the grace of God we may rise again and amend our lives. And therefore they are to be condemned who say they can no more sin as long as they live here, or deny the place of forgiveness to such as truly repent." Thomas Becon uses the Apostle Peter as an example: 'That sinners may receive remission of their sins, though they sin after they have known the truth and are baptized, it is manifest by divers places of the New Testament. Who doubteth but that Peter was both baptized and knew the truth when he confessed Christ to be the Son of the living God? . . . Yet did he fall again after that when he denied Christ . . . Did not he afterward, when he repented, obtain mercy at the hand of God? . . . Hereof doth it follow that remission of sins is not denied unto sinners, if they repent and believe."[1]

"When they say that Christ hath made no satisfaction for the sin we do after our baptism," writes William Tyndale, "say thou with the doctrine of Paul that in our baptism we receive the merits of Christ's death through repentance and faith, of which two baptism is the sign; and though when we sin of frailty after our baptism we receive the sign no more, yet we be renewed again through repentance and faith in Christ's blood; of which twain that sign of baptism, ever continued among us in baptizing our young children, doth ever keep us in mind, and call us back again unto our profession, if we be gone astray, and promiseth us forgiveness. Neither can actual sin be washed away with our works, but with Christ's blood; neither can there be any other sacrifice or satisfaction to God-ward for them save Christ's blood: forasmuch as we can do no works unto God, but receive only of His mercy with our repenting faith, through Jesus Christ our Lord and only Saviour: unto whom, and unto God our Father through Him, and

[1] Becon: *Works*, Vol. I, p. 96.

unto His Holy Spirit, that only purgeth, sanctifieth, and washeth us in the innocent blood of our redemption, be praise for ever. Amen."[1]

## PURGATORY AND PRAYERS FOR THE DEAD

As for the doctrine of purgatory, "that fiery furnace that hath burned away so many of our pence", as Latimer feelingly described it,[2] the Reformers denounced it with one voice as unscriptural and dishonouring to Christ. Their attitude is summed up in the *Homily concerning Prayer* (attributed to Bishop Jewel): "The only purgatory wherein we must trust to be saved is the death and blood of Christ, which if we apprehend with a true and steadfast faith, it purgeth and cleanseth us from all our sins, even as well as if He were now hanging upon the cross."[3] Article XXII dismisses "the Romish doctrine concerning purgatory" as "a fond thing vainly invented, and grounded upon no warranty of Scripture, but rather repugnant to the Word of God".

In his *Answer to the Fifteen Articles of the Devon Rebels* Archbishop Cranmer gives this rejoinder to the demand that prayers and masses should be offered for the souls in purgatory: "What a contumely and injury is this to Christ, to affirm that all have not full and perfect purgation by His blood that die in His faith! Is not all our trust in the blood of Christ, that we be cleansed, purged, and washed thereby? And will you have us now to forsake our faith in Christ, and bring us to the pope's purgatory to be washed therein, thinking that Christ's blood is an imperfect lee or soap that washeth not clean? If he shall die without mercy that treadeth Christ's blood under his feet, what is treading of His blood under our feet if this be not? But if according to the catholic faith, which the Holy Scripture teacheth, and the prophets, apostles, and martyrs confirmed with their blood, all the faithful that die in the Lord be pardoned of all their offences by Christ, and their sins be clearly sponged and washed away by His blood, shall they after be cast into another strong and grievous prison of purgatory, there to be punished again for that which was pardoned before? God hath promised by His Word that the souls of the just be in God's hand, and no pain shall touch them; and again he saith, 'Blessed be they

---

[1] Tyndale: *Works*, Vol. I, p. 466.    [2] Latimer: *Works*, Vol. I, p. 36.
[3] *Certain Sermons or Homilies appointed to be read in Churches* (London, 1899 edn.), p. 356.

that die in the Lord. For the Spirit of God saith that from henceforth they shall rest from their pains'.[1] And Christ Himself saith:
'He that believeth in Him that sent me hath everlasting life and
shall not come into judgment, but shall pass from death unto
life.'[2] And is God no truer of His promises but to punish that
which He promiseth to pardon? Consider the matter by your own
cases. If the king's majesty should pardon your offences, and after
would cast you into prison, would you think that he had well
observed his promise? For what is to pardon your offences but to
pardon the punishment for the same? If the king would punish
you would you take that for a pardon? Would you not allege your
pardon and say that you ought not to be punished? Who can, then,
that hath but a crumb of reason in his head, imagine of God that
He will after our death punish those things that He pardoned in
our lifetime?"[3]

Hooper states the Reformed position succinctly in the twenty-
sixth article of his *Brief and Clear Confession of the Christian Faith.*
"I do believe and confess", he says, "that Christ's condemnation is mine absolution; that His crucifying is my deliverance; His
descending into hell is mine ascending into heaven; His death is
my life; His blood is my cleansing and purging, by whom only I
am washed, purified, and cleansed from all my sins: so that I
neither receive neither believe any other purgatory, either in this
world or in the other, whereby I may be purged, but only the blood
of Jesus Christ, by the which all are purged and made clean for
ever".[4]

If purgatory is unscriptural, so also is the offering of prayers for
the dead. "In Holy Scripture," Bradford points out, "throughout
the canonical books of the Old and New Testament, we find neither
precept nor example of praying for any when they be departed this
life, but that, as men die, so shall they arise . . . 'Every man shall
receive according to that he himself doeth in this body, while he is
here alive, be it good or bad',[5] and not according to what his
executors or this chantry priest and that fraternity doth for him.
Whereby we may well see, if we will, that, as prayer for the dead is
not available or profitable to the dead, so is it not of us allowable
to be exercised. For, as they that are departed be past our prayers,
being either in joy or in misery, . . . even so we, having for it no

[1] Rev. 14:13.    [2] Jn. 5:24    [3] Cranmer: *Works*, Vol. II, pp. 181f.
[4] Hooper: *Works*, Vol. II, pp. 31f.    [5] II Cor. 5:10.

word of God, whereupon faith leaneth, cannot but sin in doing it, in that we do it 'not of faith',[1] because we have no word of God for it."[2]

"He that cannot be saved by faith in Christ's blood, how shall he look to be delivered by man's intercessions?" asks the *Homily concerning Prayer*. "Hath God more respect to man on earth than He hath to Christ in heaven? 'If any man sin', saith St. John, 'we have an advocate with the Father, even Jesus Christ the righteous, and He is the propitiation for our sins'.[3] But we must take heed that we call upon this Advocate while we have space given us in this life, lest, when we are once dead, there be no hope of salvation left unto us. For, as every man sleepeth with his own cause, so every man shall rise again with his own cause. And look, in what state he dieth, in the same state he shall be also judged, whether it be to salvation or damnation. Let us not therefore dream either of purgatory or of prayer for the souls of them that be dead; but let us earnestly and diligently pray for them who are expressly commanded in Holy Scripture, namely, for kings and rulers, for ministers of God's holy Word and sacraments, for the saints of this world, otherwise called the faithful, to be short, for all men living, be they never so great enemies to God and His people."[4]

Another custom condemned by the Reformers as contrary to the teaching of Scripture was that of praying to the saints. In particular, they rejected the practice as a violation of the sole mediatorship of our Lord Jesus Christ. John Bradford states the Reformed doctrine in the following terms: "Here we confess, teach, and believe, as before is said, according to God's holy Word, that, as all and every good thing cometh only from God the Father by the means of Jesus Christ, so for the obtaining of the same we must call upon His holy name, as He by Himself commandeth very often. But, forasmuch as God 'dwelleth in light inaccessible'[5] and 'is a consuming fire'[6] and hateth all impiety and uncleanness, and we be blind, stubble, grass, hay, and nothing but filthy, unclean, and sinful; and because that therefore, as we may not, so we dare not approach to His presence; it hath pleased this God and Father of His love to send a Spokesman and a Mediator, an Intercessor and Advocate between Him and us, even Jesus Christ, His dearly

---

[1] Rom. 14:23.
[2] Bradford: *Works*, Vol. II, p. 279.
[3] I Jn. 2:1f.
[4] *Homilies, ut supra*, p. 357.
[5] I Tim. 6:16.
[6] Heb. 12:29.

beloved Son, by whom we might have free entrance 'with boldness to come before His presence and throne of mercy, to find and obtain grace to help in time of need'.[1] For this our Mediator and Advocate is with His Father of the same substance, power, wisdom, and majesty, and therefore we may weigh well with Him in all things; and with us He is of the same substance which we are of, even flesh and man, but pure and 'without sin, in all things being tempted like unto us', and having experience of our infirmities, that He might be merciful and faithful on our behalf, to 'purge us from our sins',[2] and to bring us into such favour with the Father that we might be not only dearly beloved through Him, the only darling of the Father, but also obtain whatsoever we shall ask, according to His Word and will, in the name of this same our Mediator, Saviour, Intercessor, and Advocate.[3] So that easy it is to see that, as it is an obedient service to God the Father to call always upon Him in all our need, so to come to His presence through Christ is the honour of Christ's mediation, intercession, and advocateship. And therefore, as it cannot be but against the almighty God and Father to ask or look for anything elsewhere, at the hands of any that be departed this life, as though He were not the giver of all good things, or as though He had not commanded us to come unto Him, so we see it is manifestly against Christ Jesus our Lord, by any other saint, angel, or archangel to come and move anything at our Father's hands; as though He were not our Mediator, Advocate, and Intercessor, or else not a sufficient Mediator, Advocate, and Intercessor, or at least not so merciful, meek, gracious, loving, and ready to help as others: where He only so loved us, as the very hearts of all men and angels never were able to conceive any part of 'the height, depth, breadth, and length[4]' of the same, as it is."[5]

Archbishop Sandys appropriately cites the cases of repudiation of the worship offered by their fellow-men to Peter, Paul and Barnabas, and John: "The honour which Cornelius gave unto Peter was more than was fit to be given to a man. For Peter refused it with that reason: 'I myself am a man too'.[6] This zeal and reverence that he had to the Word made him overreach in honouring the minister of it. So did the men of Lystra honour Paul and

[1] Heb. 4:15f.
[2] Heb. 2:16ff., 4:15, 5:1ff., 1:3.
[3] Eph. 1:6, Mt. 3:17, 17:5, Jn. 14:13f.
[4] Eph.3 :18f.
[5] Bradford: *Works*, Vol. II, pp. 281f.
[6] Acts 10:25f.

Barnabas; but they said in like sort: 'O men, why do ye these things? We are men, subject to the like passions that ye be.'[1] John would have worshipped the angel likewise; but the angel refused: 'See thou do it not; I am thy fellow-servant: worship God.'[2] Here we learn how dangerously religious honour is given to any creature. It cannot be thought that either Cornelius or John would rob God of His glory, and give it to angel or man. But yet they were forbidden to do that which they did, lest they should attribute more to the messenger of God than they ought, through preposterous zeal. It is not so great a danger to honour a prince with all humility: therein men cannot so easily exceed, because the honour is civil. But the danger is in a spiritual person, lest in respect of his holy office they honour him too much."[3]

In his *Apology of the Church of England* Bishop Jewel writes: "Neither have we any other mediator and intercessor, by whom we may have access to God the Father, then Jesus Christ, in whose only name all things are obtained at His Father's hand. But it is a shameful part, and full of infidelity, that we see everywhere used in the churches of our adversaries, not only in that they will have innumerable sorts of mediators and that utterly without the authority of God's Word; so that, as Jeremiah saith, the saints be now 'as many in number or rather above the number of the cities';[4] and poor men cannot tell to which saint it were best to turn them first; and, though there be so many as they cannot be told, yet every one of them hath his peculiar duty and office assigned unto him of these folks, what thing they ought to ask, what to give, and what to bring to pass—but besides this also, in that they do not only wickedly but also shamelessly call upon the blessed virgin, Christ's mother, to have her remember that she is a mother, and to command her Son, and to use a mother's authority over Him."[5]

THE ORDER OF SALVATION

Closely linked in the Reformers' minds with the doctrine of justification was that of predestination. The Apostle describes the spiritual state of fallen man in terms of being "dead in trespasses and sins".[6] Man, as we have seen, commensurably with this teaching, is able neither to save himself nor even to contribute in the

---

[1] Acts 14:13ff.	[2] Rev. 22:8f.
[3] Sandys: *Works*, p. 272.	[4] Jer. 2:28, 11:13.
[5] Jewel: *Works*, Vol. III, p. 65.	[6] Eph. 2:1.

smallest degree to his salvation. His will is enslaved; his god is the god of this world. Like Lazarus, swathed from head to foot with burial wrappings and corrupting in the tomb, he is bound by his sins and his nature is corrupted in the death of separation from the true God. Like Lazarus, too, his only hope of being raised to newness of life is through the dynamic utterance of the divine voice of his Creator. Salvation, therefore, from beginning to end is the sovereign work of almighty God. God's bestowal of grace, however, is not capricious, haphazard, or dependent on an unpredictable development of events. Those who through His grace are brought to salvation have been chosen from all eternity and "predestinated according to the purpose of Him who worketh all things after the counsel of His own will".[1] They are taken up into the scheme of God's everlasting purpose. All is of God, from eternity to eternity. It is on this truth that the Christian's eternal security in Christ rests. Article XVII, "Of Predestination and Election", is concerned with this theme: "Predestination to life," it declares, " is the everlasting purpose of God whereby (before the foundations of the world were laid) He hath constantly decreed by His counsel secret to us, to deliver from curse and damnation those whom He hath chosen in Christ out of mankind, and to bring them by Christ to everlasting salvation, as vessels made to honour."

This leads to a statement of the order or sequence of the whole course of salvation: "Wherefore they which be endued with so excellent a benefit of God be called according to God's purpose by His Spirit working in due season: they through grace obey the calling: they be justified freely: they be made sons of God by adoption: they be made like the image of His only-begotten Son Jesus Christ: they walk religiously in good works, and at length, by God's mercy, they attain to everlasting felicity." This doctrine is a source of unfailing assurance to the believer and a constant spur to holy living; it also enables him to take a proper view both of himself and of God, and causes him to ascribe all the praise and the glory of his salvation to the sovereign goodness of divine grace. Thus the Article proceeds to affirm that "the godly consideration of predestination and our election in Christ is full of sweet, pleasant, and unspeakable comfort to godly persons and such as feel in themselves the working of the Spirit of Christ, mortifying the works of the flesh and their earthly members, and drawing up their

[1] Eph. 1:11.

mind to high and heavenly things, as well because it doth greatly establish and confirm their faith of eternal salvation to be enjoyed through Christ, as because it doth fervently kindle their love towards God."

The order of salvation is, indeed, a matter of some importance for those who wish to have some understanding of the nature and the sequence of God's dealings with His creatures in bringing them to newness of life. This order is expressed in its fullest scope in Rom. 8:29f., where the Apostle says that whom God did foreknow "He also did predestinate to be conformed to the image of His Son; . . . moreover, whom He did predestinate them He also called; and whom He called them He also justified; and whom He justified them He also glorified." Nothing could emphasize more effectively that God alone is the author of man's salvation in its entirety. The Reformers teach that in the experience of justification there is a succession from repentance to faith, and from faith to love. "Note now the order," says Tyndale in his *Answer to Sir Thomas More's Dialogue*: "first God giveth me light to see the goodness and righteousness of the law, and mine own sin and unrighteousness; out of which knowledge springeth repentance. Now repentance teacheth me not that the law is good and I evil, but a light that the Spirit of God hath given me, out of which light repentance springeth. Then the same Spirit worketh in mine heart trust and confidence to believe the mercy of God and His truth, that He will do as He hath promised; which belief saveth me. And immediately out of that trust springeth love toward the law of God again. And whatsoever a man worketh of any other love than this, it pleaseth not God, nor is that love godly. Now love doth not receive this mercy, but faith only, out of which faith love springeth; by which love I pour out again upon my neighbour that goodness which I have received of God by faith. Hereof ye see that I cannot be justified without repentance; and yet repentance justifieth me not. And hereof ye see that I cannot have a faith to be justified and saved, except love spring thereof immediately; and yet love justifieth me not before God. For my natural love to God again doth not make me first see and feel the kindness of God in Christ, but faith through preaching. For we love not God first, to compel Him to love again; but He loved us first, and gave His Son for us, that we might see and love again.[1] . . . And when we say, faith only

[1] I Jn. 4:10.

justifieth us, that is to say, receiveth the mercy wherewith God justifieth us and forgiveth us, we mean not faith which hath no repentance, and faith which hath no love unto the laws of God again, and unto good works, as wicked hypocrites falsely belie us."[1]

Again, in *The Parable of the Wicked Mammon*, Tyndale analyses the apostolic method of proclamation and instruction: "This order useth Paul in all his epistles," he writes: "first, he preacheth the law, and proveth that the whole nature of man is damned, in that the heart lusteth contrary to the will of God . . . Then preacheth he Christ, the Gospel, the promises, and the mercy that God hath set forth to all men in Christ's blood; which they that believe, and take it for an earnest thing, turn themselves to God, begin to love God again, and to prepare themselves to His will, by the working of the Spirit of God in them. Last of all, exhorteth he to unity peace, and soberness; to avoid brawlings, sects, opinions, disputing and arguing about words; and to walk in the plain and single faith and feeling of the Spirit; and to love one another after the example of Christ, even as Christ loved us; and to be thankful, and to walk worthy of the Gospel and as it becometh Christ; and with the example of pure living to draw all to Christ."[2]

The ultimate stage in the order of salvation is the glorification of the redeemed. The doctrine of election places the believer in a position free from all doubt and uncertainty concerning his final destiny, for it reveals, as we have already been reminded by Article XVII, that in accordance with God's everlasting purposes those who are Christ's will at length, by God's mercy, attain to everlasting felicity. Preaching on Lk. 1:74 ("that we being delivered out of the hand of our enemies might serve Him without fear") Archbishop Sandys says: "Him we must serve 'without fear' . . . The believing Christian, the regenerate child of God, who through faith in Christ is certain of his deliverance from the devil and from hell, assured of remission of sins and of life everlasting in the death and resurrection of Jesus Christ our Saviour, he serveth in the reverent fear of love, and not in that dreadful fear of death and everlasting damnation, wherewith the reprobate mind is daunted. He feareth not death, for he is sure of life: he feareth not damnation, for he is assured of salvation: he believeth that which Christ hath promised, and doubteth nothing of the

---

[1] Tyndale: *Works*, Vol. III, pp. 195f.
[2] Tyndale: *Works*, Vol. I, pp. 96f.

3*

obtaining of that which Christ hath procured for him. He is surely
persuaded with St. Paul that 'neither death, nor life, nor tribulation, nor affliction, nor anything present, or to come, shall separate
him from the love of God which is in Christ Jesus'.[1] He feareth
therefore neither the sting of death nor the power of Satan.[2] But
this certainty of God's love towards him in Christ, and the testimony of his love towards God again, casteth out all fear of eternal
punishment. 'For ye have not', saith the Apostle, 'received again
the spirit of bondage unto fear, but ye have received the Spirit of
adoption, by which we cry Abba, Father'. This Spirit testifieth
with our spirit that God is our gracious Father; and if He our
Father, we His children; and if His children, heirs of His glorious
kingdom.[3] . . . And this certainty of our salvation the Spirit of God
testifieth to our spirit, whereby we put away all servile fear of
punishment, being assured of God's constant favour and eternal
love towards us; who never leaveth unfinished that which He hath
begun, nor forsaketh him whom he hath chosen."[4]

If our salvation is altogether the work of God, then there is no
possibility of its failing. "He hath begun a good work in you, He
will finish it," declares Jewel, commenting on I Thess. 5:24
('Faithful is He that calleth you, who also will do it') and bringing
together a chain of scriptural promises. "He will lead you from
virtue to virtue, from strength to strength, from glory to glory.
He hath called you, He will also keep you faithful until the day of
the appearing of our Lord Jesus Christ. You are Christ's sheep.
No man shall take you out of His hands. He hath not lost one of all
them whom His Father had given Him. He knoweth His sheep.
None shall be confounded that put their trust in Him. There is no
condemnation to them that be in Christ Jesus. He is faithful, He
will perform this unto you; not for your merits, but for His own
name, and for His mercy's sake. Because He is faithful, He will
not despise the work of His own hands."[5] Again, commenting on
II Thess. 2:13, he writes: "God hath chosen you from the beginning: His election is sure for ever. The Lord knoweth who are His.
You shall not be deceived with the power and subtlety of antichrist, you shall not fall from grace, you shall not perish. This is the
comfort which abideth with the faithful when they behold the fall
of the wicked . . . Although all the world should be drowned with

---

[1] Rom. 8:38.          [2] I Cor. 15:55.          [3] Rom. 8:15ff.
[4] Sandys: *Works*, pp. 184ff.          [5] Jewel: *Works*, Vol. II, pp. 885f.

the waves of ungodliness, yet will I hold by the boat of His mercy, which shall utterly preserve me. If all the world be set on fire with the flame of wickedness, yet will I creep into the bosom of the protection of my Lord; so shall no flame hurt me. He hath loved me, He hath chosen me, He will keep me."[1]

JUSTIFICATION BEFORE CHRIST'S ADVENT

The question naturally arose concerning the justification of the Old Testament saints who lived before the coming of Christ. If salvation is through faith alone in the atoning work of Christ, what standing can they have? To this question the Reformers have but one answer, namely, that the saints of the old dispensation had the same faith in Christ as Saviour as we have, only they believed in the promises of God yet to be fulfilled, whereas we look back on the fulfilment of these promises in Christ. Ours, indeed, is the fuller knowledge, for we enjoy the light of the new covenant; but the new covenant is identical in heart and essence with the old, and it is one and the same Redeemer in whom we trust. "They believed in Abraham's Seed which was promised," says Latimer: "which faith stood them in good stead, and they were all as well saved through that same belief as we now through our belief. For it is no difference between their belief and ours, but this: they believed in Christ who was to come, and we believe in Christ who is come already. Now their belief served them as well as ours doth us. For at that time God required no further at their hands than was opened unto them. We have in our time a further and more perfect knowledge of Christ than they had."[2]

In his famous Sermon of the Plough Latimer declares, with reference to Christ as "the Lamb slain from the foundation of the world"[3] and as "a continual sacrifice",[4] that "all men that trusted in the death of Christ shall be saved, as well they that came before as they that came after; for He was a continual sacrifice, as I said, in effect, fruit, operation, and virtue, as though He had from the beginning of the world, and continually should to the world's end, hang still on the cross; and He is as fresh hanging on the cross now, to them that believe and trust in Him, as He was fifteen hundred years ago when He was crucified."[5] This is genuinely biblical

---

[1] Jewel; *Ibid.*, p. 933.
[2] Latimer: *Works*, Vol. I, p. 378.
[3] Rev. 13:8.
[4] Cf. Dan. 8:11f., Vg. *juge sacrificium.*
[5] Latimer: *Ibid.*, p. 73.

existentialism (to use a term of our twentieth century): while the unique once-for-all character of Christ's redeeming death is stressed over and over again by the Reformers, yet it is a present reality "in effect, fruit, operation, and virtue" throughout every age of human history.

"All these fathers, martyrs, and other holy men whom St. Paul spoke of[1] had their faith surely fixed in God, when all the world was against them," writes Cranmer in the *Homily of Faith*. "They did not only know God to be Lord, maker, and governor of all men in the world, but also they had a special confidence and trust that He was and would be their God, their comforter, aider, helper, maintainer, and defender. This is the Christian faith which these holy men had, and we also ought to have. And although they were not named Christian men, yet was it a Christian faith that they had; for they looked for all benefits of God the Father through the merits of His Son Jesus Christ, as we now do. This difference is between them and us: for they looked when Christ should come, and we be in the time when He is come. Therefore saith St. Augustine: 'The time is altered, but not the faith.'[2] For we have both one faith in one Christ. The same Holy Ghost also that we have had they, saith St. Paul . . . God gave them then grace to be His children, as He doth us now. But now, by the coming of our Saviour Christ, we have received more abundantly the Spirit of God in our hearts, whereby we may conceive a greater faith and a surer trust than many of them had. But in effect they and we be all one: we have the same faith that they had in God, and they the same that we have. And St. Paul so much extolleth their faith because we should no less, but rather more, give ourselves wholly unto Christ both in profession and living, now when Christ is come, than the old fathers did before His coming."[3]

It is the doctrine of justification, finally, which unlocks for us the whole purpose of Holy Scripture; for it must not be forgotten that the revelation of the Written Word is integrally connected with the divine scheme for the redemption of mankind. In the reading of Scripture we meet with two things: firstly, the laws and requirements of God, in comparison with which we stand condemned as guilty sinners and rebellious law-breakers and become aware of our urgent need for justification before God; and, secondly, we are

---

[1] In Heb. 11.      [2] Augustine: *Tract. in Joann.*, XLV.
[3] Cranmer: *Works*, Vol. II, p. 138.

confronted with the gracious promises of God's covenant and Gospel, and are assured that these promises are given, as William Tyndale says, in his *Prologue to the Prophet Jonah*, "unto a repenting soul that thirsteth and longeth after them, of the pure and fatherly mercy of God, through our faith only, without all deserving of our deeds or merits of our works, but for Christ's sake alone, and for the merits and deservings of His works, death, and passions that He suffered altogether for us, and not for Himself". These two points affirms Tyndale, "if they be written in thine heart, are the keys which so open all the Scriptures unto thee that no creature can lock thee out, and with which thou shalt go in and out, and find pasture and food everywhere".[1]

[1] Tyndale: *Works*, Vol. I, pp. 463f.

# III

# SANCTIFICATION

Unless we esteem vilely of our own election, unless we refuse to satisfy the will, to obey the commandment, to follow the example, and to answer the vocation in which God hath called us, we must be holy.

*Edwin Sandys*

Blessed shall we be if ever God make us worthy of that honour to shed our blood for His name's sake.

*John Hooper*

# III
## SANCTIFICATION

"Deeds are the fruits of love; and love is the fruit of faith." So wrote William Tyndale;[1] and this saying of his sums up the attitude of the Reformers to the subject of sanctification. The believer's love is the natural response to the prior love of God and it necessarily expresses itself in holy living. As we saw in the last chapter, so far from having no place for good works, the Reformers insisted on good works as an essential mark of the life that is truly Christian. What they consistently denied was that a man's works could in any way contribute towards the achievement of his justification before God: only the unique redeeming work of Christ could avail for that. But what they no less consistently affirmed was that, as St. James stresses, good works are the outward proof of a genuine faith in Christ, and that where such works are absent the profession of faith must be dismissed as spurious. Holiness of life must be *natural* to him who has a new nature through the inward operation of the Holy Spirit: a good tree must be expected to bring forth good fruit. Sanctification, therefore, was regarded by the Reformers as essential and, inasmuch as regeneration is altogether the work of God, inevitable for the man who has been freely justified by faith in Christ Jesus. They also saw it as obligatory because of the commandments of God to His people. Sanctification, moreover, is peculiarly the work of the Holy Spirit. Thus in the Catechism of 1553 the answer to the question why the Holy Spirit is called holy is: "Not only for His own holiness; but for that by Him are made holy the chosen of God, and members of Christ. And therefore have the Scriptures termed Him the Spirit of sanctification or making holy."[2]

The extreme peril of unholy living, which is in effect an open denial of the transforming power of God which the Christian professes to experience, is emphasized, as we have already seen,[3] by Thomas Cranmer in the *Homily of Faith*, where he insists not only that "true faith doth ever bring forth good works", but also that "thy deeds and works must be an open testimonial of thy faith".[4]

[1] Tyndale: *Works*, Vol. I, p. 57.  [2] *Liturgies of King Edward VI*, p. 514.
[3] Pp. 36f. above.  [4] Cranmer: *Works*, Vol. II, p. 140.

"Your duty," exhorts Thomas Becon, "is to live well, to practise good works, to exercise all godly acts, to lead a virtuous conversation, and in all your life through the study of innocency to seek the glory of God. Now shall your conversation declare and show by external works whether your repentance be unfeigned or not, whether your faith and love toward God be sincere, true, and proceeding from a godly heart or not. For if your repentance, faith, and love be Christian and unfeigned, then shall good works ensue and follow agreeable to the same." In response to a request for information concerning the good works which God has prepared for us to walk in, he enumerates the following: "He that believeth truly in Christ abuseth not the name of God, profaneth not the sabbath day, dishonoureth not the magistrates of the public weal, contemneth not the ministers of God's Word, despiseth not his parents and superiors, killeth not, committeth not adultery, stealeth not, beareth no false witness, coveteth not his neighbour's goods." To this list of negatives he then adds a number of positive virtues which a Christian should display: "He mortifieth old Adam. He maketh the body subject to the spirit with the moderate use of eating and drinking. He exerciseth himself in godly meditations, in reading the Holy Scriptures, in offering up prayers and thanks continually to God. He succoureth the poor members of Christ. He leaveth no man comfortless. He goeth about to hurt no man, but studieth to profit all men. He wisheth and procureth no less goodness to other than he doth to himself. To be short, all his whole lifetime he doeth nothing else than die to sin and live unto righteousness." He too insists that "so long as we continue in our old wickedness, and amend not our manners, certainly neither true repentance nor Christian faith is in us, and, to say the truth, neither have we any part of Christ or Christ's merits, but pertain still to Satan and his sinful synagogue."[1]

Preaching on Lk. 1:74f. ("That being delivered out of the hands of our enemies, we might serve Him without fear, in holiness and righteousness before Him all the days of our life"), Archbishop Sandys instructs his hearers that "the greater and better part of Holy Scripture either setteth forth God's goodness towards us or our duty towards Him", and that "the great benefit we receive from God is our redemption in Christ", while "the duty which we owe to Him again is in holiness and righteousness of life continually

[1] Becon: *Works*, Vol. I, pp. 8off.

to serve Him". He admonishes that "we were not redeemed and bought with a price to be idle and do nothing, but to glorify Him in body and spirit that hath bought us".[1] In asserting that there is a distinction between the terms "holiness" and "righteousness" as used in the verse on which he is preaching, he explains that "holiness hath relation to the former table[2] and righteousness to the latter: in holiness is set forth our duty towards God, in righteousness towards man. We must serve God in holiness in respect of Himself: we must serve man in righteousness in respect of God . . . Holiness", he proceeds, "is the end of our election: 'He chose us before the foundation of the world that we might be holy.'[3] Our holiness is a thing which God doth greatly desire: 'This is the will of God, even your holiness'.[4] Unto holiness we are not only constrained by His commandment, but allured also by His example: 'Be holy, because I am holy.'[5] Unto this we are called: 'For God did not call us unto uncleanness, but unto holiness'.[6] So that, unless we esteem vilely of our own election, unless we refuse to satisfy the will, to obey the commandment, to follow the example, and to answer the vocation in which God hath called us, we must be holy."[7]

THE PRACTICAL NATURE OF HOLINESS

The Reformers conceived of holiness or sanctification, not as a detached state of mystical experience, but as something essentially practical relating to the everyday life and the whole life of the Christian. "To fear God is in true holiness to serve God; to work righteousness is not to hurt but to help our neighbour, to do to others as we would be done unto ourselves," says Sandys in another sermon. ". . . If the fear of God were planted in our hearts, we would learn after so many admonitions to lead a better life; we would practise such lessons as we have been so long in learning; we would not live in such careless security as we do; the Gospel would take better effect in us, and bring forth more plentiful fruit; we would at length cast away impiety and worldy concupiscence, and live a sober, just, and godly life; we would repent and forsake sin, lest sin procure God's speedy wrath; the ministers would be more diligent in feeding of the flock, the people more ready

---

[1] Cf. I Cor. 6:20.
[2] The reference is to the two tables of the decalogue.
[3] Eph. 1:4.        [4] I Thess. 4:3.        [5] I Pet. 1:1
[6] I Thess. 4:7.        [7] Sandys: *Sermons*, pp. 177, 182, 190. 6.

to hear the voice of the shepherd, the magistrates more careful over the commonwealth, the subjects more obedient to frame themselves to live under law; the rich would not suffer the giver of their riches to go on begging; the poor would endeavour to get spiritual treasures and to be rich in Christ; finally, we would not feed our bellies so daintily, nor so vainly and superfluously clothe our bodies, but use temperance in diet and sobriety in apparel; having what to eat and wherewith to be clothed, we would be content."[1]

The Christian's religion, indeed, is something which must extend to and inform every sphere of his experience. It is not one aspect among many to be confined to a single compartment of existence. "When we know God," counsels Jewel, "let us glorify Him as our God; let us so live that our words, our deeds, and our whole life may testify that the kingdom of God is among us." There is a logic in the wholeness of the Christian's dedication: "Since Christ suffered all His whole body to be tormented for us, since He suffered all His members to be crucified for our sakes, let us apply ourselves and all our members to serve and please Him in holiness and upright living all the days of our lives." This is the logic of response to the love of God in Christ Jesus. But, again, the reality of the believer's union with Christ also demands it: "Let us consider that we are flesh of God's flesh, bones of his bones, and members of His members. And therefore let us give over our whole bodies, let us give over all our members, let us give over our eyes, our ears, our tongues, our hearts unto the homage and service of God."[2]

The Christian, moreover, will not regard the things and entities with which he is surrounded and of which he makes use as ends in themselves, but as belonging to God's creation and therefore as a means for him to glorify God. "Consider not therefore the beauty, strength, wealth, commodity, and pleasure of any creature in itself," exhorts Pilkington, "for then it will surely deceive thee: but lift up thy mind to Him that made them for thy use and commodity, and praise Him for His great care that He takes for thee, in making of them and giving thee the use of them." The Christian knows that "there can be no true love, which is not grounded in God and for His sake: for where God only is sought for, there is love and truth itself; wheresoever He is not, there is neither truth

---

[1] Sandys: *Works*, pp. 279f.
[2] Jewel: *Works*, Vol. II, pp. 1034, 1062, 1068.

nor true love." He knows that "that love which is grounded on wordly causes, when the world changes, it fails too". Accordingly, "he that loveth his God earnestly rejoiceth in nothing so much as when he seeth those things prosper whereby God's glory may be showed forth. He careth more for that than for his own pleasure and profit. And when such things go backward it grieveth him more than any worldly loss that can fall unto himself."[1]

Being fully assured of the absolute sovereignty of almighty God over all the affairs of the universe, and over his own life, the Christian man is undismayed by adversities and persecutions: "When danger comes, the godly-wise man will commit himself wholly to God, looking for help and deliverance at His hands," says Pilkington again; "or else patiently bears it without any dismaying, whatsoever God lays on him: for he knows well that things are not ruled by fortune, nor that any thing can fall on him without the good will of his good God and loving father. But the wordly-wise man, when he sees worldly wit, power, and polity fail, he thinks all the world fails, and things be without recovery: he trusteth not in God, and therefore no marvel if he be left desolate." This unshakeable assurance that God is sovereign at all times and over all things will mean that nothing that happens to him will deflect the Christian from the path of duty or deter him from glorifying God. "God, of His great goodness, for the better exercising of our faith hath thus ordered the course of things that, although, when we look into the world, we shall find many things to withdraw us from doing our duties to His Majesty, yet by His Holy Spirit He hath given us faith and hope of His promised goodness, that nothing should discourage us from doing our duties: for we have Him on our side that hath all things at His commandment, and whose purpose none can withstand."[2]

Sanctification, while it is the effect of the Holy Spirit's work in the believing heart, is at the same time a matter of Christian consistency: a man's life and conduct must tally with his profession of faith; otherwise he is a walking contradiction, inviting the contempt of the world and dishonouring to God. This is well brought out by Bishop Jewel in the following short chain of quotations from his sermons: "Good brethren, let us consider that as many of us as say we know God's way, we know God's Word and His Gospel,

---

[1] Pilkington: *Works*, pp. 230, 240, 351.
[2] Pilkington: *Works*, pp. 245, 351f.

if virtue follow not, if honest conversation and upright living
follow not this our profession, we shame God and dishonour His
holy name. *Dicunt se nosse Deum*, saith St. Paul, *sed factis negant*:
'They say they know God', saith he, they say they know His holy
Word and Gospel, 'but in their deeds they deny God'[1] . . . Therefore, if we have the Word of God as a song to delight our ears, if
we turn the truth of God's Gospel into riot and wantonness, if we
confess God with our lips and deny Him in our deeds, if we say
we know God's law, we know His commandments, and yet live
not thereafter, we do not praise God and confess His name,
but we shame God and dishonour His holy name; we cause the
people to think evil of God's Word and slander His Gospel.
And this is the cause why the common sort of people judge that not
to be the Gospel, which is this day preached and taught unto them;
because such as profess the Gospel live not after the Gospel; because such as say they know God's way walk not in God's way . . .
We are the children of God, the brethren of Christ, and heirs of the
everlasting kingdom, we are Christian men, we profess God's
Gospel: let us therefore remember that we must walk as becometh
the servants of Christ: we must live like the professors of God's holy
Gospel . . . This day we have heard God's Gospel preached unto
us, this day we have learned out of the Word of God, that, if we
be Christians, we should live like Christians; if we be the children
of God, we should live as becometh the children of God, without
envy, without hatred, without strife or malice . . . This is our profession, this is our religion: hereunto are we called of God, appointed
by Christ, and commanded by His holy Word . . . Let us show
ourselves in our works to be the children of God and the brethren
of Christ: let us not show ourselves Christians in name, and not in
deed: let us not love in word alone, but in deed and in verity: let
us not requite evil with evil, one mischief with another, but let us
(according to St. Paul's rule) 'overcome evil with good', hatred with
love, and so fulfil the law of God.[2] . . . It is not enough to change
our religion, it is not sufficient to alter our faith; but we must also
change our old life, we must walk in newness of life, we must walk
in holiness, we must walk as becometh the professors of a new
religion, as becometh them that are of a right faith, as becometh
all such as confess God and His Gospel."[3]

---

[1] Tit. 1:16.          [2] Rom. 12:21; cf. I Cor. 4:12; I Pet. 2:21 ff.
[3] Jewel: *Works*, Vol. II, pp. 1056, 1060, 1075, 1091.

In their doctrine of sanctification, however, the Reformers were not perfectionists. It is only when at last, at His appearing, we see Christ face to face that we shall be fully like Him. The prospect of this glorious consummation is a powerful incentive to pure living here and now.[1] Sanctification is the process of being "conformed to the image of the Son", of being "changed into the same image from glory to glory, even as by the Spirit of the Lord".[2] And this transformation of the Christian into the divine image involves the putting off of "the old man" and the putting on of "the new man";[3] it involves a conflict between the two contrary forces of the flesh and the Spirit.[4] The nature and implications of this conflict are expounded by John Bradford in his two brief treatises on *The Old Man and the New* and on *The Flesh and the Spirit*. " 'The old man' ", he says, "is like to a mighty giant, such a one as was Goliath; for his birth is now perfect. But 'the new man' is like unto a little child, such a one as was David; for his birth is not perfect until the day of his general resurrection. 'The old man' therefore is more strong, lusty, and stirring than is 'the new man', because the birth of 'the new man' is but begun now, and the 'old man' is perfectly born. And as 'the old man' is more stirring, lusty, and stronger than 'the new man', so is the nature of him clean contrary to the nature of 'the new man', as being earthly and corrupt with Satan's seed; the nature of 'the new man' being heavenly, and blessed with the celestial seed of God. So that one man, inasmuch as he is corrupt with the seed of the serpent, is an 'old man', and inasmuch as he is blessed with the seed of God from above, he is a 'new man'. And as, inasmuch as he is an 'old man', he is a sinner and an enemy to God; so, inasmuch as he is regenerate, he is righteous and holy and a friend to God, the seed of God preserving him from sin, so that he cannot sin as the seed of the serpent."

For this reason it is possible to speak of the same man as "always just and always sinful:[5] just in respect of God's seed and his regeneration; sinful in respect of Satan's seed and his first birth. Between these two men therefore there is continual conflict and war most deadly; 'the flesh and the old man' fighting against 'the

---

[1] I Jn. 3:2f.      [2] Rom. 8:29, II Cor. 3:18.
[3] Col. 3:9f.      [4] Gal. 5:16ff.
[5] The expression is reminiscent of Luther's *"simul justus et peccator"*.

Spirit and the new man', and 'the Spirit and the new man' fighting against 'the flesh and the old man' ''. If the believer should fall into sin, he is distinguished from the unbeliever in that he does not continue in sin: "This is the difference between God's children who are regenerate and elect before all time in Christ and the wicked castaways, that the elect lie not still continually in their sin as do the wicked, but at length do return again by reason of God's seed, which is in them hid as a spark of fire in the ashes; as we may see in Peter, David, Paul, Mary Magdalene, and others". The very experience of the conflict between the flesh and the Spirit is a distinguishing mark of the children of God: "This battle and strife none have but the elect 'children of God': and they that have it are the elect 'children of God' 'in Christ before the beginning of the world', whose salvation is as certain and sure as is God Himself; for they are given to Christ, a faithful Shepherd, who hath so prayed for them lest they should perish that we know His prayer is heard: yea, He promiseth so to keep them that 'they shall not perish'.[1] And therefore they ought to rejoice, and herethrough to comfort themselves in their conflicts, which are testimonials, and most true, that they are the elect and dear 'children of God'; for else they could not nor should not feel any such strife in them."[2]

In his *Meditation of the Presence of God* Bradford affirms: "There is nothing that maketh more to true godliness of life than the persuasion of Thy presence, dear Father, and that nothing is hid from Thee, but all to Thee is open and naked, even the very thoughts, which one day Thou wilt reveal and open . . . Grant me that I may always have in mind that day wherein hid works of darkness shall be illumined."[3] This and other Meditations were composed by Bradford while he was in prison awaiting execution. The one "On Following Christ" (which is reminiscent of Thomas à Kempis) reminds us that the pursuit of holiness and Christlikeness is not without cost: "Many would come to Thee, O Lord, but few will come after Thee. Many would have the reward of Thy saints, but very few will follow their ways: and yet we know, or at least we should know, that the entrance to Thy kingdom and paradise is not from a paradise, but from a wilderness; for we come not from pleasure to pleasure, but from pain to pleasure, or from

---

[1] Jn. 10:28, 17:9ff.        [2] Bradford: *Works*, Vol. I, pp. 297ff.
[3] Cf. Heb. 4:12ff.

pleasure to pain, as Thy story of the rich glutton and Lazarus doth something set forth." Again, in his *Admonition to Lovers of the Gospel*, he warns against those who are "unwilling to drink of God's cup of afflictions, which he offereth common with His Son Christ our Lord", who "walk two ways, that is, they seek to 'serve God and mammon', which is impossible", who "open their eyes to behold present things only", who "judge of religion after reason, and not after God's Word", who "follow the more part, and not the better", who "profess God with their mouths, but 'in their hearts they deny Him', or else they would sanctify Him' by serving Him more than men", who "part-stake with God who would have all, giving part to the world". These, says Bradford, "will have Christ, but none of His cross; which will not be: they will be counted to 'live godly in Christ', but yet they 'will suffer no persecution' ".[1]

A STATE OF ACTIVITY

Sanctification manifests itself outwardly in Christian living. While it springs from the inward working of the Holy Spirit in the heart, yet it is essentially a state of activity, not of passivity. The Christian is under a solemn responsibility to be active in holiness to the glory of God. Discoursing on the opening petition of the Lord's Prayer, Latimer explains that it is a challenge to us, not to God, to be holy: "I do not desire that His name be hallowed of Himself, for it needeth not; He is holy already: but I desire that He will give us His Spirit, that we may express Him in all our doings and conversations, so that it may appear by our deeds that God is even such a one indeed as Scripture doth report Him."[2] In justification the sinner is roused from death to newness of life by the sovereign working of almighty God. As Sandys says: "Man never brought one stone to this building; man never laid one finger to this work: it is the only building and work of God, who in tender compassion hath both begun and finished it."[3] In sanctification, however, while it is still the gracious work of God in soul and life, and all the glory still belongs to God alone, man is invited to be a fellow-worker with God. He who has become a new creation in Christ has been brought into the midstream of God's purposes, and it is his privilege and duty to be a collaborator in the

[1] Bradford: *Works*, Vol. I, pp. 193, 252f., 409.
[2] Latimer: *Works*, Vol. I, p. 345.       [3] Sandys: *Works*, p. 181.

fulfilment of these purposes. He is placed in a position of answerability for the quality of his living. Hence the Apostle's warning to take heed how we build upon the one foundation (I Cor. 3:10f.). "Let everyone be watchful over his life, that his conversation may be according to his profession," says Sandys on another occasion. "If we walk disorderly, we shall not walk alone: our example will draw others after it; and their sins we shall answer for. Lucifer fell not alone: he drew company from heaven with him. Jeroboam, being sinful, made Israel to sin . . . We profess Christ and true Christianity: let us not through our lewd life be a slander to our Saviour and a shame to His Gospel."[1]

If the Christian should always be on his guard not to lead others astray by the example he sets, he should also beware of the company he keeps, lest he himself should be led astray by the bad example of others. This is a warning which Pilkington gives when he bids us "beware what company we join ourselves unto: for sin in one man is of so great force that it defiles all the company he is in . . . What is a more dangerous thing than to keep company with unthrifts?" he asks. "Have not many, who before they knew such unthriftiness were sober and honest, but after they have been tangled with such evil men sold house and land, some became beggars, and many hanged? Have not many honest young men, by keeping company with swearers and whore-hunters, become open blasphemers, and given themselves to all unhappiness? So, in companying with papists, and to please the world, many have forsaken the truth which they knew and professed, and are become open enemies and persecutors of God and His people. Did not Solomon fall to idolatry with marrying heathen wives? Did not God forbid marriage with the heathen, lest they should entice us to idolatry? Was not Samson overcome in keeping company with Delilah? What a proud presumption then is this to think, I am strong enough, wise enough to take heed to myself, in what company soever I shall come! For except you be wiser than Solomon or stronger than Samson, thou shalt be overcome as they were . . . If thou sit by, hear the truth spoken against, and will not defend it to thy power, thou art guilty to thy Lord God: for Christ saith, 'He that is not with Me is against Me'.[2] If thou speak in God's cause, thou shalt be in danger of thy life and goods, or both. These things well considered would make them who have the fear of God in them to

---

[1] Sandys: *Works*, p. 397.　　　　　　　[2] Mt. 12:30.

mark this lesson well, and fly evil company: for whatsoever the evil man, who is defiled in soul, touches, it is defiled."[1]

But activity in holiness does not mean *activism*. Ostentation, the doing of our good deeds to be seen of men and to gain a reputation for holiness, is the negation of true sanctification, because it seeks glory for self instead of glory for God. God is not deceived by outward display: He looks on the heart to see what is the true reality of our conduct; He examines our living at its very roots. "The life of a Christian man is inward between him and God," writes Tyndale, "and properly is the consent of the Spirit to the will of God and to the honour of God. And God's honour is the final end of all good works." And again: "God looketh not first on thy works as the world doth, as though the beautifulness of the works pleased Him as it doth the world, or as though He had need of them. But God looketh first on thy heart, what faith thou hast to His words, how thou believest Him, trustest Him, and how thou lovest Him for His mercy that He hath showed thee: He looketh with what heart thou workest, and not what thou workest."[2]

## HOLINESS AND PRAYER

Nor does activity in holiness mean that kind of activism which displays itself in being so restlessly busy and so constantly in the public eye that the inner life of private holiness is neglected. Indeed, this inner holiness is like the oil without which the flame of outward holiness cannot burn. And its chief exercise is that of prayer. "Prayer hath one property before all other good works," declares Latimer: "for with my alms I help but one or two at once, but with my faithful prayer I help all. I desire God to comfort all men living, but specially *domesticos fidei*, 'those which be of the household of faith'.[3] Yet we ought to pray with all our hearts for the others, who believe not, that God will turn their hearts and renew them with His Spirit; yea, our prayers reach so far that our very capital enemy ought not to be omitted." He accordingly emphasizes "what an excellent thing prayer is, when it proceedeth from a faithful heart; it doth far pass all the good works that men can do".[4]

Latimer was speaking of what he knew, for he was a true man of prayer. Augustine Bernher, who had been his servant and afterwards himself became a minister of the Gospel, tells (in his

---

[1] Pilkington: *Works*, p. 169f.  [2] Tyndale: *Works*, Vol. I, pp. 90, 100.
[3] Cf. Gal. 6:10.  [4] Latimer: *Works*, Vol. I, pp. 338f.

Dedication to the Duchess of Suffolk of Latimer's sermons on the Lord's Prayer) of the Reformer's "earnestness and diligence in prayer, wherein oftentimes so long he continued kneeling that he was not able to rise without help". He would pray that "as God had appointed him to be a preacher and professor of His Word, so also He would give him grace to stand unto His doctrine until his death". And "the other thing, the which most instantly with great violence of God's Spirit he desired, was that God of His mercy would restore the Gospel of His Son Christ unto this realm of England once again; and these words 'once again, once again' he did so inculcate and beat into the ears of the Lord God, as though he had seen God before Him, and spake unto Him face to face". There was also a third "principal matter" with which his prayers were occupied, namely, "the preservation of the queen's Majesty that now is, [that is, Elizabeth I] whom in his prayer accustomably he was wont to name, and even with tears desired God to make her a comfort to this comfortless realm of England".

"Were these things desired in vain?" asks Bernher. "Did God despise the prayers of His faithful soldier? No, assuredly; for the Lord did most graciously grant all these his requests. First, concerning profession, even in the most extremity, the Lord graciously assisted him: for when he stood at the stake, without Bocardo gate at Oxford, and the tormentors about to set fire upon him and that most reverend father Doctor Ridley, he lifted up his eyes towards heaven with a most amiable and comfortable countenance, saying these words, *Fidelis est Deus, qui non sinit nos tentari supra id quod possumus*, 'God is faithful, who doth not suffer us to be tempted above our strength':[1] and so afterwards by and by shed his blood in the cause of Christ; the which blood ran out of his heart in such abundance that all those who were present, being godly, did marvel to see the most part of the blood in his body so to be gathered to his heart, and with such violence to gush out, his body being opened by the force of the fire. By the which thing God most graciously granted his request, the which was, to shed his heart's blood in the defence of the Gospel. How mercifully the Lord heard his second request, in restoring His Gospel once again to this realm, these present days can bear record." As for Latimer's third request, "it was most effectuously granted to the great praise of God, the furtherance of His Gospel, and to the unspeakable comfort of this

[1] I Cor. 10:13.

realm. For when matters were even desperate, and the enemies mightily flourished and triumphed, God's Word banished, . . . suddenly the Lord called to remembrance His mercy and made an end of all these miseries, and appointed her for whom that same grey-headed father Latimer so earnestly prayed in his captivity, . . . to restore the temple of God again".[1]

Latimer, then, was not engaging in abstract theoretical speculation when he affirmed: "Truly, it is the greatest comfort in the world to talk with God, and to call upon Him, in this prayer that Christ Himself hath taught us; for it taketh away the bitterness of all afflictions. Through prayer we receive the Holy Ghost, who strengtheneth us and comforteth us at all times, in all trouble and peril."[2] Yet Latimer knew, with the saints of every age, that prayer is the most difficult and the most opposed of all the occupations of a Christian. "The flesh resisteth the work of the Holy Ghost in our hearts, and lets [that is, hinders] it, lets it," he says on another occasion. "We have to pray ever to God. O prayer, prayer! that it might be used in this realm, as it ought to be of all men, and specially of magistrates, of counsellors, of great rulers; to pray, to pray that it would please God to put godly policies in their hearts."[3]

Prayer, then, is an exercise of holiness. It is obvious that we cannot expect our prayers to be acceptable to God if our inward intention is not to forsake sin but to continue in unholy living. As Paul admonishes Timothy, the hands we lift up in prayer must be *holy* hands (I Tim. 2:8). "Only in thy prayer away with the purpose of sinning," writes Bradford, "for he that prayeth with a purpose to continue in any sin cannot be heard; his own conscience presently condemneth him; he can have no true testimony or assurance of God hearing him . . . God condemned in the old law all spotted sacrifices: away therefore with the spots of purposing to continue in sin. Bid adieu, when thou goest to prayer, bid adieu, I say, and farewell to thy covetousness, to thy uncleanness, swearing, lying, malice, drunkenness, gluttony, idleness, pride, envy, garrulity, slothfulness, negligence, &c. If thou feelest thy wilful and perverse will unwilling thereunto, out of hand complain it to the Lord, and for His Christ's sake pray Him to reform thy wicked will, put Him in remembrance of His promise sung by the angels *Hominibus bona voluntas*, that by Christ it should be to His glory

---

[1] Latimer: *Works*, Vol. I, pp. 322f.

[2] Latimer: *Ibid.*, p. 444.          [3] Latimer: *Ibid.*, p. 228.

to give "to men a good will", to consent to His will, and therein to delight night and day. The which is that happiness which David singeth of in his first psalm: therefore more earnestly crave it, and cease not till thou get it: for at length the Lord will come in an acceptable time, I warrant thee, and give it thee, and whatsoever else thou shalt ask to His glory, in the name and faith of His dear Christ, who is 'the door of the tabernacle' whereat the acceptable sacrifices of God were offered."[1]

As the New Testament constantly teaches, prayer is to be offered in the name and for the sake of Jesus Christ. It is the merit of His atoning work, not any worthiness of our own, that makes it possible for us to come in prayer into the presence of almighty God and to address Him as our heavenly Father. In short, our holiness is His holiness. "What thing is it that maketh our prayer acceptable to God?" asks Latimer when preaching before Edward VI. "Is it our babbling? No, no; it is not our babbling, nor our long prayer; there is another thing than it. The dignity and worthiness of our words is of no such virtue. For whosoever resorteth unto God not in the confidence of his own merits, but in the sure trust of the deserving of our Saviour Jesus Christ and in His passion; whosoever doth invoke the Father of heaven in the trust of Christ's merits, which offering is the most comfortable and acceptable offering to the Father; whosoever, I say, offereth up Christ, which is a perfect offering, he cannot be denied the thing he desireth, so that it be expedient for him to have it."[2]

"Remember," says Bradford again, "how that the children of God have been diligent in prayers always from the beginning, as well in their needs corporal as spiritual. Remember that their prayers have not been in vain, but graciously have they obtained their requests as well for themselves as for others. Remember that God is now the same God, and no less rich in mercy and plentiful to them that truly call upon him:[3] and therefore in very many places doth He command us to call upon Him: so that except we will heap sin upon sin, we must needs use prayer. His promises are both universal towards all men, and most free without respect of our worthiness, if so be we acknowledge our unworthiness, and make our prayers in the faith and name of Jesus Christ, who is our Mediator, and sitteth on the right hand of His Father, praying for

---

[1] Bradford: *Works*, Vol. I, pp. 22f.
[2] Latimer: *Works*, Vol. I, p. 172.          [3] Cf. Rom. 10:12.

us, being the same Christ He hath been in times past, and so will
be unto the end of the world, to help all such as come to Him."[1]

Like Latimer, and indeed all the Reformers, Bradford made a
daily practice of prayer. In his introduction to Bradford's Sermon
on Repentance, his friend Thomas Sampson gives some description of Bradford as a man of prayer. "His manner was," he says,
"to make himself a catalogue of all the grossest and most enormous
sins which in his life of ignorance he had committed, and to lay the
same before his eyes when he went to private prayer, that by the
sight and remembrance of them he might be stirred up to offer
to God the sacrifice of a contrite heart, seek assurance of salvation
in Christ by faith, thank God for his calling from the ways of
wickedness, and pray for increase of grace to be conducted in holy
life acceptable and pleasing to God. Such a continual exercise of
conscience he had in private prayer, that he did not count himself
to have prayed to his contentment, unless in it he had felt inwardly
some smiting of heart for sin and some healing of that wound by
faith, feeling the saving health of Christ, with some change of mind
into the detestation of sin, and love of obeying the will of God . . .
Without such an inward exercise of prayer our Bradford did not
pray to his full contentment, as appeareth by this: he used in the
morning to go to the common prayer in the college where he
was, and after that he used to make some prayer with his pupils in
his chamber; but, not content with this, he then repaired to his
own secret prayer and exercise in prayer by himself, as one that
had not yet prayed to his own mind: for he was wont to say to his
familiars, 'I have prayed with my pupils, but I have not yet prayed
with myself.' "

To this account Sampson adds a warning against the empty
formalism of perfunctory prayer: "Let those secure men mark this
well, who pray without touch of breast, as the Pharisee did;[2] and
so that they have said an ordinary prayer, or heard a common
course of prayer, they think they have prayed well, and, as the
term is, they have served God well; though they never feel sting for
sin, taste of groaning, or broken heart, nor of the sweet saving
health of Christ, thereby to be moved to offer the sweet sacrifice of

[1] Bradford, *Works*, Vol. I, p. 22.
[2] See the parable of the Pharisee and the publican, Lk. 18:10ff., in
which, in contrast to the self-righteous Pharisee, the publican "smote
upon his breast, saying, 'God be merciful to me a sinner' ".

thanksgiving, nor change or renewing of mind: but as they came secure in sin and senseless, so they do depart without any change or affecting of the heart; which is even the cradle in which Satan rocketh the sins of this age asleep, who think they do serve God in these cursory prayers made only of custom, when their heart is as far from God as was the heart of the Pharisee. Let us learn by Bradford's example to pray better, that is, with the heart and not with the lips alone."[1]

The following chain of prayers excerpted from the writings of John Bradford will give some indication of the true sanctity and spirituality of this martyr of the Reformation: "O give me plentifully Thy Spirit, whom Thou has promised to 'pour out upon all flesh', that thus I may with Thy saints talk with Thee night and day, for Thy only beloved Son's sake, Jesus Christ our Lord . . . O that I might feel now Thy Spirit so to affect me, that both with heart and mouth I might heartily and in faith pray unto Thee . . . O good Father, for Thy mercy's sake, give me the true love of mankind; but yet so that I may love man for Thee and in Thee, and always prefer Thy glory above all things, through Christ our Lord . . . O that I might find such favour in Thy sight, dear Father, that Thou wouldest work in me by Thy Holy Spirit a true knowledge of all good things, and hearty love to the same, through Jesus Christ our Lord and only Saviour . . . O help us, and grant that we, being ignorant of things to come, and of the time of our death which to Thee is certain, may so live and finish our journey here that we may be ready, and then depart, when our departing may make most to Thy glory and our comfort through Christ . . . O wonderful passions which Thou sufferedst! In them Thou teachest me, in them Thou comfortest me; for by them God is my Father, my sins are forgiven: by them I should learn to fear God, to love God, to hope in God, to hate sin, to be patient, to call upon God, and never to leave Him for any temptation's sake, but with Thee still to cry, yea, even when very death shall approach, 'Father, into Thy hands I commend my spirit' . . . Forasmuch as the dullness of our hearts, blindness, and corruption are such that we are not able to arise up unto Thee by faithful and hearty prayer, according to our great necessity, without Thy singular grace and assistance; grant unto us, gracious Lord, Thy holy and sanctifying Spirit to work in us this good work, with a pure and clean mind,

[1] Bradford: *Works*, Vol. I, pp. 33f.

with an humble and lowly heart, with grace to weigh and consider
the need and greatness of that we do desire, and with an assured
faith and trust that Thou wilt grant us our requests, because Thou
art good and gracious even to young ravens calling upon Thee,
much more then to us for whom Thou hast made all things, yea,
and hast not spared Thine own dear Son; because Thou hast
commanded us to call upon Thee; because Thy throne whereunto
we come is a throne of grace and mercy; because Thou hast given
us a mediator Christ, to bring us unto Thee, being 'the way' by
whom we come, being 'the door' by whom we enter, and being our
'head' on whom we hang, and hope that our poor petitions shall not
be in vain, through and for His name's sake . . . Endue us with
Thy Holy Spirit, according to Thy covenant and mercy, as well to
assure us of pardon, and that Thou dost accept us into Thy favour
as Thy dear children in Christ and for His sake, as to write Thy
law in our hearts, and so to work in us that we may now begin and
go forwards in believing, living, fearing, obeying, praying, hoping,
and serving Thee, as Thou dost require most fatherly and most
justly of us, accepting us as perfect through Christ and by imputa-
tion. And, moreover, when it shall be Thy good pleasure and most
to Thy glory, deliver us, we beseech Thee, out of the hands of
Thine adversaries by such means, be it death or life, as may make
to our comfort most in Christ. In the mean season and for ever
save us and govern us with Thy Holy Spirit and His eternal consolation . . . Dear Father, therefore I pray thee, remember even
for Thine own truth and mercy's sake this promise and everlasting
covenant, which in Thy good time I pray thee to write in my heart,
that I may 'know Thee to be the only true God and Jesus Christ
whom Thou hast sent'; that I may love Thee with all my heart for
ever; that I may love Thy people for Thy sake; that I may be holy
in Thy sight through Christ; that I may always not only strive
against sin, but also overcome the same daily more and more, as
Thy children do; above all things desiring 'the sanctification of Thy
name', 'the coming of Thy kingdom', 'the doing of Thy will here
on earth, as it is in heaven', through Jesus Christ our Redeemer,
Mediator, and Advocate. Amen."[1]

Prayer is described by Bishop Pilkington as "a sovereign salve
for all sores" and "a sure anchor in all storms". "Happy is that
man that diligently useth it at all times," he says. "But he that will

[1] Bradford: *Works*, Vol. I, pp. 174, 175, 177, 189, 199, 200f., 204.

4.

so effectually pray that he may obtain the thing he desireth, must first prostrate himself in the sight of his God, . . . forsaking himself as unable to help himself, condemning himself as unworthy to receive such a blessing at the Lord's hand; and yet nothing doubting but that his God, that never forsaketh them that unfeignedly fly unto Him, will deal with him in mercy and not in justice, deliver him and comfort him, not for any goodness that He findeth in him, but of His own mere pity, love, grace, and mercy . . . He that findeth anything in himself, to help and comfort himself withal, needeth not to pray; but he that seeth and feeleth his present want and necessity, he will beg earnestly, crave eagerly, confessing where his relief is to be had. No man will pray for that thing which he hath or thinketh himself to have: but we ever ask, desire, beg, and pray for that we want. Let us therefore in all our supplications and prayers unto the Lord first confess our beggarly poverty and unableness to help ourselves, the want of His heavenly grace and fatherly assistance; and then our gracious God will plenteously pour His blessings into our empty souls, and fill them with His grace. If we be full already, there is no room left to take any more: therefore we must know ourselves to be empty and hungry, or else we shall not earnestly desire this heavenly comfort from above, which is requisite in all prayer."[1]

## LOVING ONE'S NEIGHBOUR

The Gospel of the Reformers was certainly not deficient in social emphasis. While, the thrust of the Gospel is initially spiritual, directed to the innermost core of man's being and designed to satisfy his spiritual need, which is the seat of all his needs, yet the Reformers had a clear perception that the faith of Christ in its outworkings must penetrate to and govern every sphere of human life and experience. The man who is saved by Christ is saved in the whole of his being and in all his relationships. It is not for him either to seal off any part of his life from the rule of God or to seal himself off from his fellow-men in individualistic isolation. Love, as we have been reminded, is the fruit of faith; and that love must, in accordance with the divine law, extend not only to God but also to one's neighbour. The frequency with which the Reformers insist on the Christian's responsibility to his neighbour, and that means to all other men, is most noteworthy. This responsibility is,

[1] Pilkington: *Works*, pp. 405, 411f.

at the profoundest level, to bring the good news of Jesus Christ
to others; but it is also to do one's utmost to come to the aid of all,
including one's enemies, who are in trouble or distress of any kind.
The logic of this, for the Christian, is that Christ by His amazing
grace in coming to our aid has set us an example which we are
bound to follow. The spirit of Christ's love and humility should
be seen in all His followers. "How did our most blessed Saviour
Christ utterly neglect and cast away, as I may so speak, His own
glory, honour, and worship, to seek our health, comfort, and
salvation!" exclaims Thomas Becon. "This ready assistance and
help ought also to be in us, if we pertain unto Christ. For we
ought to have that care for our neighbour that Christ had for us,
or else walk we not according to charity."[1]

"But whom must we love?" inquires Archbishop Sandys.
" 'Thou shalt love thy neighbour.' And who is our neighbour?
Not he only to whom we are joined by familiar acquaintance, by
alliance, or nearness of dwelling; but whosoever doth need our
help, he is our neighbour, be he Jew or Gentile, Christian or
infidel, yea, friend or enemy, he is our neighbour. To him we
ought to be near to do him good. It is frivolous for thee to object,
'He is mine enemy, he hath many ways wronged me, he hath raised
slanderous reports of me, he hath practised against me, spoiled
and robbed me: how can I love him?' If Christ loved His friends
only, He had never loved thee, whosoever thou art. Look upon
Him whose hands were stretched out upon the cross for His
enemies, and for thee when thou wast His foe. No man proposeth
him as a pattern to be followed whom in his heart he doth mislike.
Thou mislikest thine enemy because he hateth thee: if thou hate
him, then dost thou imitate the very thing which thou hatest. Love
thy neighbour therefore without exception, and love him as thyself . . . We never weary in doing good to ourselves; but to do good
to others we have no sooner begun but we are even tired. Ourselves we love not in word and show, but in truth and in deed . . .
The name of strife and contention would never be heard of if we
were thus affected towards others. The only breach of peace is
the want of love: he that loveth all men will have peace with
all men."[2]

Becon explains somewhat more fully what love of one's neighbour involves for the Christian: "If ye perceive him to be ignorant

[1] Becon: *Works*: Vol. I, p. 223.     [2] Sandys: *Works*, pp. 205f.

of the law of God, teach him God's Word, bring him unto Christ, teach him where, of whom, and by what means he shall obtain health and salvation," he exhorts. "Declare to him what the true and Christian faith is, and of what great strength, virtue, efficacy, and power it is. Exhort him unto the true good works which God approveth by His Word, and leaveth not unrewarded. Charge him to fly unto the name of God, as unto a strong bulwark, in all his adversity and trouble. Furthermore, if ye perceive that he is given altogether to wickedness and will not gladly hear any wholesome admonition, yet cease not to pray for him, as Abraham did for the filthy Sodomites and Moses for the disobedient Jews.[1] Yea, though he be your extreme enemy and seeketh your life yet wish him well unto you, pray for him, and desire God to forgive him, as Christ and Stephen did.[2] Again, if ye perceive that he is poor and hath need of your help, fail not to succour his misery and to help him in his need, even to the uttermost of your power. To make an end, if ye perceive that your neighbour hath need of anything that ye are able to do for him, I charge you in God's behalf that ye with all expedition help and comfort him."[3]

In a letter to Bullinger dated 27 January (probably in 1546) John Hooper expresses his desire "to serve my godly brethren *in* Christ, and the ungodly *for* Christ: for I do not think that a Christian is born for himself, or that he ought to live to himself, but that whatever he has or is he ought altogether to ascribe, not to himself, but to refer it to God as the author, and regard everything that he possesses as common to all, according as the necessities and wants of his brethren may require."[4] By way of illustration that the Reformers loved their neighbours in practice as well as in theory, we may turn to Latimer's first sermon on the Lord's Prayer in the course of which, having described how he was converted through Bilney's faithful witness, he says that he used to go with Bilney to visit the prisoners in the tower at Cambridge: "for he was ever visiting prisoners and sick folk."[5] On another occasion, when correcting the misconception of the so-called "religious" or monastic life, Latimer declares: "Religion, pure religion, I say, standeth not in wearing of a monk's cowl, but in righteousness,

---

[1] Gen. 18:23ff., Ex. 32:31f.  [2] Lk. 23:34, Acts 7:60.
[3] Becon: *Works*, Vol. I, pp. 227f.
[4] Hooper: in *Original Letters relative to the English Reformation*, Vol. I, p. 34.  [5] Latimer: *Works*, Vol. I, p. 335.

justice, and well-doing, and, as St. James saith, in visiting the orphans, and widows that lack their husbands, orphans that lack their parents; to help them when they be poor, to speak for them when they be oppressed: herein standeth true religion, God's religion, I say."[1]

With reference to the petition, "Give us this day our daily bread", in this same sermon, Latimer advises his hearers that to offer such a prayer (indeed, he might equally well have said *any* prayer) is to take one's place as a beggar: "Here we be admonished of our estate and condition, what we be, namely, beggars. For we ask bread: of whom? Marry, of God. What are we then? Marry beggars: the greatest lords and ladies in England are but beggars before God. Seeing then that we all are but beggars, why should we then disdain and despise poor men?" And in pointing out the implication of the plural pronoun "us" he explains: "When I say, 'Give *us* this day our daily bread', I pray not for myself only, if I ask as He biddeth me; but I pray for all others. Wherefore say I not, 'Our Father, give me this day my daily bread'? Because God is not my God alone: He is a common God. And here we be admonished to be friendly, loving, and charitable one to another: for what God giveth, I cannot say, 'This is my own'; but I must say, 'This is ours'. For the rich man cannot say, 'This is mine alone; God hath given it unto me for my own use'. Nor yet hath the poor man any title unto it, to take it away from him. No, the poor man may not do so; for when he doth so he is a thief before God and man. But yet the poor man hath title to the rich man's goods; so that the rich man ought to let the poor man have part of his riches to help and to comfort him withal.  Therefore when God sendeth unto me much, it is not mine, but ours; it is not given unto me alone, but I must help my poor neighbours withal."[2]

So, too, Tyndale, with his gift for saying things felicitously, affirms that "neighbour is a word of love; and signifieth that a man should be ever nigh, and at hand, and ready to help in time of need".[3] He also draws attention to the logical foundation on which the love of one's neighbour rests. The man who has God's Spirit understands, he says, "that good works are nothing but fruits of love, compassion, mercifulness, and of a tenderness of heart which a Christian man hath to his neighbour; and that love springeth of

---

[1] Latimer: *Op. cit.*, p. 392. Cf. Jas. 1:27.    [2] Latimer: *Ibid.*, pp. 397f.
[3] Tyndale: *Works*, Vol. I, p. 85.

that love which he hath to God, to His will and commandments; and he understandeth also that the love which man hath to God springeth of that infinite love and bottomless mercy which God in Christ showed first to us". Accordingly, "a Christian man feeleth that that unspeakable love and mercy which God hath to us, and that Spirit who worketh all things that are wrought according to the will of God, and that love wherewith we love God, and that love which we have to our neighbour, and that mercy and compassion which we show on him, and also that eternal life which is laid up in store for us in Christ, are altogether the gift of God through Christ's purchasing".[1] And in his *Obedience of a Christian Man* there is this fine passage: "Christ is the cause why I love thee, why I am ready to do the uttermost of my power for thee. and why I pray for thee. And as long as the cause abideth, so long lasteth the effect: even as it is always day so long as the sun shineth. Do therefore the worst thou canst unto me, take away my goods, take away my good name; yet as long as Christ remaineth in my heart, so long I love thee not a whit the less, and so long art thou as dear unto me as mine own soul, and so long I pray for thee with all my heart: for Christ desireth it of me, and hath deserved it of me. Thine unkindness compared unto His kindness is nothing at all; yea, it is swallowed up as a little smoke of a mighty wind, and is no more seen or thought upon . . . Thus Christ is all, and the whole cause why I love thee."[2]

HOLINESS AND TEMPTATION (OR TESTING)

Temptations, so far from being obstacles, should be welcomed by the Christian as rungs in the ladder of his sanctification. They are, Latimer asserts, "a declaration of God's favour and might: for though we be most weak and feeble, yet through our weakness God vanquisheth the great strength and might of the devil". A distinguishing mark of those who love God is that "they fight against temptations and assaults of the devil". Urging us to remember that our life is a warfare, "let us be contented to be tempted", he says. ". . . For there is nothing so dangerous in the world as to be without trouble, without temptation. For look, when we be best at ease, when all things go with us according unto our will and pleasure, then we are commonly most farthest off from God. For our nature is so feeble that we cannot bear tranquillity;

---

[1] Tyndale: *Works*, Vol. I, pp. 108f.          [2] Tyndale: *Ibid.*, p. 298.

we forget God by and by: therefore we should say, *Proba me*, 'Lord, prove me, and tempt me' "—remembering always that "God will not suffer us to be tempted further than we shall be able to bear", and that ahead there is the crown of everlasting life awaiting us.[1]

The endurance of suffering and persecution for Christ's sake is a special test of the reality of the faith which a man professes and also a means of his sanctification. If ever any knew the purifying power of fiery trials it was the Reformers of the sixteenth century. "It is good and needful for us to have afflictions and exercises," preaches Latimer; "for, as St. Augustine saith, *Sanguis Christian-orum est veluti semen fructuum evangelicorum*: 'The blood of Christians is, as it were, the seed of the fruit of the Gospel.' For when one is hanged here, and another yonder, then God goeth sowing of His seed. For like as the corn that is cast into the ground riseth up again and is multiplied, even so the blood of one of those who suffer for God's Word's sake stirreth up a great many. And happy is he to whom it is given to suffer for God's holy Word's sake! For it is the greatest promotion that a man can have in this world to die for God's sake, or to be despised or contemned for His sake."[2] Christ our Saviour promised unto us that we should be sufferers here in this world, and then in the world to come we shall have life everlasting. Therefore let us be content; for though it be a hard journey, yet there shall be a good end of it. Like as when a man goeth a great journey, and laboureth very sore, but in the end he cometh to good cheer, then all his labour is forgotten; so we shall come at the end to that felicity which no eyes have seen, no ears have heard, nor heart perceived, which God hath prepared for His elect."[3]

In preaching on the parable of the great banquet (Mt. 22) Latimer characteristically describes the various courses which the heavenly King has prepared for those who come to the marriage of His Son, and in doing so likens the sufferings of our present pilgrimage to "certain sauces" which give us a relish for Christ. "This feast, this costly dish," he says, "hath its sauces; but what be they? Marry, the cross, affliction, tribulation, persecution, and all manner of miseries: for like as sauces make lusty the stomach to receive meat, so affliction stirreth up in us a desire to Christ. For when we be in quietness we are not hungry, we care not for Christ:

---

[1] Latimer: *Works*, Vol. I, pp. 434ff.    [2] Latimer: *Ibid.*, p. 361.
[3] Latimer: *Ibid.*, p. 490. Cf. I Cor. 2:9.

but when we be in tribulation, and cast into prison, then we have a desire to Him; then we learn to call upon Him; then we hunger and thirst after Him; then we are desirous to feed upon Him. As long as we be in health and prosperity we care not for Him; we be slothful, we have no stomach at all; and therefore these sauces are very necessary for us ... Therefore it cometh of the goodness of God when we be put to taste the sauce of tribulation: for He doth it to a good end, namely, that we should not be condemned with this wicked world. For these sauces are very good for us; for they make us more hungry and lusty to come to Christ and feed upon Him."[1]

"Although persecution be great," says Pilkington in his Exposition of the Prophet Haggai, "yet God strengthens His to die for His truth in most quiet peace to the shame of their persecutors. Where there is no striving there is no victory; where there is no victory, there is no praise nor reward: therefore God of His great love, that His people may have most noble victories and greatest reward, suffereth them to be troubled by the devil and his ministers, but not to be overcome." And again, when expounding Obadiah 17, he declares: "Thus is this ever true, that in Zion, the true church of Christ, shall be the 'Holy One', Christ, sanctifying all that believe in Him; there shall be 'holiness' in faith, religion, and manners, to the praise of God; there shall be also 'a sanctuary and holy place' with assemblies, in spite of their foes; and persecution does not hurt, but rather increase and further true religion, though not in the greater yet in the better part of men. For whosoever the Holy Ghost does inflame with an earnest zeal to His religion, they cannot keep it within them; they cannot abide to see their God and His Word blasphemed; they will burst out and declare their faith."[2]

Bishop Jewel comments as follows on the "joy of the Holy Ghost" (I Thess. 1:6): "This is that which passeth all natural sense and wisdom. Many seem to take in good part and abide patiently afflictions, loss of goods, imprisonment, and loss of life. But no man can rejoice in the suffering of these things, but the child of God; no man, but whom Christ hath chosen out of the world, but whose name is written in the book of life, but he in whom the Spirit beareth witness with his spirit that he is the child of God.

[1] Latimer: *Works*, Vol. I, pp. 463ff.
[2] Pilkington: *Works*, pp. 158f., 264.

He knoweth that through many tribulations he must enter into rest. He knoweth the wicked could have no power over him unless it were given them from above. He knoweth that all is done for the best to them that love God, and that God can dispose means, if it were so expedient, to bring to nought all the devices of the ungodly." And in commenting on I Thess. 3:3 ("that no man should be moved with these afflictions; for ye yourselves know that we are appointed therunto") he says: "Think not that you shall enjoy the pleasures of this world, if you be the faithful servants of Christ. Christ shed His blood for thee, that thou shouldest not refuse to give thy blood for Him. Drink the cup of bitter gall whereof Christ began to thee, and carry thy cross, that thou mayest follow after Him. If thou be ashamed of Christ, He shall be ashamed of thee before His Father in heaven: the cross cannot hurt thee, for Christ hath sanctified it in His blood. Behold not the sword which striketh thee, but think on the crown of glory which thou shalt receive. Gold is clearer after it hath been put into the fire: be thou gold, and the fiery persecution shall not hurt thee. Let not the fear of death put out thy faith. Trust in the Lord, be strong, and He shall stablish thy heart. Be rooted and built in Christ and stablished in the faith. Then shall thy heart rejoice, and no man shall take thy joy from thee."[1]

## THE CAPTIVITY EPISTLES OF THE ENGLISH REFORMATION

No documents of the English Reformation are more moving, or more replete with the spirit of true Christian sanctity, than are the letters which were written by Latimer, Ridley, Cranmer, and their colleagues while they were in prison awaiting the time of their martyrdom. What more searching test of a Christian man's sanctification could there be than to be called upon, as these and many others were at this time, to endure the squalor and solitude of prolonged imprisonment, with the expectation of a cruel death at the end, because of the evangelical faith which he professes? The letters of these men show them to have been more than conquerors through Jesus Christ their Lord; for they are distinguished by a spirit not merely of equanimity but also of joy and wonder that

[1] Jewel: *Works*, Vol. II, pp. 823f., 844.

4*

their Master should have honoured them by permitting them to
suffer in this way for His cause. There is no note of regret, no
plea for deliverance. Here, then, is their testimony, freely given
under these harsh circumstances.

"We are still involved in the greatest dangers, as we have been
for almost the last eighteen months," Bishop Hooper writes to the
Swiss Reformer Henry Bullinger on 11 December 1554. "The
enemies of the Gospel are every day giving us more and more
annoyance; we are imprisoned apart from each other, and treated
with every degree of ignominy. They are daily threatening us with
death, which we are quite indifferent about; in Christ Jesus we
boldly despise the sword and the flames. We know in whom we
have believed, and we are sure that we shall lay down our lives in a
good cause. Meanwhile aid us with your prayers, that He who hath
begun a good work in us will perform it even unto the end. We are
the Lord's; let Him do what seemeth good in His eyes . . . I have
a most faithful guardian and defender of my salvation in our heavenly Father through Jesus Christ, to whom I have wholly committed myself. To His faithfulness and protection I commend
myself: if He shall prolong my days, may He cause it to be for the
glory of His name; but if He wills that my short and evil life should
be ended, I can say with equal complacency, His will be done!"[1]

To his wife, Anne Hooper, he writes (13 October 1553) that,
seeing "we live for this life amongst so many and great perils and
dangers, we must be well assured by God's Word how to bear
them, and how patiently to take them, as they be sent to us from
God", and that "all troubles and adversity that chance to such as
be of God by the will of the heavenly Father can be none other but
gain and advantage". In accordance with the apostolic injunction
to the Colossians, as being risen with Christ, to "seek those things
which are above, where Christ sitteth on the right hand of God"
(Col. 3:1), he affirms that "the Christian man's faith must be always
upon the resurrection of Christ, when he is in trouble; and in that
glorious resurrection he shall not only see continual and perpetual
joy and consolation, but also the victory and triumph over all
persecution, trouble, sin, death, hell, the devil, and all other
persecutors and tyrants of Christ and of Christ's people, the tears
and weepings of the faithful dried up, their wounds healed, their

[1] Hooper: in *Original Letters relative to the English Reformation,* Vol. I,
pp. 105f.

bodies made immortal in joy, their souls for ever praising the Lord, and conjunction and society everlasting with the blessed company of God's elect in perpetual joy".[1]

In another letter (undated) "to certain godly persons, professors, and lovers of the truth", Hooper refers to the act of parliament, passed in November 1553, whereby the Reformed religion was outlawed, and tenderly advises them how they should conduct themselves now that "the wicked idol the mass is stablished again by law". "We must give God thanks," he says, "for that truth He hath opened in the time of His blessed servant King Edward the Sixth, and pray unto Him that we deny it not, nor dishonour it with idolatry, but that we may have strength and patience rather to die ten times than to deny Him once. Blessed shall we be if ever God make us worthy of that honour to shed our blood for His name's sake . . . Let us pray to our heavenly Father that we may know and love His blessed will and the glorious joy prepared for us in time to come, and that we may know and hate all things contrary to His blessed will and also the pain prepared for the wicked men in the world to come."[2] On 14 June 1554, in a similarly addressed letter, he writes: "I do not care what extremity this world shall work or devise, praying you in the bowels of Him that shed His precious blood for you, to remember and follow the knowledge ye have learned of His truth. Be not ashamed nor afraid to follow Him; beware of this sentence, that it take no place in you: 'No man (saith Christ) that putteth his hand to the plough and looketh backward is meet for the kingdom of God'.[3] . . . Seeing the price of truth in religion hath been always the displeasure and persecution of the world, let us bear it, and Christ will recompense the charges abundantly. It is no loss to lack the love of the world and to find the love of God, nor no harm to suffer the loss of worldly things and find eternal life. If man hate and God love, man kill the body and God bring both body and soul to eternal life, the exchange is good and profitable. For the love of God use singleness towards Him. Beware of this foolish and deceitful collusion, to think a man may serve God in spirit, secretly to his conscience, although outwardly with his body and bodily presence he cleave, for civil order, to such rites and ceremonies as now be used contrary to God and His Word.[4]"

[1] Hooper: *Later Writings*, pp. 580ff.    [2] Hooper: *Ibid.*, p. 589.
[3] Lk. 9:62.    [4] Hooper: *Ibid.*, p. 596.

True to his Master's example and instruction, Hooper does not
neglect to pray for those who persecute and despitefully use him
—who, in his own words, written in a letter dated 2 September
1554 to friends of his in London, "have taken all wordly goods and
lands from me and spoiled me of all that I had, have imprisoned
my body, and appointed not one-halfpenny to feed and relieve me
withal. But I do forgive them," he continues, "and pray for them
daily in my poor prayer unto God, and from my heart I wish their
salvation, and quietly and patiently bear their injuries, wishing no
farther extremity to be used towards us. Yet, if it seem contrary
best unto our heavenly Father, I have made my reckoning, and
fully resolve myself to suffer the uttermost that they are able to do
against me, yea, death itself, by the aid of Christ Jesus, who died
the most vile death of the cross for us wretches and miserable
sinners. But of this I am assured, that the wicked world, with all
its force and power, shall not touch one of the hairs of our heads
without leave and licence of our heavenly Father, whose will be
done in all things. If He will life, life be it; if He will death, death
be it. Only we pray that our wills may be subject unto His will . . .
Dearly beloved, if we be contented to obey God's will, and for His
commandment's sake to surrender our goods and ourselves to be at
His pleasure, it maketh no matter whether we keep goods and life,
or lose them. Nothing can hurt us that is taken from us for God's
cause, and nothing can at length do us good that is preferred
contrary unto God's commandment."[1]

On 21 January 1555, less than three weeks before his martyrdom, Hooper wrote a last letter to his friends, from which we take
the following: "Now is the time of trial, to see whether we fear
more God or man. It was an easy thing to hold with Christ while the
prince and world held with Him: but now the world hateth Him,
is the true trial who be His. Wherefore in the name, and in the
virtue, strength, and power of His Holy Spirit, prepare yourselves
in any case to adversity and constancy. Let us not run away when
it is most time to fight . . . Imprisonment is painful: but yet
liberty upon evil conditions is more painful. The prisons stink; but
yet not so much as sweet houses where the fear and true honour of
God lacketh. I must be alone and solitary: it is better so to be, and
have God with me, than to be in company with the wicked. Loss
of goods is great; but loss of God's grace and favour is greater . . .

---

[1] Hooper: *Later Writings,* p. 598.

It is better to make answer before the pomp and pride of wicked men than to stand naked in the sight of all heaven and earth before the just God at the latter day. I shall die then by the hands of the cruel man: he is blessed that loseth his life full of mortal miseries and findeth the life full of eternal joys. It is a grief to depart from goods and friends; but yet not so much as to depart from grace and heaven itself. Wherefore there is neither felicity nor adversity of this world that can appear to be great, if it be weighed with the joys or pains in the world to come. I can do no more but pray for you; do the same for me for God's sake. For my part (I thank the heavenly Father) I have made my accounts, and appointed myself unto the will of the heavenly Father: as He will, so I will, by His grace."[1] On 9 February, having been taken from his prison in London, John Hooper was burnt at the stake in the cathedral city of Gloucester, where he had formerly been bishop.

On 1 July 1555 John Bradford was burned at Smithfield after a long period of imprisonment in the Tower of London. During the previous year he had sent from his cell a letter "to certain godly men" which concluded with the following sentiments: "O that we considered often and indeed what we have professed in baptism! Then the cross and we should be well acquainted together, for we are 'baptized into Christ's death'[2] . . . O that we considered what we be, where we be, whither we are going, who calleth us, how He calleth us, to what felicity He calleth us, whereby He calleth us! . . . O Lord God, 'open Thou our eyes' that we may see the hope whereunto Thou hast called us. Give us eyes of seeing, ears of hearing, and hearts of understanding . . . O dear Father, kindle in us an earnest desire to be with Thee in soul and body, to praise Thy name for ever, with all Thy saints, in Thy eternal glory. Amen."[3]

"Away with dainty niceness!" he says in his *Exhortation to the Brethren in England*, dated 11 February 1555. "Will ye think the Father of heaven will deal more gently with you in this age than He hath done with others, His dearest friends, in other ages? What way, yea, what storms and tempests, what troubles and dis-quietness found Abel, Noah, Abraham, Isaac, Jacob, and good Joseph! Which of these had so fair a life and restful times as we have had? Moses, Aaron, Samuel, David the king, and all the good

---

[1] Hooper: *Later Writings*, pp. 618f.    [2] Rom. 6:3.
[3] Bradford: *Works*, Vol. I, p. 382.

kings, priests, prophets in the Old Testament, at one time or other, if not throughout their life, did feel a thousand parts more misery than we have felt hitherto. As for the New Testament, Lord God! how great was the affliction of Mary, of Joseph, of Zacharias, of Elizabeth, of John the Baptist, of all the apostles and evangelists, yea, of Jesus Christ our Lord, the dear Son and darling of God! And, since the time of the apostles, how many and great are the number of martyrs, confessors, and such as have suffered the shedding of their blood in this life, rather than they would be stayed in their journey, or lodge in any of Satan's inns, lest the storms or winds which fell in their travellings might have touched them! And, dearly beloved, let us think what we are, and how far unmeet to be matched with these; with whom yet we look to be placed in heaven . . . Ye shall see in us, by God's grace, that we preached no lies nor tales of tubs, [that is, fairy tales] but even the very true Word of God, for the confirmation whereof we, by God's grace and the help of your prayers, will willingly and joyfully give our blood to be shed, as already we have given our livings, goods, friends, and natural country: for now be we certain that we be in the highway to heaven's bliss . . . This wind will blow God's children forwards and the devil's darlings backward. Therefore like God's children, let us go on forward apace: the wind is in our backs; hoist up the sails; 'lift up your hearts and hands unto God'[1] in prayer, and keep your anchor of faith to cast out in time of trouble on the rock of God's Word and mercy in Christ by the cable of God's verity . . . Affliction, persecution, and trouble are no strange thing to God's children, and therefore it should not dismay, discourage, or discomfort us; for it is none other thing than all God's dear friends have tasted in their journey to heaven-wards."[2]

Three days earlier Bradford had written to Archbishop Cranmer and Bishops Ridley and Latimer, with whom a year previously he had shared the same cell in the Tower of London for some weeks, and who were now imprisoned in Oxford: "Our dear brother Rogers hath broken the ice valiantly, and as this day, I think, or tomorrow at the uttermost, hearty Hooper, sincere Saunders, and trusty Taylor end their course and receive their crown. The next am I, who hourly look for the porter to open me the gates after them, to enter into the desired rest. God forgive me mine unthankfulness for this exceeding great mercy, that amongst so many

[1] Lam. 3:41.        [2] Bradford: *Works*, Vol. I, pp. 417f.

thousands it pleaseth His mercy to choose me to be one in who He will suffer . . . O what am I, Lord, that Thou shouldest thus magnify me, so vile a man and miserable as always I have been! Is this Thy wont, to send for such a wretch and a hypocrite as I have been in a fiery chariot, as Thou didst for Elijah? . . . For my farewell, therefore, I write and send this unto you, trusting shortly to see you where we shall never be separated."[1]

On 24 June 1555, one week before his martyrdom, John Bradford writes to his mother: "I die not, my good mother, as a thief, a murderer, an adulterer, etc., but I die as a witness of Christ, His Gospel and verity, which hitherto I have confessed, I thank God as well by preaching as by imprisonment; and now, even presently, I shall most willingly confirm the same by fire. I acknowledge that God most justly might take me hence simply for my sins, which are many, great, and grievous: but the Lord, for His mercy in Christ, hath pardoned them all, I hope. But now, dear mother, He taketh me hence by this death, as a confessor and witness that the religion taught by Christ Jesu, the prophets, and the apostles is God's truth . . . Therefore, my good and most dear mother, give thanks for me to God that He hath made the fruit of your womb to be a witness of His glory . . . I confess to the whole world I die and depart this life in hope of a much better, which I look for at the hands of God my Father, through the merits of His dear Son Jesus Christ. Thus, my dear mother, I take my last farewell of you in this life, beseeching the almighty and eternal Father, by Christ, to grant us to meet in the life to come, where we shall give Him continual thanks and praise, for ever and ever."[2]

In these and the other letters of the martyrs there is no suggestion of self-pity or pessimism. Rather, we find that the sanctifying Spirit has brought them to the experience of that "good cheer" which accords with Christ's encouragement to His disciples: "In the world ye shall have tribulation: but be of good cheer; I have overcome the world!" (Jn. 16:33). It is this spirit of Christian joy despite affliction that shines so clearly through these letters from prison. "Dearly beloved," says Bradford in his *Exhortation to the Brethren in England*, "although to lose life and goods, or friends, for God's Gospel sake, it seem a bitter and sour thing; yet in that our 'Physician' who cannot lie (Jesus Christ I mean) doth tell us that it is very wholesome, howsoever it be untoothsome, let us with

[1] Bradford: *Works*, Vol. II, pp. 190f.     [2] Bradford: *Ibid.*, 249ff.

good cheer take the cup at His hand and drink it merrily. If the cup seem unpleasant and the drink too bitter, let us put some sugar therein, even a piece of that which Moses cast into the bitter water, and made the same pleasant:[1] I mean an ounce, yea, a dram of Christ's afflictions and cross which He suffered for us. If we call this to mind, and cast of them into our cup (considering what He was, what He suffered, of whom, for whom, to what end, and what came thereof) surely we cannot loathe our medicine, but wink, and drink it lustily."[2]

And this good cheer survived the final and most searching test of all. On the afternoon of Sunday 30 June the keeper's wife suddenly burst in, breathless and much distressed, and said (the scene is as recounted by Foxe): " 'O Master Bradford, I come to bring you heavy news.' 'What is that?' said he. 'Marry', quoth she, 'tomorrow you must be burned, and your chain is now a-buying, and soon you must go to Newgate.' With that Master Bradford put off his cap, and lifting up his eyes to heaven said: 'I thank God for it; for I have looked for the same a long time, and therefore it cometh not now to me suddenly, but as a thing waited for every day and hour: the Lord make me worthy thereof'; and so, thanking her for her gentleness, departed up into his chamber." The next day as the flames were kindled around him in the presence of a great concourse of onlookers he turned to the young apprentice, John Leaf, who was suffering with him and exclaimed: "Be of good comfort, brother; for we shall have a merry supper with the Lord this night!"[3]

Bradford had been chaplain to Ridley when the latter was Bishop of London, and when Ridley received the news of his sentence he wrote to him as follows: "Oh, dear brother, seeing the time is now come when it pleaseth the heavenly Father, for Christ our Saviour His sake, to call upon you and to bid you come, happy are you that ever you were born, thus to be awake at the Lord's calling... Where the martyrs for Christ's sake shed their blood and lost their lives, oh what wondrous things hath Christ afterward wrought to His glory and confirmation of their doctrine! If it be not the place that sanctifieth the man, but the holy man doth by Christ sanctify the place, brother Bradford, then happy and holy shall be that place wherein thou shalt suffer, and shall be with thy

---

[1] Ex. 15:23ff.                    [2] Bradford: *Works*, Vol. I, p. 431.
[3] See Bradford: *Works*, Vol. II, pp. xxxix, xlii.

ashes in Christ's cause sprinkled over withal. All thy country may rejoice of thee that ever it brought forth such a one, who would render his life again in His cause of whom he had received it . . . We do look now every day when we shall be called on, blessed be God! I ween I am the weakest many ways of our company; and yet I thank our Lord God and heavenly Father by Christ that since I heard of our dear brother Rogers' departing and stout confession of Christ and His truth even unto the death, my heart (blessed be God!) so rejoiced of it that since that time, I say, I never felt any lumpish heaviness in my heart, as I grant I have felt sometimes before. O good brother, blessed be God in thee, and blessed be the time that ever I knew thee! Farewell, farewell!"[1]

Another letter written from his cell in the Bocardo, Oxford, was addressed by Ridley to "the brethren remaining in captivity of the flesh and dispersed abroad in sundry prisons, but knit together in unity of spirit and holy religion". (The degree to which, as revealed in these letters composed by men appointed to die, the thoughts and concerns of the Reformers were turned, not inwards upon themselves and their own afflictions, but outwards to others, whether individuals or groups or the nation as a whole, is quite remarkable.) With complete conviction he affirms the rightness of their cause before God: "We never had a better or a more just cause either to contemn our life or shed our blood: we cannot take in hand the defence of a more certain, clear, and manifest truth. For it is not any ceremony for which we contend; but it toucheth the very substance of our whole religion, yea, even Christ Himself . . . If any therefore would force upon us any other God besides Him whom Paul and the apostles have taught, let us not hear him, but let us fly from him and hold him accursed. Brethren, ye are not ignorant of the deep and profound subtleties of Satan; for he will not cease to range about you, seeking by all means possible whom he may devour: but play ye the men, and be of good comfort in the Lord. And albeit your enemies and the adversaries of the truth, armed with all worldly force and power that may be, do set upon you, yet be not ye faint-hearted, and shrink not therefor: but trust unto your captain Christ, trust unto the Spirit of truth, and trust to the truth of your cause, which, as it may by the malice of Satan be darkened, so can it never be clean put out. For we have (high praise be given to God therefor!) most plainly, evidently, and

[1] Ridley: *Works*, pp. 377f.

clearly on our side all the prophets, all the apostles, and undoubtedly all the ancient ecclesiastical writers who have written until of late years past. Let us be hearty and of good courage therefore, and thoroughly comfort ourselves in the Lord."

He exhorts them, too, to think kindly and pray for the salvation of their persecutors: "Good brethren, though they rage never so fiercely against us, yet let us not wish evil unto them again; knowing that, while for Christ's cause they vex and persecute us, they are like madmen, most outrageous and cruel against themselves, heaping hot burning coals upon their own heads: but rather let us wish well unto them, 'knowing that we are thereunto called in Christ Jesu, that we should be heirs of the blessing'.[1] Let us pray therefore unto God that He would drive out of their hearts this darkness of errors and make the light of His truth to shine unto them, that they, acknowledging their blindness, may with all humble repentance be converted unto the Lord, and together with us confess Him to be the only true God, who is the Father of lights,[2] and His only Son Jesus Christ, worshipping Him in spirit and verity."[3]

Ridley's call came on 16 October of that same year, 1555, at Oxford, outside Balliol College. A little while before he wrote a letter of last farewell "to all his true and faithful friends in God". He spoke to them "as a man minding to take a far journey". It is a letter, too, of farewell to his countrymen, to his Church of England, to Cambridge, his university where he had studied and taught, to Kent and London where he had ministered as pastor and bishop, and to the peers of the realm, amongst whom he had sat in the House of Lords. "I warn you, all my well beloved kinsfolk and countrymen," he writes, "that ye be not amazed or astonished at the kind of my departure or dissolution: for I assure you that I think it the most honour that ever I was called unto in all my life; and therefore I thank my Lord God heartily for it, that it hath pleased Him to call me of His great mercy unto this high honour, to suffer death willingly for His sake and in His cause; unto the which honour He called the holy prophets, and His dearly beloved apostles, and His blessed chosen martyrs. For know ye that I doubt no more, but that the causes wherefor I am put to death are God's causes and the causes of the truth, than I doubt that the gospel which John wrote is the Gospel of Christ or that Paul's

[1] I Pet. 3:9.          [2] Jas. 1:17.          [3] Ridley: *Works,* pp. 344f.

epistles are the very Word of God. And to have a heart willing to abide and stand in God's cause and in Christ's quarrel even unto death, I assure thee (O man) it is an inestimable and an honourable gift of God, given only to the true elect and dearly beloved children of God." Here again the victorious note of "good cheer" is dominant: "All ye that be my true lovers and friends, rejoice and rejoice with me again, and render with me hearty thanks to God our heavenly Father that for His Son's sake, my Saviour and Redeemer Christ, He hath vouchsafed to call me, being else without His gracious goodness in myself but a sinful and a vile wretch, to call me (I say) unto this high dignity of His true prophets, of His faithful apostles, and of His holy, elect, and chosen martyrs: that is, to die, and to spend this temporal life in the defence and maintenance of His eternal and everlasting truth."[1]

It is, Ridley emphasizes, for their comfort that he is writing, lest the manner of his death should be a cause of confusion and sorrow to them; "Whereas", he urges them, "ye have rather cause to rejoice (if ye love me indeed) for that it hath pleased God to call me to a greater honour and dignity than ever I did enjoy before, either in Rochester or in the see of London, or ever should have had in the see of Durham, whereunto I was last of all elected and named. Yea, I count it greater honour before God indeed to die in His cause (whereof I nothing doubt) than is any earthly or temporal promotion or honour that can be given to a man in this world ... I trust in my Lord God, the God of mercies and the Father of all comfort, through Jesus Christ our Lord, that He who hath put this mind, will, and affection by His Holy Spirit in my heart, to stand against the face of the enemy in this cause, and to choose rather the loss of all my worldly substance, yea, and of my life too, than to deny His known truth, that He will comfort me, aid me, and strengthen me evermore even unto the end, and to the yielding up of my spirit and soul into His holy hands."[2]

On the night prior to his martyrdom Ridley announced to Mistress Irish, the wife of his keeper, and the others who were taking supper with them, that on the next day he was to be married, and "so showed himself to be as merry as ever he was at any time before". When Mistress Irish wept at the prospect of his painful death he gently but cheerfully comforted her with the

[1] Ridley: *Works*, pp. 397f.      [2] Ridley: *Ibid.* pp. 405f.

assurance that, "though my breakfast be somewhat sharp and painful, yet I am sure my supper shall be more pleasant and sweet"; and when his brother offered to watch all night with him he replied: "No, no, that you shall not; for I mind (God willing) to go to bed and to sleep as quietly tonight as ever I did in my life."[1]

The following day, bound back to back with Ridley at the same stake was his fellow-bishop, Hugh Latimer. Latimer, too, had endured a prolonged imprisonment prior to his martyrdom, and it was during this period that he sent a letter to an unnamed fellow-Christian who like him was a captive for the profession of the Gospel and whom he wished to encourage to persevere in steadfastness. "The wise men of the world can find shifts to avoid the cross," he writes, "and the unstable in faith can set themselves to rest with the world; but the simple servant of Christ doth look for no other but oppression in the world. And then is it their most glory, when they be under the cross of their Master Christ; which He did bear, not only for our redemption, but also for an example to us, that we should follow His steps in suffering, that we might be partakers of His glorious resurrection . . . We are now more near to God than ever we were, yea, we are at the gate of heaven; and we are a joyful spectacle become, in this our captivity, to God, to the angels, and to all His saints, who look that we should end our course with glory. We have found the precious stone of the Gospel, for the which we ought to sell all that we have in the world. And shall we exchange or lay to gage the precious treasure which we have in our hands for a few days to lament in the world, contrary to our vocation? God forbid it! But let us, as Christ willeth us in St. Luke. 'look up, and lift up our heads, for our redemption is at hand'[2] . . . Embrace Christ's cross, and Christ shall embrace you."[3]

The last of Latimer's letters that we have was written from prison in Oxford on 15 May 1555 "to all the unfeigned lovers of God's truth". It is a superb manifesto of Christian constancy and joy under persecution which deserves to be placed among the noblest documents of the literature of our profession. This venerable white-bearded saint, whose years are now three score and ten, is as bold and true-hearted in captivity as he ever was during the time of his liberty. Silenced as a preacher, he now puts

---

[1] Ridley: *Works*, pp. 292f.        [2] Lk. 21:28.
[3] Latimer: *Works*, Vol. II, pp. 429ff.

pen to paper: "Brethren," he writes, "the time is come when
the Lord's ground will be known: I mean, it will now appear who
have received God's Word in their hearts indeed, to the taking of
root therein. For such will not shrink for a little heat or sun-
burning weather, but stoutly stand and grow . . . I pray you, tell
me, if any from the beginning, yea, the best of God's friends, have
found any fairer way or weather to the place whither we are going
(I mean to heaven) than we now find and are like to find." As
Bradford had done just over three months previously,[1] Latimer
draws attention to the afflictions and sufferings which God's
servants throughout Old and New Testaments experienced: "See
whether any of them all found any other way unto the city whereunto we travel than by many tribulations," he challenges. "Besides
this," he continues, "if you should call to remembrance the primitive Church (Lord God!) we should see many that have given
cheerfully their bodies to most grievous torments rather than they
would be stopped in their journey . . . But if none of these were,
if you had no company to go with you, yet have you me, your
poorest brother and bondman in the Lord, with many other, I
trust in God. But if ye had none of the fathers, patriarchs, good
kings, prophets, apostles, evangelists, martyrs, holy saints, and
children of God, who in their journey to heaven found what you
are like to find (if you go on forwards, as I trust you will), yet have
you your general captain and master, Christ Jesus, the dear darling
and only-begotten and beloved Son of God, in whom was all the
Father's joy and delectation; ye have Him to go before you: no
fairer was His way than ours, but much worse and fouler, towards
His city of the heavenly Jerusalem. Let us remember what manner
of way Christ found: begin at His birth, and go forth until ye come
at His burial, and you shall find that every step of His journey was
a thousand times worse than yours is. For He had laid upon Him at
one time the devil, death, and sin; and with one sacrifice, never
again to be done, He overcame them all . . . Let us therefore follow
Him: for thus did He that we should not be faint-hearted; for we
may be most sure that 'if we suffer with Him we shall also reign
with Him'[2] . . . Be therefore partakers of the afflictions of Christ,
as God shall make you able to bear; and think it no small grace of
God to suffer persecution for God's truth's sake . . . And as the
fire hurteth not the gold, but maketh it finer, so shall ye be more

---

[1] See pp. 107f. above.          [2] II Tim. 2:12.

pure in suffering with Christ. The flail or the wind hurteth not the wheat, but cleanseth it from the chaff. And ye, dearly beloved, are God's wheat: fear not the fanning wind, fear not the millstone; for all these things make you the meeter for God's tooth . . . Dearly beloved, cast yourselves wholly upon the Lord, with whom all the hairs of your head be numbered, so that not one of them shall perish without His knowledge . . . No man shall once touch you without His knowlege; and when they touch you it is for your profit: God will work thereby to make you like unto Christ . . . Read the tenth psalm; and pray for me your poor brother and fellow-sufferer for God's sake: His name therefore be praised! And let us pray to God that He of His mercy will vouchsafe to make both you and me meet to suffer with good consciences for His name's sake. Die once we must; how and where, we know not. Happy are they whom God giveth to pay nature's debt (I mean to die) for His sake. Here is not our home; let us therefore accordingly consider things, having always before our eyes that heavenly Jerusalem, and the way thereto in persecution. And let us consider all the dear friends of God, how they have gone after the example of our Saviour Jesus Christ: whose footsteps let us also follow, even to the gallows (if God's will be so), not doubting, but as He rose again the third day, even so shall we do at the time appointed of God."[1]

16 October 1555 was the day (as has previously been mentioned) on which Hugh Latimer, aged but unbowed, in company with his younger colleague Nicholas Ridley, was given grace to seal his testimony with the blood of martyrdom. During the preceding imprisonment Ridley had written in affectionate terms to Latimer: "Methinketh I see you suddenly lifting up your head towards heaven, after your manner, and then looking upon me with your prophetical countenance, and speaking unto me with these or like words: 'Trust not, my son (I beseech you, vouchsafe me the honour of this name, for in so doing I shall think myself both honoured and loved of you), trust not, I say, my son, to these word-weapons, for the kingdom of God is not in words, but in power.' "[2] This same communication he had prefaced with this memorable prayer: "O heavenly Father, the Father of all wisdom, understanding, and true strength, I beseech Thee, for Thy only

---

[1] Latimer: *Works*, Vol. II, pp. 435ff.
[2] Ridley: *Works*, p. 146. Cf. I Thess. 1:5.

Son our Saviour Christ's sake, look mercifully upon me, wretched creature, and send Thine Holy Spirit into my breast; that not only I may understand according to Thy wisdom, how this pestilent and deadly dart is to be borne off, and with what answer it is to be beaten back; but also, when I must join to fight in the field for the glory of Thy name, that then I, being strengthened with the defence of Thy right hand, may manfully stand in the confession of Thy faith and of Thy truth, and continue in the same unto the end of my life: through the same our Lord Jesus Christ. Amen."[1]

When they met at the stake, Ridley had "a wondrous cheerful look" and embraced old Bishop Latimer. They then knelt together in prayer as they sought for the last time the grace of God for victory in this their final trial. After they had been chained back to back at the stake, and as the faggots were lit for their burning, Latimer uttered what has been described as "the noblest sermon he had ever composed":[2] "Be of good comfort, Master Ridley, and play the man: we shall this day light such a candle by God's grace in England as I trust shall never be put out!"[3] And so once again the grace of God was proved sufficient and His power was made perfect in the weakness of His faithful witnesses; once again the blood of Christ's martyrs was the seed of the Church.

With this testimony of the English Reformers before us, we are able to appreciate (and let us not forget that there are many in this present generation who are being called on to prove by personal experience) how true are the words written to Peter Martyr in that same year from prison by Archbishop Cranmer (who was himself to be martyred at the same spot as Latimer and Ridley on 21 March 1556) explaining how he had learnt by experience that "God never shines forth more brightly, and pours out the beams of His mercy and consolation, or of strength and firmness of spirit, more clearly or impressively upon the minds of His people, than when they are under the most extreme pain and distress, both of mind and body, that He may then more especially show Himself to be the God of His people, when He seems to have altogether forsaken them; then raising them up when they think He is bringing them down and laying them low; then glorifying them when He is thought to be confounding them; then quickening

---

[1] Ridley: *Works*, p. 142.

[2] Bishop Marcus L. Loane: *Masters of the English Reformation* (London, 1954), p. 132.        [3] Foxe: Vol. VII, pp. 459f.

them when he is thought to be destroying them."[1] What more need be said to demonstrate that the Reformers are examples to us, in their practice as well as in their preaching, in their dying as well as in their living, of that sanctification which, being the fruit of divine grace, by the evident depth of its reality adds lustre to the name of Christ?

[1] *Original Letters relative to the English Reformation*, Vol. I, p. 29.

# IV

# PREACHING AND WORSHIP

We cannot be saved without hearing of the Word: it is a necessary way to salvation. We cannot be saved without faith, and faith
cometh by hearing of the Word. . . . There must be preachers if
we look to be saved.

*Hugh Latimer*

If we take ourselves to be Christians indeed, as we be named,
let us credit the word, obey the law, and follow the doctrine and
example of our Saviour and Master Christ.

*The Book of Homilies*

# IV

# PREACHING AND WORSHIP

Prior to the Reformation, preaching had fallen into such neglect that it had virtually ceased to be a function of the Church. This was due to the widespread ignorance, indolence, and general dissoluteness of the clergy, encouraged by the all too common failure of the bishops to exercise due oversight in the dioceses for which thay had accepted responsibility. Frequently, indeed, clergy and bishops were unknown to the people because, instead of living among their people, they were absentees from their parishes and dioceses. Ecclesiastical titles and preferments could be procured through influence or purchased for money, without any thought being given to the souls of the people and their need of the Gospel. Inevitably this state of affairs led to the eclipse of preaching. No less inevitably, however, the rediscovery of the Word of God involved the rediscovery of the necessity of preaching. Christ Himself was a tireless preacher, and He had commissioned His followers to preach the Gospel to the uttermost parts of the earth. It was plain to the Reformers as they read the New Testament that preaching had been the primary function of the Apostles, just as Paul told the Corinthians that Christ had sent Him not to baptize but to preach the Gospel (I Cor. 1:17). And it was plain to them that the reinstitution of this apostolic office of preaching was essential if the Church of their day was to be renewed. Accordingly, we find that they were themselves constant preachers, diligently labouring to restore preaching to its proper prominence in the parishes of England.

A church that has ceased to preach, or that preaches error contrary to Scripture, has ceased to function as a true part of the Church of Christ. Hence Article XIX designates the preaching of the pure Word of God as a distinguishing mark of the Church of Christ. When (in 1550 or 1551—the year is uncertain) John Jewel took his degree of Bachelor of Divinity, he preached a sermon in St. Mary's Oxford, on the text: "If any man speak, let him speak as the oracles of God" (I Pet. 4:11), in which he insisted before his learned audience that a pastor should speak often, and also that what he says should be taken from the Holy Scriptures.

Pointing to the sloth and negligence against which they were contending, he reminded them of the cry of the prophet: "Woe unto me because I have kept silence", and the affirmation of the Apostle: "Woe unto me if I preach not the Gospel." "If Christ, if the apostles, if the prophets had held their peace, in what case had we now been in?" asks Jewel: "what religion had there been anywhere? what worship of God had there been? That we behold the light, that we have escaped out of bondage, that we are accounted, and be, the sons of God, all this we owe to the preaching of the Word of God". And he warns them that unless they have this in remembrance all that had so far been gained by the Reformation could well be lost. "The victory is kept by that same means as it is obtained." To take the voice of the pastor away from the church is to leave religion haphazard, blind, confused and to mingle everything with error, superstition, and idolatry. "It is the mark of a pastor, not so much to have learnt many things, as to have taught much," he asserts, and admonishes his hearers that if any of the flock of the Lord "shall perish through our default, his blood will be required at our hands." It is not for the pastor to complain that the people are deaf and ungrateful: this is no excuse for silence, but rather a challenge to preach with still more frequency and urgency. "The more serious the disease, the greater is the need for a physician." Again, the stubbornness of the people should not be allowed to upset the preacher unduly. "Let us persevere with our task and leave the success to the Lord," Jewel counsels," . . . for, as it is our duty to instruct the people with words, so it belongs to God to join to His words faith and force. Such is the power of the Word of God that to effect nothing and to profit no one is impossible." Therefore "the truth must be spoken, not lies; the Scriptures, not fables; the precepts of the most high God, not the dreams of men; for religion must be ordered, not by our judgment, but by the Word of God."[1]

It was indeed, because of the serious decay of preaching that the Books of Homilies were published (the first during Cranmer's archbishopric and the second after Elizabeth had come to the throne). Their contents were intended to be read regularly in church by those clergy who were incompetent to preach sermons. But the reading of these homilies was never meant to supplant the preaching of sermons. Their publication was designed as a temporary

[1] Jewel: *Works*, Vol. II, pp. 95off.

expedient to tide the Church over until such time as there should be an instructed and spiritual ministry. Today they remain a valuable repository of certain aspects of Reformation teaching. There is an interesting comment on the scope of the homilies in a letter from Archbishop Grindal to the Queen, dated 20 December 1576. "Where it is thought," he writes, "that the reading of godly homilies, set forth by public authority, may suffice, I continue of the same mind as I was when I attended last upon your Majesty. The reading of homilies hath its commodity, but is nothing comparable to the office of preaching. The godly preacher is termed in the Gospel *fidelis servus et prudens, qui novit famulitio Domini cibum demensum dare in tempore*, who can apply his speech according to the diversity of times, places and hearers, which cannot be done in homilies: exhortations, reprehensions, and persuasions are uttered with more affection, to the moving of the hearers, in sermons than in homilies. Besides, homilies were devised by the godly bishops in your brother's time only to supply necessity, for want of preachers, and are by the statute not to be preferred but to give place to sermons, whensoever they may be had; and were never thought in themselves alone to contain sufficient instruction for the Church of England . . . If every flock might have a preaching pastor, which is rather to be wished than hoped for, then were reading of homilies altogether unnecessary. But to supply that want of preaching of God's Word, which is the food of the soul, . . . both in your brother's time and in your time certain godly homilies have been devised, that the people should not be altogether destitute of instruction: for it is an old and true proverb, 'better half a loaf than no bread'."[1]

## THE PRIMACY OF PREACHING

In his *Catechism* Thomas Becon describes it as "the first and principal point of a bishop's and a spiritual minister's office to teach and preach the Word of God", and denounces the non-preaching parson as "a Nicholas bishop" (that is, a mock St. Nicholas' Day boy bishop) "and an idol, and indeed no better than a painted bishop on a wall; yea, he is, as the prophet saith, a 'dumb dog, not able to bark'; he is also, as our Saviour Christ saith, 'unsavoury salt, worth for nothing but to be cast out and to be trodden under foot of men'. Woe be to those rulers that set such idols and

[1] Edmund Grindal: *Remains*, pp. 382f.

white daubed walls over the flock of Christ, whom He hath purchased with His precious blood."[1] Again he writes in the Preface to his work entitled *The Demands of Holy Scripture* that, "as there cannot be a greater jewel in a Christian commonwealth than an earnest, faithful, and constant preacher of the Lord's Word, so can there not be a greater plague among any people than when they have reigning over them blind guides, dumb dogs, wicked wolves, hypocritical hirelings, popish prophets, which feed them not with the pure wheat of God's Word, but with the wormwood of men's trifling traditions".[2]

Commenting on Haggai 1:13, Bishop Pilkington says that in this verse is declared "the worthiness, authority, high title, and rule given to the preachers, for the commendation of their office. Haggai here is called 'the angel of the Lord', as some in English do translate it, or the messenger, or ambassador . . . So these names with such like are given to preachers in the Scripture, to set forth the highness of their vocation and authority that God calleth them to". The word 'angel', however, "betokens not the substance of the creature, but the office . . . This name is also given to the preachers for the heavenly comfort that they bring to man from God, whose messengers they be". Turning to verse 14, he explains that it is "the ordinary way to keep us in the fear of God and continual remembrance of the last day, often and diligently to read and hear God's Word preached unto us . . . Thus," he continues, "we see how necessary it is for us to be kept in God's school, and hear the trumpet of His Word sounding continually in our ears, to awake us up out of this deadly sleep of sin, and stir us forward to a diligent doing of our studies . . . This is the strength and power that comes by the Word of God: that where it is diligently heard and faithfully believed it maketh us altogether new men, of loiterers workers, and altogether lusty and courageous, and afraid of no displeasure, so that we may work in the Lord's house . . . This strength hath God's Word when it is worthily received, that it maketh a man to forget his own profit, yea, lands, wife, children, goods, and life, and manfully to bear death, prison, fire, and displeasure of princes, so that he may do his duty to his Lord God, and escape His displeasure . . . We may also learn what a treasure it is to have God's Word amongst us, seeing it is the ordinary way

---

[1] Becon: *Works*, Vol. II, p. 320.   [2] Becon: *Works*, Vol. III, p. 598.

that He hath ordained to bring us unto Him by; and what a grief it is to want the continual preaching of the same . . . For men fall chiefly into heresies when they trust to their own wits and learning, forsaking or not submitting their wits unto God's wisdom contained in His infallible Word and truth."[1]

Archbishop Sandys, when preaching on Acts 10:34f., says that "Cornelius teacheth us how desirous we ought to be of God's Word, how glad and ready to hear it, and how that in dutiful love we should provoke others to the hearing and embracing of it: for it is the Word of truth and salvation." The preacher has a clearly defined line of duty from which he must not deviate. He "may teach no other than he hath commission to speak, than is commanded him of God. He may not add to the written Word, neither take from it. God's law is perfect: it doth perfectly instruct and teach all things necessary to salvation. The disciples must only break those loaves unto the people which they have received at Christ's hands." The preacher in himself, however, is not important, but his message, and especially the One to whom that message points. "Respect not persons, but reverence the matter," Sandys advises: "when thou hearest the minister preaching the truth, thou hearest not him, but the Son of God, the teacher of all truth, Christ Jesus."[2]

"Despise not, good brethren, despise not to hear God's Word declared," pleads Bishop Jewel. "As you tender your own souls, be diligent to come to sermons; for that is the ordinary place where men's hearts be moved, and God's secrets be revealed. For, be the preacher never so weak, yet is the Word of God as mighty and as puissant as ever it was. If thou hear God's Word spoken by a weak man, an ignorant man, a sinner as thou thyself art, and yet wilt believe it and hear it with reverence, it is able to open thine eyes, and to reveal unto thee the high mysteries of thy salvation. Remember, we are the sons of the prophets. The kingdom of God is come amongst us. Let us not withstand the Spirit of God: let us not tread down the blood of the everlasting testament . . . It is not our doctrine that we bring you this day; we wrote it not, we found it not out, we are not the inventors of it; we bring you nothing but what the old fathers of the Church, what the apostles, what Christ our Saviour Himself hath brought before us."[3]

[1] Pilkington: *Works*, pp. 105f., 112ff.
[2] Sandys: *Works*, pp. 270ff.    [3] Jewel: *Works*, Vol. II, p. 1034.

While, as Article XXIII declares, "it is not lawful for any man to take upon upon him the office of public preaching or ministering the sacraments in the congregation, before he be lawfully called and sent to execute the same", yet it does not follow from this that the layman has no responsibilities of witness and communication. There is also such a thing as preaching by the quality of one's living. "Every private man ought to be, in virtuous living, both light and salt to his neighbour," says Tyndale when expounding Christ's words, "Ye are the salt of the earth" and "Ye are the light of the world" (Mt. 5:11ff.); "insomuch that the poorest ought to strive to overrun the bishop, and preach to him in example of living. Moreover, every man ought to preach in word and deed unto his household, and to them that are under his governance." The Christian layman, further, has an obligation to study and instruct himself in the Word of God, so much so that he is in a position to reprove false teaching, no matter from whose mouth he hears it. Thus Tyndale continues: "And though no man may preach openly, save he that hath the office committed unto him, yet ought every man to endeavour himself to be as well learned as the preacher, as nigh as it is possible. And every man may privately inform his neighbour, yea, and the preacher and bishop too, if need be. For if the preacher preach wrong, then may any man, whatsoever he be, rebuke him, first privately, and then, if that help not, complain farther. And when all is proved, according to the order of charity, and yet none amendment had, then ought every man that can to resist him, and to stand by Christ's doctrine, and to jeopard life and all for it."

This is a good example of the practical implications of the Reformed emphasis on the sovereignty of God's Word, which is placed above all human and ecclesiastical authority. Tyndale, indeed, asserts the right of the least man in the realm to reprove even the king should he decree what is contrary to the commandments of God. "Though every man's body and goods be under the king, do he right or wrong," says Tyndale, "yet is the authority of God's Word free, and above the king: so that the worst in the realm may tell the king, if he do him wrong, that he doth ... otherwise than God hath commanded him, and so warn him to avoid the wrath of God." As for the ecclesiastical authorities, he puts and answers the following questions: "Have I no power to resist the bishop or preacher that with false doctrine slayeth the souls for whom my Master and Lord Christ hath shed His blood? Be we otherwise under our bishops than Christ and His apostles and all the prophets were under the bishops of the old law? Nay, verily: and therefore we may, and also ought to do as they did, and to answer as the apostles did '*Oportet magis obedire Deo quam hominibus*—We ought to obey God rather than men'. In the Gospel every man is Christ's disciple, and a person for himself, to defend Christ's doctrine in his own person. The faith of the bishop will not help me, nor the bishop's keeping the law is sufficient for me. But I must believe in Christ for the remission of all sin, for mine own self, and in mine own person. No more is the bishop's or preacher's defending God's Word enough for me; but I must defend it in mine own person, and jeopard life and all thereon when I see need and occasion."[1] To this principle Tyndale remained inflexibly true in his life and labours as well as in his martyrdom.

LATIMER'S SERMON OF THE PLOUGH

Among the varied documents of the English Reformation none are more informative concerning the state of preaching in England at that time, and also concerning the Reformed doctrine of preaching, than are the sermons of him who was the most remarkable preacher of the day, and indeed one of the greatest preachers the Church universal has ever had, Bishop Hugh Latimer. In this chapter, therefore, we shall draw freely upon his famous sermons. Most famous of all, perhaps, is Latimer's *Sermon of the Plough*, which was preached in London on 18 January 1548. Latimer explains that God's Word is the seed, the congregation is the field in which that seed is sown, and the preacher is the ploughman: "for the preaching of the Gospel is one of God's ploughworks, and the preacher is one of God's ploughmen". Just as there is no time of the year when the ploughman on his farm has not special work to do, so too the preacher has enough to do to keep him fully occupied. "He hath first a busy work to bring his parishioners to a right faith, . . . and then to confirm them in the same faith: now casting them down with the law and with threatenings of God for sin; now ridging them up again with the Gospel and with the promises of God's favour; now weeding them by telling them their faults and making them forsake sin; now clotting them by breaking their stony hearts and by making them supple-hearted, and making

[1] Tyndale: *Works*, Vol. II, pp. 36f.

them to have hearts of flesh, that is, soft hearts, and apt for doctrine to enter in; now teaching . . .; now exhorting . . .; so that they have a continual work to do." Latimer explains further that "the preaching of the Word of God unto the people is called meat [that is, daily food]: Scripture calleth it meat; not strawberries, that come but once a year, and tarry not long, but are soon gone: but it is meat, it is no dainties." Preaching is something that the people need to be given all the year round. But "many make a strawberry of it, ministering it but once a year . . . And how few of them there be throughout this realm that give meat to their flock as they should do, the Visitors can best tell," laments Latimer.[1] "Too few, too few: the more is the pity, and never so few as now." Yet "it is God's work, God's plough, and that plough God would have still going".[2]

Latimer proceeds to warn in the sternest terms those prelates who had allowed their duty of preaching to lapse: "Ye that be prelates, look well to your office; for right prelating is busy labouring, and not lording. Therefore preach and teach, and let your plough be doing." Referring to the fact that for so long there had been so many "unpreaching prelates, lording loiterers, and idle ministers", he makes the following charge: "This much I dare say, that since lording and loitering have come up preaching hath come down, contrary to the apostles' times: for they preached and lorded not, and now they lord and preach not. For they that be lords will ill go to plough: it is no meet office for them; it is not seeming for their estate. Thus came up lording loiterers; thus crept in unpreaching prelates; and so have they long continued. For how many unlearned prelates we have now at this day! . . . For ever since the prelates were made lords and nobles the plough standeth; there is no work done, the people starve. They hawk, they hunt, they card, they dice, they pastime in their prelacies with gallant gentlemen, with their dancing minions, and with their fresh companions, so that ploughing is set aside; and by their lording and loitering preaching and ploughing is clean gone."[3]

And then came a moment when everyone present must have waited with bated breath to hear the disclosure of the name of a

---

[1] That is, those who carried out the visitations in the dioceses to report on the condition of affairs in the parishes; cf. Cranmer: *Works*, Vol. II, pp. 81f., 154f.; Hooper: *Later Writings*, pp. 117f.; Latimer: *Works*, Vol. II, pp. 240f., 242ff.

[2] Latimer: *Works*, Vol. I, pp. 59ff.    [3] Latimer: *Ibid.*, pp. 65f.

prelate who was, unlike those whom Latimer had been censuring, anything but negligent in his work. "And now I would ask you a strange question," proceeded Latimer: "who is the most diligent bishop and prelate in all England, that passeth all the rest in doing his office? I can tell, for I know him who it is ; I know him well. But now I think I see you listening and hearkening that I should name him. There is one that passeth all other, and is the most diligent prelate and preacher in all England. And will ye know who it is? I will tell you: it is the devil. He is the most diligent preacher of all other; he is never out of his diocese; he is never far from his cure; ye shall never find him unoccupied; he is ever in his parish; he keepeth residence at all times; ye shall never find him out of the way; call for him when you will, he is ever at home; the diligentest preacher in all the realm, he is ever at his plough: no lording nor loitering can hinder him; he is ever applying his business; ye shall never find him idle, I warrant you. And his office is to hinder religion, to maintain superstition, to set up idolatry, to teach all kinds of popery . . . Where the devil is resident and hath his plough going, there away with books, and up with candles; away with Bibles, and up with beads; away with the light of the Gospel, and up with the light of candles, yea, at noon-days. Where the devil is resident, that he may prevail, up with all superstition and idolatry: censing, painting of images, candles, palms, ashes, holy water, and new ser-vice of men's inventing, as though man could invent a better way to honour God with than God Himself hath appointed. Down with Christ's cross, up with purgatory pickpurse . . . Away with clothing the naked, the poor, and impotent; up with decking of images and gay garnishing of stocks and stones: up with man's traditions and his laws, down with God's traditions and His most holy Word."

"Oh that our prelates would be as diligent to sow the corn of good doctrine as Satan is to sow cockle and darnel," cries Latimer. The prelates, however, "take their pleasures. They are lords, and no labourers: but the devil is diligent at his plough. He is no un-preaching prelate; he is no lordly loiterer from his cure, but a busy ploughman; so that among all the prelates, and among all the pack of them that have cure, the devil will go for my money, for he still applieth his business. Therefore, ye unpreaching prelates, learn of the devil: to be diligent in doing of your office, learn of the devil: and if you will not learn of God, nor good men, for shame learn of the devil; '*ad erubescentiam vestram dico*—I speak it for your shame': if you will not learn of God, nor good men, to be diligent in your office, learn of the devil!"[1] Not only is such a sermon graphically revealing to us of the evil times on which preaching had fallen before God raised up the Reformers, but we can also well sense with what gripping effectiveness Latimer's boldness of metaphor together with his homeliness of speech must have struck the ears of his audience.

## "GOD'S INSTRUMENT OF SALVATION"

From the New Testament (as has already been briefly mentioned) the Reformers learnt that preaching is not just an option or an extra but a divinely appointed necessity for the Church. Latimer calls it categorically "God's instrument of salvation"; and again on another occasion he says: "Take away preaching, and take away salvation"[2]; or again, in his second sermon on the Lord's Prayer, he declares: "This office of preaching is the office of salvation; for St. Paul saith, '*Visum est Deo per stultitiam praedicationis salvos facere credentes*' 'It hath pleased God to save believers by the foolishness of preaching'. How can men then believe but by and through the office of preaching? Preachers are Christ's vicars."[3] When preaching before King Edward VI on 12 April 1549, Latimer is insistent that "we cannot be saved without hearing of the Word: it is," he declares, "a necessary way to salvation. We cannot be saved without faith, and faith cometh by hearing of the Word. '*Fides ex auditu.*' 'And how shall they hear without a preacher?' I tell you, it is the footstep of the ladder of heaven, of our salvation. There must be preachers, if we look to be saved."[4]

With characteristic humour—and his humour is never without point or purpose—he tells his distinguished audience the story of a "gentlewoman of London": "One of her neighbours met her in the street, and said, 'Mistress, whither go ye?' 'Marry', said she, 'I am going to St. Thomas of Acres to the sermon; I could not sleep all this last night, and I am going now thither; I never failed of a good nap there!' And so," Latimer observes, "I had rather ye should go a napping to the sermons than not to go at all. For with what mind soever ye come, though ye come for an ill purpose, yet peradventure ye may chance to be caught before ye go; the preacher

[1] Latimer: *Works*, Vol. I, pp. 70ff.     [2] Latimer: *Ibid.*, pp. 178, 155.
[3] Latimer: *Ibid.*, p. 349.     [4] Latimer: *Ibid.*, p. 200; cf. pp. 418, 470ff.

may chance to catch you on his hook . . . It is declared in many places of Scripture how necessary preaching is," he explains; "as this, '*Evangelium est potentia Dei ad salutem omni credenti*—The preaching of the Gospel is the power of God to every man that doth believe'. He means God's Word opened: it is the instrument, and the thing whereby we are saved . . . Here you may see how necessary this office is to our salvation. This is the thing that the devil wrestleth most against: it hath been all his study to decay this office. He worketh against it as much as he can: he hath prevailed too much, too much in it. He hath set up a state of unpreaching prelacy in this realm this seven hundred year." And so he admonishes his hearers: "Beware, beware, ye diminish not this office."[1]

Nor should preachers imagine that the pulpit is the only fitting place from which to deliver a sermon: the message is to be proclaimed under all circumstances and wherever opportunity may offer. Latimer cites the example of Christ, who preached from a boat. "It was a goodly pulpit that our Saviour Christ had gotten Him here," he remarks: "an old rotten boat, and yet He preached His Father's will, His Father's message, out of this pulpit. He cared not for the pulpit, so He might do the people good." Accordingly, "a good preacher may declare the Word of God sitting on a horse, or preaching in a tree. And yet if this should be done the unpreaching prelates would laugh it to scorn. And though it be good to have the pulpit set up in churches, that the people may resort thither, yet I would not have it superstitiously used, but that in a profane place the Word of God might be preached sometimes; and I would not have the people offended withal, no more than they be with our Saviour Christ's preaching out of a boat. And yet to have pulpits in churches, it is very well done to have them, but they would be occupied; for it is a vain thing to have them as they stand in many churches."[2] As he points out in a sermon preached at Stamford on 9 November of the following year (1550), "Christ knew what a charge hangeth upon this necessary office of preaching, the office of salvation, and therefore most earnestly applied it Himself."[3]

Advice concerning the manner of preaching is given by Pilkington in his *Exposition upon Nehemiah*. "Good natures," he says, "are

[1] Latimer: *Works*, Vol. I, pp. 201ff.    [2] Latimer: *Ibid.*, pp. 206f.
[3] Latimer: *Ibid.*, p. 292.

moved rather with the glad tidings of the Gospel than sharpness of the law . . . A gentle kind of preaching is better to win weak minds than terrible thundering of vengeance. Yet is the law most necessary to be taught, to pull down froward hearts, and bring them to knowledge of themselves . . . Both be good and necessary; but the Gospel more comfortable, and the law fearful. Fear maketh a man many times to fly from ill, but love maketh him willingly to do good . . . If thou wouldst have a man earnest in anything, rather draw him to it by love than drive him to it by fear: bring him once to love it earnestly, and nothing shall make him afraid to stand to it manfully . . . That preacher, therefore, who will win most unto God shall rather do it by gentleness than by sharpness, by promise than by threatenings, by the Gospel than by the law, by love than by fear: though the law must be interlaced to throw down the malice of man's heart; the flesh must be bridled by fear, and the spirit comforted with loving kindness promised."[1]

In his *Obedience of a Christian Man* Tyndale warns against assigning to some outward action or ceremony the importance that properly belongs to preaching. He refers to Gal. 3:2, where St. Paul says that the Holy Spirit is received by the hearing of faith, that is, the believing response to preaching; and to Acts 10:44, which tells how, while Peter was preaching, the Holy Spirit fell on Cornelius and his household. "Putting on of the hands is an indifferent thing," he asserts. "For the Holy Ghost came by preaching of the faith."[2] The same is the case with the sacraments; for the proper function of the sacraments is a *preaching* function. "The sacraments which Christ ordained preach God's Word unto us," says Tyndale, "and therefore justify and minister the Spirit to them that believe . . . Dumb ceremonies are no sacraments, but superstitiousness. Christ's sacraments preach the faith of Christ, as His apostles did, and thereby justify . . . And hereby mayest thou know the difference between Christ's signs or sacraments and antichrist's signs or ceremonies: that Christ's signs speak, and antichrist's be dumb." The reason for this is that the symbols ordained by Christ are annexed to the promises of God. "Where no promise of God is, there can be no faith nor justifying nor forgiveness of sins: for it is more than madness to look for anything of God save what He hath promised. How far He hath promised, so far is He bound to them that believe, and further not. To have a faith,

---

[1] Pilkington: *Works*, pp. 354f.     [2] Tyndale: *Works*, Vol. I, pp. 274f.

therefore, or a trust in anything where God hath not promised is plain idolatry."

Accordingly, Tyndale deplores the notion that "the wagging of the bishop's hand over us" blesses us and puts away our sins. "If my sins be full done away in Christ, how remaineth there any to be done away by such fantasies?" he asks. "The apostles knew no ways to put away sin or to bless us but by preaching Christ . . . The bishops therefore ought to bless us in preaching Christ, and not to deceive us and to bring the curse of God upon us with wagging their hands over us."[1]

While it is true that the preacher's task is a ceaseless one, and calls for courage and perseverance, yet any success that may follow his preaching is owed entirely to the secret working of God. Preachers are required to be faithful in calling sinners to repentance and faith. But, as Latimer emphasizes, "they can do no more but call; God is He that must bring in; God must open the hearts". This is illustrated by the story of Lydia (Acts 16:14). "Paul could but only preach; God must work; God must do the thing inwardly."[2] And so Latimer says of his own preaching: "It lieth not in me to make it fruitful: if God work not in your hearts, my preaching can do you but little good. I am God's instrument but for a time; it is He that must give the increase."[3] Pilkington emphasizes the same truth in these words: "God requires nothing of thee but thy labour: the increase belongs to God alone to give as He thinks good. St. Paul, comparing himself with the other apostles, saith, he 'laboured more than any of the rest, and filled all places and countries with the Gospel betwixt Jerusalem and Illyricum'[4]; but he never tells how many he converted to the faith, for that is the work of God, and neither he who grafts nor he who waters is anything, but God who gives the increase."[5]

The objection is anticipated that, if salvation is the result of the hidden work of God in the heart, and if, further, He knows and keeps His elect in accordance with His inscrutable purpose, then there is really no need of preachers, since God is able to save His elect apart from preaching. "A goodly reason!" retorts Latimer. "God can save my life without meat and drink: need I none therefore? God can save me from burning, if I were in the fire: shall I

---

[1] Tyndale: *Works*, Vol. I, pp. 283ff.   [2] Latimer: *Works*, Vol. I, p. 285.
[3] Latimer: *Ibid.*, p. 155.   [4] I Cor. 15:10, Rom. 15:19.
[5] Pilkington: *Works*, p. 45. See I Cor. 3:7.

run into it therefore? No, no; I must keep the way that God hath
ordained, and use the ordinary means that God hath assigned, and
not seek new ways. This office of preaching is the only ordinary
way that God hath appointed to save us all thereby."[1]

Latimer addresses himself also to another question that might
occur to the minds of his hearers, namely, whether they must
conclude that their forefathers, who were deprived of evangelical
preaching and afflicted with false doctrine, were therefore in a state
of damnation. To this Latimer offers the following response: "It
is with the false doctrine as it is with fire: the nature of fire is to
burn and consume all that which is laid in the fire that may be
burned. So the nature of false doctrine is to condemn, to bring to
everlasting damnation." Yet there have been exceptions to this rule,
as Scripture shows, for example, in the case of the burning bush
which was not consumed, and of the three young men who passed
unscathed through Nebuchadnezzar's fiery furnace. The nature
of false doctrine is indeed "to consume, to corrupt, and bring to
everlasting sorrow: yet let us hope," says Latimer, "that our forefathers were not damned, for God hath many ways to preserve
them from perishing; yea, in the last hour of death God can work
with His Holy Ghost and teach them to know Christ His Son for
their Saviour; though they were taught other ways before, yet God
can preserve them from the poison of the false doctrine." And he
reminds the congregation that in the time of Ahab, when true
religion had been overthrown and the prophets of Baal were
supreme, Elijah, who believed that he was the last servant of the
true God left in the land, was assured by God that there were no
less than seven thousand in Israel who had not bowed the knee to
Baal. "Therefore," Latimer continues, "let us hope that though the
doctrine of this time was false and poisoned, yet for all that God
hath had His. He hath had seven thousand, that is to say, a great
number amongst them which took no harm by the false doctrine,
for He wonderfully preserved them."

But this suggests the earlier objection once again: "Seeing then
that God can save men and bring them to everlasting life without
the outward hearing of the Word of God, then we have no need to
hear the Word of God; we need not to have preachers amongst us:
for like as He hath preserved them, so He will preserve us too,
without the hearing of God's Word." This Latimer dismisses as a

[1] Latimer: *Works*, Vol. I, p. 306.

foolish reason. "In our time," he explains, "God hath sent light into the world; He hath opened the gates of heaven unto us by His Word; which Word be opened unto us by His officers, by His preachers: shall we now despise the preachers? Shall we refuse to hear God's Word, to learn the way to heaven, and require Him to save us without His Word? No, no; for when we do so we tempt God, and shall be damned world without end."[1]

### THE PROPERTIES OF A GOOD PREACHER

What, then, are "the properties of every good preacher"? As defined by Latimer, they are: "to be a true man; to teach, not dreams nor inventions of men, but *viam Dei in veritate*, 'the way of God truly'; and not to regard the personage of man."[2] Nor must the faithful preacher expect popularity, but rather opposition and hatred, and even death. "Take this for a sure conclusion," Latimer had written to King Henry VIII on 1 December 1530, "that there where the Word of God is truly preached, there is persecution, as well of the hearers as of the teachers . . . For the world loveth all that are of the world, and hateth all things that are contrary to it . . . And the Holy Scripture doth promise nothing to the favourers and followers of it in this world but trouble, vexation, and persecution."[3] In one of the sermons we are pointed to the examples of John the Baptist and Christ and His Apostles: "But, I pray you, what thanks had they for their calling, for their labour? Verily this: John the Baptist was beheaded; Christ was crucified; the apostles were killed: this was their reward for their labours. So all the preachers shall look for none other reward; for no doubt they must be sufferers, they must taste of these sauces: their office is, *arguere mundum de peccato*, 'to rebuke the world of sin', which no doubt is a thankless occupation." But "they must spare nobody; they must rebuke high and low when they do amiss; they must strike them with the sword of God's Word: which no doubt is a thankless occupation; yet it must be done, for God will have it so".[4]

Again, when preaching on the Christian's armour (Eph. 6:10f.), Latimer says of St. Paul: "Now, when he hath done, and set out all his mind, at the last he cometh and desireth them to pray for him: but for what? Not to get a fat benefice or a bishopric. No, no; St. Paul was not a hunter for benefices. He saith, 'Pray that I may have

---

[1] Latimer: *Works*, Vol. I, pp. 525ff.    [2] Latimer: *Ibid.*, p. 292.
[3] Latimer: *Works*, Vol. II, p. 303.    [4] Latimer: *Works*, Vol. I, p. 468.

utterance and boldness to speak': for when a preacher's mouth is stopped, so that he dare not rebuke sin and wickedness, no doubt he is not meet for his office."[1] Pilkington also emphasizes the need for outspokeness from the pulpit without respect of persons, when expounding Haggai 1:12: "The preacher," he says, "must not be afraid to rebuke sin in all sorts and degrees of men, as here Haggai did rebuke both Zerubbabel, the chief ruler in the commonwealth, and Joshua the high priest and chief in religion, and also the whole people beside, and threatens the plagues indifferently to all without any flattery or respect of person . . . For as God, a most righteous judge, will punish all sin, so must His preachers indifferently warn and rebuke all sorts of sinners; or else God will require their blood at their hands, if they perish without their warning, as Ezekiel saith."[2]

This principle of boldness and outspokeness in preaching without any respect of persons was certainly no academic matter removed from reality where Hugh Latimer was concerned. For him to preach boldly in his country diocese might have been comparatively easy; but to stand in the pulpit and without favour or hesitation to proclaim the truth of God before and to the king and his court in London called for the highest moral courage. This courage sprang from the conviction that God's revealed truth must be communicated to all without distinction, coupled with the internal dynamic of the Holy Spirit. Thus when preaching before the king Latimer declares: "All things written in God's book are most certain, true, and profitable for all men; for in it is contained meet matter for kings, princes, rulers, bishops, and for all states."[3] In another such sermon he tells how he had been advised not to say anything when preaching that might antagonize the sovereign —advice which a faithful minister of God's Word could not entertain for a moment if it meant covering over the truth. "You that be of the court, and especially ye sworn chaplains," preaches Latimer, "beware of a lesson that a great man taught me at my first coming to the court. He told me for good-will; he thought it well. He said to me, 'You must beware, howsoever ye do, that ye contrary not the king; let him have his sayings; follow him; go with him'. Marry, out upon this counsel! Shall I say as he says? Say

[1] Latimer: *Works*, Vol. I, p. 507.
[2] Pilkington: *Works*, pp. 98f. The reference is to Ezek. 3:18.
[3] Latimer: *Works*, Vol. I, p. 87.

your conscience, or else what a worm shall ye feel gnawing; what a remorse of conscience shall ye have when ye remember how ye slacked your duty!" In the same sermon he solemnly implores the young ruler so to order things "that preaching may not decay: for surely, if preaching decay, ignorance and brutishness will enter again".[1] And so Latimer the old bishop preached, with all due homage, but without servile fear, before Edward the young king, concerned not for his own safety or advancement but for the eternal welfare of his illustrious hearers.

But if there is a congregation more likely even than the sovereign and his court to intimidate the preacher and to tempt him to soften or turn aside from the message that is laid upon him, it is a gathering of his fellow bishops and clergy. Latimer, however, was no less courageous when preaching before Convocation. Thus in a sermon delivered in 1536, after describing how until recent times the clergy had without check led the people into error and idolatry and superstition, he asks: "Be these the faithful dispensers of God's mysteries, and not rather false dissipators of them? whom God never put in office, but rather the devil set them over a miserable family, over an house miserably ordered and entreated. Happy were the people if such preached seldom!" That same afternoon he addresses them in a manner that might fittingly apply to many a protracted ecclesiastical assembly of our own day. "The end of your Convocation shall show what ye have done," he says; "the fruit that shall come of your consultation shall show what generation ye be of. For what have ye done hitherto, I pray you, these seven years and more? What have ye engendered? What have ye brought forth? What fruit has come of your long and great assembly? What one thing that the people of England hath been the better of a hair, or yourselves either more accepted before God or better discharged before the people committed unto your care? . . . I am bold with you, but I speak Latin and not English, to the clergy, not to the laity; I speak to you being present, and not behind your backs. God is my witness, who knoweth my heart and compelleth me to say what I say." So he challenges them again: "I pray you in God's name, what did you do, so great fathers, so many, so long a season, so oft assembled together?" And he answers his own question by taunting them with having achieved two things: firstly, burning the body of a dead man whose will was considered to contain

---

[1] Latimer: *Works*, Vol. I, pp. 231f., 269.

heretical opinions; and, secondly, wishing to burn a live man, Latimer himself, because he had refused to "subscribe to certain articles that took away the supremacy of the king".[1] "Take away these two noble acts," Latimer continues scathingly, "and there is nothing else left that ye went about"—though then he thinks of a third "noble act", namely, an attempt to fasten a charge of heresy on the Dutch scholar Erasmus. "Ye have oft sat in consultation, but what have ye done?" he persists. "Ye have had many things in deliberation, but what one is put forth whereby either Christ is more glorified or else Christ's people made more holy? I appeal to your conscience."[2]

In one of his sermons before Edward VI Latimer propounds an example from Scripture of preaching which proved to be powerful and effective: this was the sermon of Jonah to the Ninevites. "They believed God's preacher, God's officer, God's minister, and were converted from their sin," he tells his congregation. "They believed that, as the preacher said, if they did not repent and amend their life, the city would be destroyed within forty days. This was a great fruit: for Jonah was but one man, and he preached but one sermon, and it was but a short sermon, as touching the number of words; and yet he turned the whole city, great and small, rich and poor, king and all." By way of contrast, he draws attention to the fact that, though there were many preachers in England who preached sermons which were both many and long, yet the people did not repent and turn from their sin. Why this difference between England and Nineveh? "In this sermon of Jonah is no great curiousness, no great clerkliness, no great affectation of words nor of painted eloquence." Jonah simply proclaimed that there were yet forty days, and then Nineveh would be destroyed. "This was no great curious sermon," says Latimer, "but this was a nipping sermon, a pinching sermon, a biting sermon; it had a full bite, it was a nipping sermon, a rough sermon, and a sharp biting sermon." Pointedly, Latimer asks whether they did not marvel

---

[1] The body burned was that of William Tracy—"a very good man," says Latimer, "reported to be of an honest life while he lived, full of good works, good both to the clergy and also to the laity." Latimer, whose preaching because of its boldness in attacking the errors prevalent in the church had become distasteful to those antagonistic to the Reformation, which was still in its early stages, had recently been made Bishop of Worcester.     [2] Latimer: *Works*, Vol. I, pp. 37, 45f.

that the Ninevites refrained from casting Jonah into prison. "But," he adds, "God gave them grace to hear him, and to convert and amend at this preaching . . . But in England if God's preacher, God's minister, be anything quick, or do speak sharply, then he is a foolish fellow, he is rash, he lacketh discretion. Nowadays if they cannot reprove the doctrine that is preached, then they will reprove the preacher that he lacketh due consideration of the times, and that he is of learning sufficient, but he wanteth discretion."

Latimer is speaking feelingly, for he himself had been accused of preaching indiscreetly and even seditiously. Not that he had no patience with discretion; but he was unwilling to use discretion at the expense of truth. "I know that preachers ought to have a discretion in their preaching," he says, "and that they ought to have a consideration and respect to the place and the time that he preacheth in; as I myself will say here what I would not say in the country for no good. But what then? Sin must be rebuked; sin must be plainly spoken against. And when should Jonah have preached against Nineveh if he should have forborne for the respects of the times, or the place, or the state of things there?" Sin had to be rebuked there and judgment denounced against the unrepentant, just as in London where Latimer was preaching. The city of Nineveh believed the Word of God proclaimed through God's preacher; and Christ, when rebuking the wickedness of His generation, declared that the people of Nineveh would rise up against the Jews in the last day and testify against them [Mt. 12:41]. So, too, Latimer dealt faithfully with his generation and earnestly uttered this warning: "I say, Nineveh shall arise against England, thou England; Nineveh shall arise against England, because it will not believe God, nor hear His preachers that cry daily unto them, nor amend their lives, and especially their covetousness."[1]

LATIMER'S EXAMPLE

In Hugh Latimer we have a noble model of a Christian preacher who diligently applied himself to the fulfilment of his high calling and was faithful even unto death. But we will let his servant Augustine Bernher (who himself became a preacher of the Word) speak from first-hand knowledge of "that same reverend father and most constant martyr of Christ, Dr. Hugh Latimer, my most

[1] Latimer: *Works*, Vol. I, pp. 240ff.

dear master: for whose most painful travels, faithful preachings, true carefulness for his country, patient imprisonment, and constant suffering all the whole realm of England hath great cause to give unto the eternal God most high laud and praise . . . Did not God appoint him," asks Bernher, "even in King Henry's days, to be a singular instrument to set forth His truth, and by his preaching to open the eyes of such as were deluded by the subtle and deceitful crafts of the popish prelates?" When he was released from the Tower,[1] "did he give himself up to the pleasures of the world, to delicateness, or idleness? No, assuredly; but even then most of all he began to set forth his plough,[2] and to till the ground of the Lord, and to sow the good corn of God's Word, behaving himself as a faithful messenger of God, being afraid of no man; telling all degrees their duties faithfully and truly, without respect of persons or any kind of flattery." Bernher tells us that besides all his labours in preaching, and despite his advancing years, "every morning ordinarily, winter and summer, about two of the clock in the morning he was at his book most diligently". With prophetic instinct he foresaw the troubles with which England was to be afflicted, and "he ever affirmed that the preaching of the Gospel would cost him his life, to the which thing he did most cheerfully arm and prepare himself".

On the accession of Mary, therefore, the arrival of a royal messenger bearing letters summoning Latimer to London was not unexpected. Indeed, the old bishop was not only ready for him but had actually refused to avail himself of an opportunity which had been given him to escape to safety (which might have spared his opponents some embarrassment, in view of the love and veneration with which Latimer was held by the people). "My friend," he said, "you be a welcome messenger to me; and be it known unto you and to the whole world that I go as willingly to London at this present, being called by my prince to render a reckoning of my doctrine, as ever I was to any place in the world; and I do not

---

[1] Latimer had been imprisoned in the Tower of London during the concluding part of Henry VIII's reign. His inability to sign the notorious Six Articles of 1539 was followed by his resignation of the bishopric of Worcester and his silencing as a preacher until the accession of Edward VI in 1547.

[2] An echo of Latimer's famous Sermon of the Plough, preached in London at the beginning of 1548; cf. pp. 127 ff. above.

doubt but that God, as He hath made me worthy to preach His Word before two excellent princes, [that is, Henry VIII and Edward VI] so He will enable me to witness the same unto the third, [that is, Mary] either to her comfort or to her discomfort eternally." In relating "how patiently he took his imprisonment, and how boldly and willingly he in the end adventured his life in the defence of the glorious Gospel of Jesus Christ", Bernher mentions one thing in particular, namely, that Latimer "being in prison, comfortless and destitute of all worldly help, most of all did rejoice in this, that God had given him grace to apply his office of preaching, and assisted him without fear or flattery to tell unto the wicked their faults and admonish them of their wickedness, neither allowing nor consenting to anything that might be prejudicial or hurtful unto the Gospel of Christ, although the refusal thereof did cast him in danger of his life".[1]

The dark and blood-stained period of Mary's reign, when the preaching of the Gospel was forbidden in the land and preachers were silenced either by death or exile, was succeeded at last by the dawn of the Elizabethan era when preaching began to come into its own once again. The joy that this new day brought is reflected in a letter written from London on 8 August 1559 to the Swiss Reformer Henry Bullinger by Thomas Lever, who after Mary's death had returned with other preachers from exile on the Continent. He describes how they "preached the Gospel in certain parish churches, to which a numerous audience eagerly flocked together", and how, when they "solemnly treated of conversion to Christ by true repentance, many tears from many persons bore witness that the preaching of the Gospel is more effectual to true repentance and wholesome reformation than anything that the whole world can either imagine or approve".[2]

THE REFORM OF WORSHIP

If the rediscovery of the Bible as the authoritative Word of God led to the rediscovery of the necessity of preaching the Gospel to which it bears witness, it also caused the Reformers to become aware of the urgent need for reforming the Church's worship in accordance with the supreme standard of Holy Scripture. And as God had raised up William Tyndale as the primary agent for the

[1] Latimer: *Works*, Vol. I, pp. 319ff.
[2] *Zurich Letters*, Second Series, p. 30.

great work of translating the Scriptures into the English language, and Hugh Latimer as the outstanding preacher of God's Word in those days, so also He had His man prepared to undertake the tremendous task of bringing the worship of the Church of England into line with Holy Scripture. That man was Thomas Cranmer, to whom, under God, more than to anyone else, the treasury of Christian worship which is the English Book of Common Prayer is owed. As a liturgiologist, Cranmer has remained without peer right up to the present moment. His library, containing the works of the early fathers, the medieval authors, and contemporary Reformed theologians, was the envy of scholars and universities. In erudition he was phenomenal. "There was no book," says Strype, "either of the ancient or modern writers, especially upon the point of the eucharist, which he had not noted with his own hand in the most remarkable places: no councils, canons, decrees of popes, which he had not read and well considered." His exact knowledge of authors old and new was the result of his indefatigable reading and made him a formidable opponent in theological controversy.[1] In his controversy with Gardiner, Cranmer took trouble to point out that he was not dependent on the opinions of other men: "I," he writes, "having exercised myself in the study of Scripture and divinity from my youth (whereof I give most hearty lauds and thanks to God), have learned now to go alone, and do examine, judge, and write all such weighty matters myself; although, I thank God, I am neither so arrogant nor so wilful that I will refuse the good advice, counsel, and admonition of any man, be he man or master, friend or foe."[2]

The principles which guided Cranmer and his colleagues as they addressed themselves to the task of reforming the worship of the Church of England are set forth in the two treatises, entitled *Concerning the Service of the Church* and *Of Ceremonies, Why some be abolished and some retained*, which are prefaced to the Book of Common Prayer and which are, almost certainly, from the pen of Cranmer himself. First and foremost, the great foundation, upon which all else must stand, was that of Holy Scripture. This principle of principles, that "it is not lawful for the Church to ordain anything that is contrary to God's Word written", is the master-key to the understanding of the work of the Reformers in the

[1] Strype: *Memorials of Archbishop Cranmer*, Vol. III, pp. 375f.
[2] Cranmer: *Works*, Vol. I, p. 224.

construction of the Prayer Book. Accordingly, attention is drawn in the first place to the ordering of the ancient fathers of the Church "that all the whole Bible (or the greatest part thereof) should be read over once every year; intending thereby that the clergy, and especially such as were ministers in the congregation, should (by often reading and meditation in God's Word) be stirred up to godliness themselves, and be more able to exhort others by wholesome doctrine, and to confute them that were adversaries to the truth; and, further, that the people (by daily hearing of Holy Scripture read in the church) might continually profit more and more in the knowledge of God, and be the more inflamed with the love of His true religion". This, then, is the primary and supreme principle in the reform of Christian worship: the authority of Holy Scripture as the measuring-rod by which all forms of worship must be ruled.

In the second place, we find that there is a thorough respect for the scriptural catholicity of the ancient Church and a desire to reinstate the purer order of the past after centuries of corruption and deterioration. It is important to realize that the Reformers did not view themselves as innovators, but as restorers: their aim was to *re*form what during the intervening generations had become *de*formed. In declaring *"Renovatores modo sumus, non Novatores"*, Lancelot Andrewes at the beginning of the seventeenth century was but defending the Church of England as it had been renewed by his predecessors.[1] By the beginning of the sixteenth century the Church had reached a state which may aptly be described in the terms of Christ's denunciation of the religious situation of Judaism in His day: the commandments of God had been laid aside and replaced by the commandments of men to such an extent that the Word of God had been rendered null and void through the prevalence of human traditions (Mk. 7:6f.). "These many years past," writes Cranmer, "this godly and decent order of the ancient fathers [that is, the daily reading of Scripture] hath been so altered, broken, and neglected, by planting in uncertain stories and legends, with multitude of responds, verses, vain repetitions, commemorations, and synodals, that commonly when any book of the Bible was begun after three or four chapters were read out all the rest were unread." Holy Scripture had, indeed, been virtually smothered by a mass of man-made importations.

[1] Lancelot Andrewes: *Works*, Vol. III (Oxford, 1843), p. 26.

WORSHIP IN THE VERNACULAR

Another principle of liturgical reform was that the services of the Church should be conducted in the language of the people, so that all could understand and participate intelligently in public worship. Hence the complaint that, "whereas St. Paul would have such language spoken to the people in the church as they might understand, and have profit by hearing the same, the service in this Church of England these many years hath been read in Latin to the people, which they understand not; so that they have heard with their ears only, and their heart, spirit, and mind have not been edified thereby". It was to remedy this serious defect that the Book of *Common* Prayer was constructed, setting forth worship in which all the congregation could join in common, because it was in their own native language. As Article XXIV declares, "it is a thing plainly repugnant to the Word of God and the custom of the primitive Church to have public prayer in the church, or to minister the sacraments, in a tongue not understanded of the people".

In 1549, when replying to the Devon rebels who had demanded, amongst other things, the restoration of the Latin mass, Cranmer insisted that in public worship everything that is done "should be the act of the people and pertain to the people, as well as to the priest. And standeth it with reason," he argues, "that the priest should speak for you, and in your name, and you answer him again in your own person, and yet you understand never a word, neither what he saith nor what you say yourselves? The priest prayeth to God for you, and you answer *Amen*, you wot not whereto. Is there any reason herein? Will you not understand what the priest prayeth for you, what thanks he giveth for you, what he asketh for you? Will you neither understand what he saith, nor let your hearts understand what your own tongues answer? Then must you needs confess yourself to be such people as Christ spake of when He said, 'These people honour Me with their lips, but their hearts be far from Me'. Had you rather be like pies [that is, magpies] or parrots, that be taught to speak, and yet understand not one word that they say, than be true Christian men that pray unto God in heart and in faith? . . . I have heard suitors murmur at the bar because their attorneys have pleaded their cases in the French tongue, which they understood not. Why then be you offended that the priests, who plead your cause before God, should speak such language as you may understand? If you were before the king's highness, and should choose one to speak for you all, I am sure you would not choose one that should speak Greek or Hebrew, French or Italian, no, nor one that should speak Latin neither. But you would be glad to provide such a one as should speak your own language, and speak so loud that you might both hear him and understand him, that you might allow or disallow what he said in your names. Why do you then refuse to do the like unto God? When the priest desireth anything of God for you, or giveth thanks for you, how can you in your heart confirm his sayings when you know not one word that he saith? For the heart is not moved with words that be not understood."

Referring to the admonition given by Paul to the Corinthians— "If the trumpet give an uncertain sound, who shall prepare himself to the battle? So likewise ye?, except ye utter by the tongue words easy to be understood, how shall it be known what is spoken? for ye shall speak into the air" (I Cor. 14:8f.)—Cranmer writes: "Even so should the priests be God's trump in His Church: so that if he blow a certain blast that the people may understand, they be much edified thereby; but if he give such a sound as is to the people unknown, it is clearly in vain, saith St. Paul, for he speaks to the air; but no man is the better or edified thereby, nor knoweth what he should do by what he heareth . . . . Be you such enemies to your own country," he asks the rebels, "that you will not suffer us to laud God, to thank Him, and to use His sacraments in our own tongue, but will enforce us contrary as well to all reason as to the Word of God?"[1]

William Whitaker, writing in Elizabeth's reign, declared that he could "recognize no greater holiness in one language than another". and denied that "the majesty of sacred things can be diminished by any vernacular tongues, however barbarous". At the same time he affirmed that "nothing can be more dignified, majestic, or holy than the Gospel". To the objection that by the use of the vernacular "the mysteries of the sacraments are horribly profaned, which should be carefully concealed from the common people", he answered that "neither Christ nor the apostles ever commanded that those mysteries should be concealed from the people". To conceal the design and purpose of the sacraments is to

[1] Cranmer: *Works*, Vol. II, pp. 169f.

render them meaningless and unfruitful. "These therefore should not be concealed, but explained to God's people; and the hiding of them is an antichristian device to fill the people with a stupid admiration of they know not what."[1] He adduces evidence to show, also, that "it was the custom of the primitive Church for the whole people to combine their desires and assent with the prayers of the minister, and not, as with the papists (amongst whom the priest alone performs his service in an unknown tongue), to remain silent or murmur their own indefinite prayers to themselves".[2]

It was, naturally, a matter of acute distress to the Reformers when Mary, on her accession in 1553, set aside the Book of Common Prayer and caused the nation to revert to the traditions of medievalism, including the use of Latin in the services of the church. Thus we find Ridley writing from his prison cell as follows: "As for the darkness that Satan now bringeth upon the Church of England, who needeth to doubt thereof? Of late time, our Saviour Christ, His apostles, prophets, and teachers, spoke in the temple to the people of England in the English tongue, so that they might be understood plainly and without any hardness of the godly and such as sought for heavenly knowledge in matters which, of necessity of salvation, pertained to the obtaining of eternal life. But now those things which once were written of them for the edifying of the congregation are read on a strange tongue without interpretation, manifestly against St. Paul's commandment;[3] so that there is no man able to understand them who hath not learned that strange and unknown tongue." The conduct of worship in English made it possible for all "to join their hearts and lips in prayer together". Now, however, to Ridley's sorrow, the services of the Church "are commanded to be hid and shut up from them in a strange tongue, whereby it must needs follow that the people neither can tell how to pray nor what to pray for; and how can they join their hearts and voices together," he asks, "when they understand no more what the voice signifieth than a brute beast."[4]

The use of the English language is, as this quotation from Ridley shows, closely bound up with another principle of Christian worship, namely, that it should be congregational. It is not the

---

[1] Whitaker: *Disputation on Holy Scripture*, pp. 250ff.
[2] Whitaker: *Ibid.*, p. 271.    [3] See I Cor. 14:5, 28.
[4] Ridley: *Works*, pp. 349f.

preserve of a priest functioning in isolation from the people. Nor are the people intended to be uncomprehending spectators or mere attenders. They are there *to worship*, and they should therefore be able to participate intelligently in the services, to "join their hearts and voices together" in the united adoration of Almighty God. It is for the minister to lead, not to monopolize, the worship of the Church.

It was necessary, further, that the services of the Church which had become encumbered and complicated with a multiplicity of regulations should be simplified and set free from everything that hindered the spontaneous approach to God in prayer and praise. The desirability of having certain rules for the proper ordering of public worship was, of course, admitted. Paul's clear injunction was that everything should be done decently and in order (I Cor. 14:40). The rules now proposed, however, were, in contrast to those they were replacing, "few in number" and "plain and easy to be understood". The Book of Common Prayer is introduced as "an order for prayer and for the reading of Holy Scripture much agreeable to the mind and purpose of the old fathers, and a great deal more profitable and commodious than that which of late was used". The reason for its being more profitable is that "here are left out many things, whereof some are untrue, some uncertain, some vain and superstitious", and that "nothing is ordained to be read but the very pure Word of God, the Holy Scriptures, or that which is agreeable to the same, and that in such a language and order as is most easy and plain for the understanding both of the readers and hearers". It is more commodious "for the shortness thereof, and for the plainness of the order, and for that the rules be few and easy".

In explaining why some ceremonies were abolished and some retained, it is pointed out that "the great excess and multitude" of ceremonies "hath so increased in these latter days that the burden of them was intolerable". The complaint of Augustine in his day, more than a thousand years previously, is cited, to the effect that ceremonies had "grown to such a number that the estate of Christian people was in worse case concerning that matter than were the Jews". Augustine had counselled that "such yoke and burden should be taken away".[1] "But," it is asked, "what would St. Augustine have said if he had seen the ceremonies of late days

[1] See Augustine: Letter LV, to Januarius.

used among us, whereunto the multitude used in his time was not to be compared?" The excess of ceremonies in the years prior to the Reformation was "so great, and many of them so dark, that they did more confound and darken than declare and set forth Christ's benefits unto us". The Reformers could be content "only with those ceremonies which do serve to a decent order and godly discipline". Accordingly, "the most weighty cause of the abolishment of certain ceremonies was, that they were so far abused, partly by the superstitious blindness of the rude and unlearned, and partly by the insatiable avarice of such as sought more their own lucre than the glory of God, that the abuses could not well be taken away, the thing remaining still".

At the same time, however, there was no wholesale jettisoning of what was old. There were some, indeed, in the Church at that time who advocated abandoning all that belonged to the past and starting again entirely *de novo*. But to such it is rejoined that "surely where the old may be well used, there they cannot reasonably reprove the old only for their age, without betraying of their own folly". On the contrary, "in such a case they ought rather to have reverence unto them for their antiquity". There is no special virtue attaching to "innovations and new-fangledness", which ought rather "always to be eschewed". And there was in fact no just excuse for offence since the ceremonies abandoned were those which were the "most abused, and did burden men's consciences without any cause"; while those retained were "neither dark nor dumb ceremonies, but are so set forth that every man understands what they do mean, and to what use they do serve". These were retained also in the interests of "discipline and order".

The Reformers were careful to explain that it was only their own house of the Church of England that they were setting in order. It was by no means their desire to dictate to other nations and churches as to the precise manner in which they ought to worship. "In these our doings," they say, "we condemn no other nations, nor prescribe anything but to our own people only: for we think it convenient that every country should use such ceremonies as they shall think best to the setting forth of God's honour and glory, and to the reducing of the people to a most perfect and godly living, without error of superstition." Reformed churches in other countries were to be free to order their worship in accordance with the requirements of their own particular circumstances, though always in obedience to the supreme rule of the Word of God.[1]

PRINCIPLES OF REFORMED WORSHIP

The principles, then, by which the Reformers were guided as they redrafted the public worship of the Church of England may be summarized under the following heads:

1. *Scripturalness*. All Christian worship must be governed by the revelation of God's Word, which is the touchstone of all doctrine and worship.

2. *Catholicity*. What is the best from the treasury of devotion of the past is not to be rejected, remembering always that that only is truly catholic which is in harmony with the apostolic witness of the New Testament.

3. *Purity*. All that is false and superstitious must be discarded, and those things originally good in themselves which have become corrupted and distorted must be reformed.

4. *Simplicity*. An excessive number of rules and rites is to be avoided. True worship is itself essentially a simple act, and it is a spiritual tragedy when the simplicity characteristic of the New Testament becomes lost under a burdensome accumulation of man-made traditions and elaborations.

5. *Intelligibility*. To worship without the understanding is not to worship at all, but to lapse into superstition; and therefore it is essential that Christian worship should be in that language which is understood by all the people.

6. *Commonness*. The people are not spectators but participants, for Christian worship is the prerogative of clergy and people together, not of one in isolation from the other, and therefore it must be congregational, or common, worship.

7. *Orderliness*. God is God of order, not disorder, and as the proper end of all worship is the glory of God, so, in accordance with the apostolic injunction, all things should be done in decent and orderly fashion.

The achievement of the Reformers in the restoration of public worship which conformed to these principles is well described by Nicholas Ridley in his farewell letter from prison. "This Church of England," he writes, "had of late, [that is, under Edward VI]

[1] The preceding quotations are from the Preface to the Book of Common Prayer.

of the infinite goodness and abundant grace of Almighty God, great substance, great riches of heavenly treasure, great plenty of God's true and sincere Word, the true and wholesome administration of Christ's holy sacraments, the whole profession of Christ's religion truly and plainly set forth in baptism, the plain declaration and understanding of the same taught in the holy catechism, to have been learned of all true Christians. This church had also a true and sincere form and manner of the Lord's supper, wherein, according to Jesus Christ's own ordinance and holy institution, Christ's commandments were executed and done. For upon the bread and the wine set upon the Lord's table thanks were given, the commemoration of the Lord's death was had, the bread in the remembrance of Christ's body torn upon the cross was broken, and the cup in the remembrance of Christ's blood shed was distributed, and both communicated unto all that were present and would receive them, and also they were exhorted of the minister so to do. All was done openly in the vulgar tongue, so that everything might be both easily heard and plainly understood of all the people, to God's high glory, and the edification of the whole church. This church had of late the whole divine service, all common and public prayers ordained to be said and heard in the common congregation, not only framed and fashioned to the true vein of Holy Scripture, but also all things so set forth according to the commandment of the Lord and St. Paul's doctrine, for the people's edification, in their vulgar tongue. It had also holy and wholesome homilies in commendation of the principal virtues which are commended in Scripture; and likewise other homilies against the most pernicious and capital vices that useth (alas) to reign in this realm of England. This church had, in matters of controversy, articles so penned and framed after the Holy Scripture and grounded upon the true understanding of God's Word, that in short time, if they had been universally received, they should have been able to have set in Christ's Church much concord and unity in Christ's true religion, and to have expelled many false errors and heresies, wherewith this church (alas) was almost overgone."[1]

With the termination of the unhappy Marian interlude the Reformed order of worship was restored in England, and under Elizabeth's illustrious rule the Book of Common Prayer was the

[1] Ridley: *Works*, pp. 399f.

focal point of religious unity in the nation—not that there were not disputes, and demands for revision from certain quarters, but the points at issue concerned matters of subsidiary importance (such as the wearing of the surplice, the sign of the cross in baptism, kneeling to receive communion, and the giving of a ring in marriage) and did not threaten the significant general unanimity over the worship of the Prayer Book and the principles on which they were based. The persecutions and burnings under Mary did more, in fact, to establish the Reformed faith than to uproot it, as the virile Protestantism which flourished once more during Elizabeth's reign shows. The principles of the English Reformation were vigorously reaffirmed in the famous *Apology of the Church of England*, written in 1562 by John Jewel, Bishop of Salisbury. Jewel's defence of the manner in which the worship of the Church of England had been reformed fully confirms what has been already said. "We receive and embrace all the canonical Scriptures, both of the Old and New Testament," he declares, "giving thanks to our God who hath raised up unto us that light which we might ever have before our eyes, lest either by the subtlety of man or by the snares of the devil we should be carried away to errors and lies." The Scriptures are, indeed, "the very sure and infallible rule whereby may be tried whether the Church doth stagger and err, and whereunto all ecclesiastical doctrine ought to be called to account"; and he pointedly adds (for the Council of Trent was still in session) that "against these Scriptures neither law nor ordinance nor any custom ought to be heard: no, though Paul himself or an angel from heaven should come and teach the contrary".[1]

After vindicating the Reformed doctrine of the sacraments (a subject with which we deal in chapter VI), Jewel continues: "As touching the multitude of vain and superfluous ceremonies, we know that Augustine did grievously complain of them in his own time; and therefore have we cut off a great number of them, because we know that men's consciences were cumbered about them, and the churches of God overladen with them. Nevertheless, we keep still and esteem not only those ceremonies which we are sure were delivered to us from the apostles, but some others too besides, which we thought might be suffered without hurt to the Church of God: because we had a desire that all things in the holy congregation might (as Paul commandeth) 'be done with comeliness and

[1] Jewel: *Works*, Vol. III, p. 62. Cf. Gal. 1:8f.

in good order'; but as for all those things which we saw were either very superstitious, or unprofitable, noisome, or mockeries, or contrary to the Holy Scriptures, or else unseemly for honest or discreet folks, as there be an infinite number nowadays where papistry is used, these, I say, we have utterly refused without all manner of exception, because we would not have the right worshipping of God any longer defiled with such follies."[1]

## INVOCATION OF SAINTS AND IMAGES

Of the superstitions against which the Reformers protested one of the most widely practised was the invocation of the saints. Thomas Becon describes, with irony, the situation which prevailed under the Roman Church: "If it be done of a good intent, they say, all is well whatsoever we do. If we fast the blessed saints' evens and worship them with a *Paternoster*, *Ave*, and creed, they will do for us whatsoever we ask. St. George will defend us in battle against our enemies. St. Barbara will keep us from thundering and lightning. St. Agasse [Agatha] will save our house from burning. St. Antony will keep our swine. St. Luke will save our ox. St. Job will defend us from the pox. St. Gertrude will keep our house from mice and rats. St. Nicholas will preserve us from drowning. St. Loye will cure our horse. St. Dorothy will save our herbs and flowers. St. Sith [Osyth] will bring again whatsoever we lose. St. Apolline will heal the pain of our teeth. St. Sweetlad and St Agnes will send us maids good husbands. St. Peter will let us in at heaven-gates—with a thousand such-like."[2]

It is noteworthy that in the Litany, that admirable and comprehensive form of public intercession in the Book of Common Prayer, all invocations addressed to the Virgin Mary, angels, and saints—so characteristic of unreformed worship—were completely removed. Throughout the length of the Prayer Book all prayers are offered to God through Jesus Christ, and through no other mediator. Bishop Jewel explains that, as no mortal creature "can be justified by his own deserts in God's sight", therefore "our only succour and refuge is to fly to the mercy of our Father by Jesu Christ, and assuredly to persuade our minds that He is the obtainer of forgiveness for our sins, and that by His blood all our spots of sin be washed clean".[3]

[1] Jewel: *Works*, Vol. III, p. 65.     [2] Becon: *Works*, Vol. II, p. 536.
[3] Jewel: *Works*, Vol. III, p. 66.

Similarly with the worshipping or honouring of inanimate objects, such as images and relics, for, as Tyndale points out, all creatures other than angels and men "are in honour less than man, and man is lord over them". They are not made after the image of God as man is, nor have they been bought at the price of Christ's blood as man has. "The honour of them is to do man service, and man's dishonour is to do them honourable service, as unto his better." The sumptuous clothing and decking of images with rich garments and costly jewels is a sin both against God and against one's neighbour. "It followeth," says Tyndale, "that we cannot, but unto our damnation, put a coat worth an hundred coats upon a post's back and let the image of God and the price of Christ's blood [sc. our fellow-man] go up and down thereby naked. For if we care more to clothe the dead image made by man and the price of silver, than the lively image of God and the price of Christ's blood, then we dishonour the image of God and Him that made him, and the price of Christ's blood, and Him that bought him."[1]

The distinction made by the papists between different degrees of worship or reverence—*dulia* to angels, saints, and images, *hyperdulia* to the Virgin Mary, and *latria* to God—is without substance, for it is a distinction which is opposed to the plain teaching of Scripture, as the Reformers show in many places in their writings. It is God alone to whom, as our Creator and Redeemer, we owe all worship and honour. In Tyndale's words: "God hath created and made us unto His own likeness, and our Saviour Christ hath bought us with His blood. And therefore we are God's possession, of duty and right, and Christ's servants only, to wait on His will and pleasure, and ought therefore to move neither hand nor foot, nor any other member, either heart or mind, otherwise than He hath appointed. God is honoured in His own person when we receive all things, both good and bad, at His hand, and love His law with all our hearts, and believe, hope, and long for all that He promiseth."[2]

In the *Homily against Peril of Idolatry* Bishop Jewel, whose work it is believed to be, speaks of "the corruption of these latter days" which has "brought into the church infinite multitude of images" and describes how these have been "decked with gold and silver, painted with colours, set . . . with stone and pearl, clothed . . . with

[1] Tyndale: *Answer to Sir Thomas More's Dialogue*, in *Works*, Vol. III, p. 59.  [2] Tyndale: *Op. cit.*, p. 57.

silks and precious vestures", and have been the cause of great harm to "the simple and unwise, occasioning them thereby to commit most horrible idolatry".[1] There follows a lengthy demonstration that such practices are contrary both to the worship enjoined in God's Word and also to the teaching of the "holy and ancient learned fathers and doctors", and a refutation of the arguments put forward to justify the use of images in the worship of the Church. Particularly significant is the example of the Apostles and of Christ Himself; for Peter forbade Cornelius to fall down and worship him (Acts 10:25f.), Paul and Barnabas restrained the people of Lystra from sacrificing to them (Acts 14:18), John was rebuked by the angel when he wished to worship him and admonished to worship God (Rev. 19:10, 22:8), and Christ, when Satan offered Him all the kingdoms of the world on condition that He would bow down and worship him, repelled the tempter by quoting from Holy Writ, "Thou shalt worship the Lord thy God, and Him only shalt thou serve" (Mt. 4:8ff., Dt. 6:13)[2]. "Whereas", writes Jewel, "all godly men did ever abhor that any kneeling and worshipping or offering should be used to themselves when they were alive, for that it was the honour due to God only, . . . yet we like madmen fall down before the dead idols or images of Peter and Paul, and give that honour to stocks and stones which they thought abominable to be given to themselves being alive." On the strength of the examples given, and especially that of Christ, the following exhortation is offered: "Therefore, above all things, if we take ourselves to be Christians indeed, as we be named, let us credit the word, obey the law, and follow the doctrine and example of our Saviour and Master Christ, repelling Satan's suggestion to idolatry and worshipping of images, according to the truth alleged and taught out of the Testament and Gospel of our said heavenly Doctor and Schoolmaster Jesus Christ."[3]

The conclusion of this matter is that true religion and pleasing of God consists, "not in making, setting up, painting, gilding, clothing, and decking of dumb and dead images, . . . nor in kissing of them, capping, kneeling, offering to them, in censing of them, setting up of candles, hanging up of legs, arms, or whole bodies of wax before them, or praying and asking of them or of saints things belonging only to God to give". "Let us take heed and be

[1] *Book of Homilies* (London, 1899), p. 180.
[2] Cf. pp. 67f.     [3] *Book of Homilies*, pp. 193f.

wise," we are counselled, "and let us have no strange gods, but one only God, who made us when we were nothing, the Father of our Lord Jesus Christ, who redeemed us when we were lost, and with His Holy Spirit, who doth sanctify us. For 'this is life everlasting, to know Him to be the only true God, and Jesus Christ whom He hath sent'.[1] Let us honour and worship for religion's sake none but Him; and Him let us worship and honour as He will Himself, and hath declared by His Word that He will be honoured and worshipped; not in or by images or idols, which He hath most straitly forbidden, neither in kneeling, lighting of candles, burning of incense, offering up of gifts unto images and idols, to believe that we shall please Him; for all these be abomination before God; but let us honour and worship God *in spirit and truth*, [Jn. 4:24] fearing and loving Him above all things, trusting in Him only, calling upon Him and praying to Him only, praising and lauding of Him only, and all other in Him and for Him."[2]

WORSHIP IN SPIRIT AND TRUTH

God, who is Himself Spirit and Truth, cannot, indeed, be worshipped appropriately except in spirit and in truth, and He may be worshipped in this way in any place and under any circumstances; for, as another of the Homilies, that *Of the Right Use of the Church*, reminds us, He who is "the Lord of heaven and earth, whose seat is in heaven and the earth His footstool, cannot be enclosed in temples or houses made with man's hand, as in dwelling-places able to receive or contain His majesty". This Scripture clearly testifies (cf. Acts 7:48f., 17:24). Nevertheless, it was with the divine sanction that the temple of old was erected in Jerusalem and was spoken of as God's holy temple and the house of prayer; and, further, it was the practice of both Christ and His Apostles to worship and preach in synagogues wherever they went. This example, not to speak of the practice of the Christian Church throughout the centuries, assures us that God approves the material church building as a place "for the people of God to resort together unto, there to hear God's holy Word, to call upon His holy Name, to give Him thanks for His innumerable and unspeakable benefits bestowed upon us, and duly and truly to celebrate His holy sacraments; in the unfeigned doing and accomplishing of which standeth that true and right worshipping of God

[1] Jn. 17:3.  [2] *Book of Homilies*, pp. 281f.

aforementioned''. It is urged, moreover, that "all godly men and women ought, at time appointed, with diligence to resort unto the house of the Lord, there to serve Him and to glorify Him, as He is most worthy and we most bound".[1]

We are exhorted also to learn the lesson, not only from the Israelites of old but also from Christ Himself, who drove out with a scourge the profaners of God's temple because they had turned the house of prayer into a den of thieves,[2] that the place of public prayer is to be used and treated with reverence. To neglect to come to God's house, or on coming to behave irreverently in church, is to invite the displeasure of God upon ourselves—the same displeasure as was forcibly shown by Christ against those who profaned the sacred precincts in His day. If we dread the punishment of Almighty God, then (proceeds the Homily) "let us amend this our negligence and contempt in coming to the house of the Lord, this our irreverent behaviour in the house of the Lord; and restoring thither diligently together, let us there, with reverent hearing of the Lord's holy Word, calling on the Lord's holy Name, giving of hearty thanks unto the Lord for all His manifold and inestimable benefits daily and hourly bestowed upon us, celebrating also reverently of the Lord's holy sacraments, serve the Lord in His holy house, as becometh the servants of the Lord, 'in holiness and righteousness before Him all the days of our life':[3] and then we shall be assured after this life to 'rest in His holy hill' and to dwell in His tabernacle',[4] there to praise and magnify His holy name in the congregation of His saints,[5] in the holy house of His eternal kingdom of heaven, which He hath purchased for us by the death and shedding of the precious blood of His Son our Saviour Jesus Christ."[6]

The worship of Almighty God, Creator, Redeemer, and Judge, was for the Reformers not merely an indescribable privilege but also a most solemn responsibility. They approached God with love and joy indeed, but with awe too, for they were ever conscious of His infinite majesty and holiness. To come before God without seriousness was great wickedness.

This seriousness is impressively shown in the three longer exhortations of the Communion service. This sacrament which, being the sacrament of the body and blood of Christ, is to be "received

---

[1] *Book of Homilies*, pp. 163ff.  [2] Mt. 21:12f.  [3] Lk. 1:75.
[4] Ps. 15:1.  [5] Ps. 149:1.  [6] *Book of Homilies*, pp. 171ff.

in remembrance of His meritorious cross and passion, whereby alone we obtain remission of our sins and are made partakers of the kingdom of heaven," is "so divine and comfortable a thing to them who receive it worthily" and "so dangerous to them that will presume to receive it unworthily", that those proposing to partake of it are urged "so to search and examine your own consciences (and that not lightly and after the manner of dissemblers with God; but so) that ye may come holy and clean to such a heavenly feast, in the marriage garment required by God in Holy Scripture, and be received as worthy partakers of that holy Table". To this end the following counsel is then given: "First, to examine your lives and conversations by the rule of God's commandments, and whereinsoever ye shall perceive yourselves to have offended, either by will, word, or deed, there to bewail your own sinfulness, and to confess yourselves to Almighty God, with full purpose of amendment of life. And if ye shall perceive your offences to be such as are not only against God but also against your neighbours, then ye shall reconcile yourselves unto them, being ready to make restitution and satisfaction, according to the uttermost of your powers, for all injuries and wrongs done by you to any other; and being likewise ready to forgive others that have offended you, as ye would have forgiveness of your offences at God's hand: for otherwise the receiving of the Holy Communion doth nothing else but increase your damnation."

The second of these exhortations is addressed to those who show themselves negligent to come to the Lord's Table. "Ye know," says the minister, "how grievous and unkind a thing it is, when a man hath prepared a rich feast, decked his table with all kinds of provision, so that there lacketh nothing but the guests to sit down; and yet they who are called (without any excuse) most unthankfully refuse to come. Which of you in such a case would not be moved? Who would not think a great injury and wrong done unto him? Wherefore, most dearly beloved in Christ, take ye good heed, lest ye, withdrawing yourselves from this holy supper, provoke God's indignation against you." The congregation is reminded that those who, in the parable, for a variety of pretexts refused to accept the invitation to the banquet were not excused, but were "counted unworthy of the heavenly feast", which is the plainest and most solemn of warnings.[1]

[1] Lk. 14:15f.

Again, in the third exhortation, appointed for the time of communion, the people are reminded of the apostolic admonition that those who eat that bread and drink that cup unworthily are guilty of the body and blood of the Lord, and eat and drink their own condemnation, thereby inviting the punishment of God upon themselves (I Cor. 11:27f.); and they are then solemnly exhorted in the following terms: "Judge therefore yourselves, brethren, that ye be not judged of the Lord; repent you truly of your sins past; have a lively and steadfast faith in Christ our Saviour; amend your lives, and be in perfect charity with all men; so shall ye be meet partakers of those holy mysteries, And above all things ye must give most humble and hearty thanks to God, the Father, the Son, and the Holy Ghost, for the redemption of the world by the death and passion of our Saviour Christ, both God and man; who did humble Himself, even to the death upon the cross, for us, miserable sinners, who lay in darkness and the shadow of death; that He might make us the children of God, and exalt us to everlasting life ... To Him therefore, with the Father and the Holy Ghost, let us give (as we are most bounden) continual thanks; submitting ourselves wholly to his Holy will and pleasure, and studying to serve Him in true holiness and righteousness all the days of our life."

The marks of earnestness, profundity, and devotion are characteristic of the approach of the Reformers to Christian worship— an approach which is summed up to perfection in the beautiful "prayer of humble access" in the service of Holy Communion, which reads: "We do not presume to come to this Thy table, O merciful Lord, trusting in our own righteousness, but in Thy manifold and great mercies. We are not worthy so much as to gather up the crumbs under Thy table. But Thou art the same Lord, whose property is always to have mercy: Grant us therefore, gracious Lord, so to eat the flesh of Thy dear Son Jesus Christ, and to drink His blood, that our sinful bodies may be made clean by His body, and our souls washed through His most precious blood, and that we may evermore dwell in Him, and He in us." By their example and by their writings, and particularly by the Book of Common Prayer, the Reformers recall us to worship that is scriptural, that is evangelical, and that is serious.

# V

# MINISTRY

We are but God's servants, God's messengers, appointed to lead and guide you. Thus therefore ought every man to esteem the preachers of God's Gospel, as messengers, as servants, as ministers of Christ; thus ought every man to think and judge of them.

*John Jewel*

# MINISTRY

We have seen in the preceding chapter how the Reformers re-instated evangelical preaching and gave it a place of honour as God's primary instrument of salvation. The central place which preaching enjoyed in their doctrine of the ministry is nowhere more strikingly demonstrated than in the Ordinal of the Church of England. Prior to the Reformation, and still today in the Roman Catholic Church, the emphasis in ordination is overwhelmingly on the sacerdotal function of the ministry. Indeed, that the minister is regarded as essentially an offerer of sacrifices is apparent from the title itself, *sacerdos*, of the office to which he is ordained. In the ordination service the bishop defines the foremost duty of the priest (*sacerdos*) as to offer the sacrifice of the mass; he vests him with the chasuble, with the words: "Receive the sacerdotal vest-ment"; he prays that by an immaculate benediction he may trans-form the bread and wine into the body and blood of God's Son, and anoints the hands of the candidate with oil for this express pur-pose; and he then delivers to him a paten on which is the unconse-crated host and a chalice containing wine mixed with water, with these words: "Receive power to offer sacrifice to God and to cele-brate mass both for the living and for the dead." This delivery of the instruments of his ministry (*porrectio instrumentorum*) together with the authorization to function as a sacrificing priest constitutes the essence of valid ordination in the Roman rite.

## THE ENGLISH ORDINAL

The Reformers, however, rejected this whole concept of the Christian ministry as a sacerdotal priesthood. In the first English Ordinal, published in 1550, not only the bread and the cup but also, significantly, a Bible is delivered to the candidate, who is given authority "to preach the Word of God and to minister the holy sacraments". The candidate, in short, is being ordained to the ministry of the Word and sacraments. There is no mention of the offering of sacrifices. All the ceremonial referred to above is omitted. But in the 1552 Ordinal (which is in all essentials the same as that of 1662 in the present Prayer Book) the handing over of paten and chalice to the ordinand is discontinued, so that any possible excuse for misconstruction or misrepresentation may be removed. The sole "instrument" of his ministry is now the Bible: not, however, that it is regarded as no longer a ministry of the sacraments, but rather that the sacraments, as visible words, are rightly included within the ministry of the Word. Thus the bishop still says to him: "Take thou authority to preach the Word of God and to minister the holy sacraments . . . " The prayer at the end of the service is focussed on the Word of God: the Heavenly Father is desired to send His blessing on those newly ordained, "that they may be clothed with righteousness", that "Thy Word spoken by their mouths may have such success that it may never be spoken in vain", and that "we may have grace to hear and receive what they shall deliver out of Thy most holy Word, or agreeable to the same, as the means of our salvation".

So also, in the earlier part of the service, the bishop in describing the office to which they are called makes no mention of any sacerdotal function: their calling, he reminds them, is "to be messengers, watchmen, and stewards of the Lord; to teach and to premonish, to feed and provide for the Lord's family; to seek for Christ's sheep that are dispersed abroad, and for His children who are in the midst of this naughty world, that they may be saved through Christ for ever". "Seeing," he exhorts them, "that you cannot by any other means compass the doing of so weighty a work, pertaining to the salvation of man, but with doctrine and exhortation taken out of the Holy Scriptures, and with a life agreeable to the same; consider how studious ye ought to be in reading and learning the Scriptures, and in framing the manners both of yourselves and of them that specially pertain unto you, according to the rule of the same Scriptures." And he expresses his "good hope" that "you have clearly determined, by God's grace, to give yourselves wholly to this office whereunto it hath pleased God to call you: so that . . . you will continually pray to God the Father, by the mediation of our only Saviour Jesus Christ, for the heavenly assistance of the Holy Ghost; that, by daily reading and weighing of the Scriptures, ye may wax riper and stronger in your ministry . . ."

The emphasis is no different in the consecration of an archbishop or bishop. As when he was ordained priest, so now again the one to be consecrated declares that he is "persuaded that the Holy Scriptures contain sufficiently all doctrine required of necessity for eternal salvation through faith in Jesus Christ", and that he is "determined out of the same Holy Scriptures to instruct the people committed to [his] charge, and to teach or maintain nothing as required of necessity to eternal salvation, but that which [he] shall be persuaded may be concluded and proved by the same". He promises that he will "faithfully exercise himself in the same Holy Scriptures, and call upon God by prayer for the true understanding of the same, so as [he] may be able by them to teach and exhort with wholesome doctrine, and to withstand and convince the gainsayers". And he affirms that he is "ready, with all faithful diligence, to banish and drive away all erroneous and strange doctrine contrary to God's Word, and both privately and openly to call upon and encourage others to the same".

There is, again, no hint of any sacerdotal function in the episcopal office to which he is being called. It is the pastoral obligations of the office that are stressed—the setting of an example of godly living to others, the maintenance of due discipline in his diocese, faithfulness in "ordaining, sending, or laying hands upon others", and the showing of gentleness and mercy "for Christ's sake to poor and needy people and to all strangers destitute of help". For him as bishop, no less than as presbyter, the Bible is the "instrument" of his ministry. The Book is handed to him with an admonition to be, in the first place, loyal to God's Word: "Give heed unto reading, exhortation, and doctrine. Think upon the things contained in this Book. Be diligent in them, that the increase coming thereby may be manifest unto all men. Take heed unto thyself and to doctrine, and be diligent in doing them; for by so doing thou shalt both save thyself and them that hear thee." And, in the second place, he is admonished to be faithful as a pastor of God's people: "Be to the flock of Christ a shepherd, not a wolf; feed them, devour them not. Hold up the weak, heal the sick, bind up the broken, bring again the outcasts, seek the lost. Be so merciful, that you be not too remiss; so minister discipline, that you forget not mercy: that when the chief Shepherd shall appear you may receive the never-fading crown of glory." As John Jewel wrote to Josiah Simler, "we require our bishops to be pastors, labourers, and watchmen".[1]

In the Preface to his *Defence of the True and Catholic Doctrine of the Sacrament* Archbishop Cranmer describes the sacerdotalism of the papal Church, and the distinctive doctrines associated with

[1] *Zurich Letters*, Vol. I, p. 50.

it, as the very tap-root of the tree of error which he and his fellow Reformers felt it essential to extirpate. "The rest," he says, "is but leaves and branches, the cutting away whereof is but like topping and lopping of a tree or cutting down of weeds, leaving the body standing and the roots in the ground; but the very body of the tree, or rather the roots of the weeds, is the popish doctrine of transubstantiation, of the real presence of Christ's flesh and blood in the sacrament of the altar (as they call it), and of the sacrifice and oblation of Christ made by the priest for the salvation of the quick and the dead. Which roots if they be suffered to grow in the Lord's vineyard, they will overspread all the ground again with the old errors and superstitions. These injuries to Christ be so intolerable that no Christian heart can willingly bear them. Wherefore, seeing that many have set to their hands and whetted their tools to pluck up the weeds and to cut down the tree of error, I, not knowing otherwise how to excuse myself at the last day, have in this book set to my hand and axe with the rest, to cut down this tree and to pluck up the weeds by the roots, which our heavenly Father never planted." And he testifies concerning his responsibilities as a minister of Christ: "I know in what office God hath placed me, and to what purpose, that is to say, to set forth His Word truly unto His people to the uttermost of my power, without respect of person or regard of anything in the world, but of Him alone. I know what account I shall make to Him hereof at the last day, when every man shall answer for his vocation and receive for the same good or ill, according as he hath done. I know how antichrist hath obscured the glory of God and the true knowledge of His Word, overcasting the same with mists and clouds of error and ignorance through false glosses and interpretations. It pitieth me to see the simple and hungry flock of Christ led into corrupt pastures, to be carried away blindfold they know not whither, and to be fed with poison in the stead of wholesome meats."

These words of Cranmer provide an admirable commentary on the Reformed doctrine of the ministry. The objective, achieved so successfully in the English Ordinal and Book of Common Prayer, was the actual uprooting of the tree of sacerdotalism and the establishment of a ministry whose chief office was the setting forth of God's Word truly to the people in preaching, in the administration of the sacraments of the Gospel, and in pastoral labour. Humanly speaking, the attainment of this goal was due to the initiative of Cranmer, acting in his capacity as head minister of the Church of England, more than to any other single factor or person.

The Reformed position is well summed up in the Catechism composed by Alexander Nowell, Dean of St. Paul's, early in Elizabeth's reign and sanctioned for general use in the Church at that time. In response to the inquiry whether the Lord's supper was "ordained to this end that Christ's body should be offered in sacrifice to God the Father for sins", the following answer is given: "It is not so offered. For He, when He did institute His supper, commanded us to eat His body, not to offer it. As for the prerogative of offering for sins, it pertaineth to Christ alone, as to Him who is the eternal Priest; who also when He died upon the cross once made that only and everlasting sacrifice for our salvation, and fully performed for ever. For us there is nothing left to do but to take the use and benefit of that eternal sacrifice bequeathed us by the Lord Himself, which we chiefly do in the Lord's supper."[1]

This view of the ministry does no more than reflect the plain teaching of the New Testament, and particularly that of the Epistle to the Hebrews. One of the main factors which contributed to the development of the sacerdotal concept of the Christian ministry was the disregard of this New Testament teaching, on the one hand, and, on the other, the adoption of the Aaronic priesthood of the Old Testament as a model or prototype of the ministry of the Christian Church. As the Epistle to the Hebrews carefully shows, however, the Aaronic order, essentially sacerdotal as it was, was of a temporary nature only, being superseded, in accordance with prophetic expectation, by the order of Melchizedek, which is permanent and final. On the coming of Christ the old order was done away for good. There is, further, a radical contrast between the two orders: the Aaronic order had a long succession of priests, mortal men who were in turn carried away by death and had to be replaced; the order of Melchizedek has but one priest, Christ Himself, who lives for evermore, with the consequence that there is now neither plurality nor succession of priests: the priests of the Aaronic order, being sinful men, had first to offer sacrifice for their own sins before offering for the people; Christ, constituting the order of Melchizedek, and being Himself without sin, offered no sacrifice for Himself but only for us, who are sinful and in need of redemption: the sacrifices of old were imperfect and anticipatory,

[1] *Nowell's Catechism*, p. 215.

and therefore were numerous, repeated day after day and year
after year; the sacrifice of Christ was perfect and final, a sacrifice,
moreover, not of some animal but of His own self, and therefore
once offered and never to be repeated. All Christian priesthood,
accordingly, is fully comprehended in Christ, and in no one else.
The New Testament does, indeed, speak of offerings other than
that of Christ, but they are offerings of response, not initiative, and
they are offered by all true members of Christ's Church, laity and
clergy alike: the offerings, namely, of gratitude, praise, and glory
to God, of what we have and what we are—in short, of our whole
being. Thus in the words of the Communion service (echoing
Rom. 12:1), "We offer and present unto Thee, O Lord, ourselves,
our souls and bodies, to be a reasonable, holy, and lively sacrifice
unto Thee." That is why the Apostle Peter declares to all members
of Christ's Church, without distinction of clergy and laity, that
they are "an holy priesthood" whose office is "to offer up spiritual
sacrifices, acceptable to God by Jesus Christ" (I Pet. 2:5, 9). This
is the proper priesthood of all believers.

Preaching on Psalm 4:5, "Offer up the sacrifices of righteousness", Archbishop Sandys speaks as follows: "Let us now consider
who are priests to offer up these sacrifices. For there can be no
sacrifice without a priest, as there can be no priest where there is no
sacrifice. In the Scriptures I find a threefold priesthood allowed of
God: a Levitical priesthood, such as that of Aaron and his sons;
a royal priesthood figured in Melchizedek, and verified in Christ;
a spiritual priesthood, belonging generally to all Christians. The
Levitical priesthood continued unto Christ, then ceased. For
being a figure of the truth which was to come, the truth being
come, it could no longer continue. Neither is there in the royal
priesthood of Melchizedek any other that hath succeeded, but only
Christ. He is 'a priest for ever according to the order of Melchizedek', a king and a priest, a God and a man, perfect, innocent,
undefiled, unspotted, severed from sinners; yet numbered,
punished, plagued with the wicked; humbled to the depth, and
exalted far above the highest heavens; without beginning, without
end, without father as man, without mother as God.[1] The third
priesthood is that which is common to all Christians: for 'He hath
made us kings and priests unto God His Father'.[2] . . . What sacrifices Aaron did offer up, and what sacrifice Christ hath presented

[1] Heb. 7: 1ff.                    [2] Rev. 1:6.

to His Father, we all know. It followeth now to be considered what kind of sacrifice we must offer. Aaron offered sacrifice which could not in itself be accepted of God, nor take away the sins of them for whom it was offered.[1] . . . But the Priest according to the order of Melchizedek hath offered the sacrifice of His own flesh, acceptable even for the worthiness of it, and by the virtue which is in it forcible and more than sufficient to wash away all sin. This He did willingly.[2] . . . He did it perfectly.[3] . . . At the hands of the minister it is required that he feed the flock committed unto his charge: this is righteousness in him, it is his sacrifice . . . We must all sacrifice unto the Lord with our goods, with our minds, and with our bodies. For all these we have received to serve Him withal . . . This is the sacrifice of righteousness, even a broken and a contrite heart.[4] The other sacrifice of the mind is praise, which consisteth in thanksgiving and petition."[5]

PRIEST AND PRESBYTER

So also Tyndale writes: "There is a word called in Latin *sacerdos*, in Greek *hiereus*, in Hebrew *cohan*, that is, a minister, an officer, a sacrificer, or a priest: as Aaron was a priest, and sacrificed for the people, and was a mediator between God and them. And in the English should it have had some other name than priest . . . Of that manner is Christ a priest for ever; and all we priests through Him, and need no more of any such priest on earth, to be a mean for us unto God. For Christ hath brought us all into the inner temple, within the veil or forehanging, and unto the mercy-stool of God, and hath coupled us unto God; where we offer, every man for himself, the desires and petitions of his heart, and sacrifice and kill the lusts and appetites of his flesh, with prayer, fasting, and all manner godly living. Another word is there in Greek, called *presbyter*, in Latin *senior*, in English an *elder*, and is nothing but an officer to teach, and not to be a mediator between God and us. By a priest, then, in the New Testament, understand nothing but an elder to teach the younger, and to bring them unto the full knowledge and understanding of Christ, and to minister the sacraments which Christ ordained, which is also nothing but to teach Christ's promises."[6]

---

[1] Heb. 10:4.   [2] Is. 53:10.
[3] Heb. 10:14, 8:12, and I Jn. 1:7 are cited here.   [4] Ps. 51:17.
[5] Sandys: *Sermons*, pp. 411ff.   [6] Tyndale: *Works*, Vol. I, pp. 255ff.

6*

In view of this emphasis on the non-sacerdotal character of the ministry it may well be asked why the term "priest" was retained by the Reformers to designate one of the ministerial orders. The fact is that "priest" is but another form of the word "presbyter", and, so far as its etymology is concerned, does not carry a sacerdotal connotation. This consideration weighed in favour of its retention—though it was not retained without much hesitancy. Over the centuries, however, it had virtually lost its association with the concept of presbytership or eldership in common parlance and had become the customary English equivalent for the Greek *hiereus* or the Latin *sacerdos*. At the same time it had long been the habit to refer to the clergy generally as priests. The Reformers, indeed, would have preferred to dispense with the term "priest" because of its objectionable associations, and, significantly, the Litany of 1544 designated the clergy as "bishops, pastors, and ministers". It was not till 1662 that this was altered to read "bishops, priests, and deacons" (thereby bringing it into line with the designations of the Ordinal). When under cross-examination in Oxford in 1554, the year prior to his martyrdom, Bishop Latimer declared, with reference to the use of the word "priest", that "a minister is a more fit name for that office, for the name of a priest importeth a sacrifice".[1]

Later in the century, Archbishop Whitgift, pointing out that "the very word itself, as it is used in our English tongue, soundeth the word *presbyter*", expressed the hope that "as heretofore use hath made it to be taken for a sacrificer, so will use now alter that signification and make it to be taken for a minister of the Gospel".[2] Richard Hooker, indeed, in what was perhaps a rather too optimistic assessment of the contemporary situation, was of the opinion that this change in signification had already been achieved. "As for the people," he wrote, "when they hear the name it draweth no more *their minds* to any cogitation of sacrifice than the name of a senator or an alderman causeth them to think upon old age or to imagine that everyone so termed must needs be ancient because years were respected in the first nomination of both. Wherefore to pass by the name, let them use what dialect they will, whether we call it a priesthood, a presbytership, or a ministry it skilleth not." None the less, he too was aware of the greater appropriateness of the term presbyter. Thus he added: "Although

[1] Latimer: *Works*, Vol. II, p. 264.  [2] Whitgift: *Works*, Vol. III, p. 351.

in truth the word *presbyter* doth seem more fit, and in propriety of speech more agreeable, than *priest* with the drift of the whole Gospel of Jesus Christ. For what are they that embrace the Gospel but sons of God? What are churches but His families? Seeing therefore we receive the adoption and state of sons by their ministry whom God hath chosen out for that purpose, seeing also that when we are the sons of God our continuance is still under their care who were our progenitors, what better title could there be given them than the reverend name of *presbyters* or fatherly guides? The Holy Ghost throughout the body of the New Testament making so much mention of them doth not anywhere call them priests."[1] In our present-day ecumenical situation the Church of South India has given a wise lead by its restoration of the term "presbyter" as the designation of one who is in full ministerial orders.

In the Christian Church, then, the ministerial office is not distinctively priestly in nature, but rather prophetic and pastoral. No man may presume to copy or participate in the unique mediatorial priesthood of Christ. It is as the great Prophet and Pastor that Christ is the minister's supreme example. "Christ was the true prophet," says Bishop Jewel when expounding I Cor. 4:1 ("Let a man so account of us as of the ministers of Christ and stewards of the mysteries of God"); "and why so? Because He preached His Father's will. 'Whatsoever I have heard of My Father', saith Christ, 'the same have I declared unto you'. St. Paul was the true servant of Christ and steward of His secrets; and why so? Because he laboured in God's vineyard, he preached, he taught more than all the rest of the apostles of Christ did . . . Therefore was he the true and faithful minister of God's mysteries, because he thus diligently always taught God's Gospel and the glory of His name; for this cause, I say, and none other, was he the steward and dispenser of God's secrets."[2] This indicates how far behind the concept of the ministry as a sacerdotal office had been left, not least significantly when speaking of the dispensing of God's mysteries. The Reformers had learnt from the New Testament that to be a faithful minister of God's mysteries no longer meant to act the part of a sacrificing priest, but to labour faithfully as shepherds of the flock of Christ and to preach and teach His truth. And this applies no less to the "holy mysteries" of the sacrament of Christ's body and

---

[1] Hooker: *Laws of Ecclesiastical Polity*, V, lxxviii, 2f.
[2] Jewel: *Works*, Vol. II, p. 1049.

blood, in which the action is not that of immolation, but of proclamation and of response to the promises of which the sacred symbols are pledges and guarantees.

The command and example of Christ must, indeed, be obligatory for His servants, as Thomas Becon insists in his *New Catechism*: "Christ commandeth His ministers to preach the Gospel, that is to say remission and forgiveness of sins, in His name, and not men's traditions and their own dreams. And as the minister of Christ ought to preach nothing but Christ's Word, so ought all his acts, deeds, and enterprise to tend unto this purpose only, to set forth the glory of God and the honour of His holy name, both in life and doctrine, both in work and word, as Christ saith: 'I have given you an example, that, as I have done, so likewise ye should do.' "[1] Becon goes on to explain that "the office and duty of a bishop or spiritual minister" consists principally in three points: "first, in teaching the Word of God and in ministering the sacraments; secondly, in praying for the people; thirdly, in leading a good life, unto the example of his parishioners." A fourth distinguishing mark was frequently added by the Reformers, namely, the maintenance of hospitality. But Becon emphasizes that "the first and principal point of a bishop's and a spiritual minister's office" is "to teach and preach the Word of God", adducing passages of Scripture to prove that this is so. He concludes, accordingly, that "such as are sent of Christ are sent to preach the Gospel", and that "if they preach not it is an evident token that Christ sent them not, but antichrist and the devil".[2]

To the minister who complains that he sees little fruit of his preaching and feels tempted to desist from it, Latimer rejoins: "Thou art troubled with what God gave thee no charge of, and leavest undone what thou art charged with. God commandeth thee to preach; and *si non locutus fueris*, if thou speak not, if thou warn not the wicked, that they turn and amend, they shall perish in their iniquities; *sanguinem autem ejus de manu tua requiram*. This text nippeth; this pincheth; this toucheth the quick: 'He shall die in his wickedness, but I will require his blood at thy hand'. If you do not your office, if ye teach not the people, and warn them not, you shall be damned for it. If you do your office, you are discharged: *tuam animam liberasti*."[3]

[1] Becon: *Works*, Vol. II, p. 318.   [2] Becon: *Ibid.*, p. 320.
[3] Latimer: *Works*, Vol. I, p. 286.

THE PASTORAL NATURE OF THE MINISTRY

The pastoral responsibilities of the ministry are effectively urged by Latimer in a sermon on Lk. 2:8f., during the course of which he derives a parable from the behaviour of the shepherds in the Christmas story: "Now these shepherds, I say, they watch the whole night, they attend upon their vocation, they do according to their calling, they keep their sheep, they run not hither and thither, spending the time in vain and neglecting their office and calling. No, they did not so. Here, by these shepherds, all men may learn to attend upon their offices and callings. I would wish that clergymen—the curates, parsons, and vicars, the bishops, and all other spiritual persons—would learn this lesson by these poor shepherds; which is this, to abide by their flocks and by their sheep, to tarry amongst them, to be careful over them, not to run hither and thither after their own pleasure, but to tarry by their benefices and feed their sheep with the food of God's Word, and to keep hospitality, and so to feed them both soul and body. For I tell you that these poor unlearned shepherds shall condemn many a stout and great learned clerk: for these shepherds had but the charge over brute beasts, and yet were diligent to keep them and to feed them; and the others have the cure over God's lambs, which He bought with the death of His Son, and yet they are so careless, so negligent, so slothful over them; yea, and the most part intendeth not to feed the sheep. They seek only their own pleasure, their own pastimes; they care for no more."[1]

Passages like this—and there are plenty of them—give us an insight into the serious and widespread state of pastoral dereliction and apathy with which the Reformers had to contend as they sought to restore a worthy conception of the ministerial office and its obligations. They even had to admonish the clergy that in times of danger their duty was not to seek their own safety, but to be with their flock so that they might minister to them in their need. "Vicars and parsons be afraid when there cometh a sickness in the town," says Latimer in another revealing sermon; "therefore they were wont commonly to get themselves out of the way, and send a friar thither who did nothing else but rob and spoil them: which doing of the vicar was damnable; for it was a diffidence and a mistrust in God. Therefore, ye vicars, parsons, or curates, what

[1] Latimer: *Works*, Vol. II, pp. 119f.

name soever ye bear, when there cometh any sickness in your town leave not your flock without a pastor, but comfort them in their distress; and believe certainly that with your well-doing you cannot shorten your lives."[1] So, too, Bishop Hooper insists that "it is every minister's office of the Church diligently (*and especially in the time of pestilence and plagues*) to call upon the people for amendment of life and to show them truly, diligently, and plainly this medicine of repentance, which consisteth of these parts: first, in knowledge of sin; then, in hatred of sin; thirdly, in forsaking of sin; fourthly, in believing the forgiveness of sins for Christ's sake; and fifthly, to live in virtuous and godly life, to honour God, and to show his obedience to God's law, that by sin is transgressed."[2]

The very high and solemn estimate which the Reformers had of the Christian ministry is well indicated by Bishop Jewel when he says that "they that exercise this ministry are the eyes of Christ, the pillars of the Church, the interpreters of God's will, the watchmen of the Lord's tower, the leaders of Christ's sheep, the salt of the earth, the light of the world". Their importance, however, is not due to any competence of their own: 'The power whereby they did conquer the world was not in them, but in the Word which they preached . . . Though men be but simple, yet the Word they deliver is mighty; though they be mortal, the Word of the Lord endureth for ever." As always, we are brought back to this position, that it is the proclamation of the Word of God that is constitutive of the Christian ministry. "If any man hide this Word," continues Jewel, "he slayeth the people: he is a dumb dog"; for the ministry of the Church "standeth in the setting forth of the mystery of our salvation, both by the preaching of the Word of God and by the due and reverent ministration of the sacraments. The principalest part of this office," he adds, "is to preach repentance, so that we may amend our lives and be converted unto God."[3]

Again, when commenting on I Thess. 3:13, Jewel says: "As the minister's duty is to teach the Word of God and divide it aright, without deceit or guile; so ought the people to receive it with reverence, and to give obedience unto it . . . Without this Word we can receive no comfort, we cannot see the light, nor grow in faith, nor abide in the Church of God. It is the Word of reconciliation.

---

[1] Latimer: *Works*, Vol. I, p. 416.
[2] Hooper: *Homily in the Time of Pestilence*, 1553, in *Works*, Vol. II, p. 174.           [3] Jewel: *Works*, Vol. II, pp. 1130f.

By it God maketh atonement between Himself and the sons of men. Therefore when the epistles, the psalms, the chapters, and the gospel are read in our hearing, let us remember whose Word we hear. Let us think thus with ourselves: These are the words of our gracious God. My God openeth His mouth from heaven above. He speaketh to me that I may be saved; He speaketh to me to keep me from error, to comfort me in the adversities and troubles of this life, and to lead me to the life to come." And, commenting on I Thess. 4:7 ("For God hath not called us unto uncleanness, but unto holiness"), he admonishes: "It behoveth every man, when he is in secret and alone to bethink himself whereunto God hath called him . . . The minister and preacher thus: I have charge given me to lead the people of God to the way of righteousness; I am called to do the work of an evangelist, to preach the Word in season and out of season, to show the people their offences, and to reprove them with all earnestness, to teach them that they deny all ungodliness, and turn wholly unto God; 'for necessity is laid upon me; and woe is me if I preach not the Gospel'."[1]

Sandys warns that it is not only possible for ministers to "destroy by ill teaching", but that "likewise there are others who, teaching well but living ill, do more harm by their life in one hour than good by their doctrine in many years";[2] and on another occasion, when preaching on Jn. 6:11f., he draws attention to the example of Christ, "in whom the first thing which we have to observe is His diligence in His office. He preached in the cities," continues Sandys, "in the temple, in the villages, in the ships, on the shores, in the wilderness: He neither spared any labour nor omitted any occasion to do good. The next thing is His pitiful affection towards the people, upon whom He looked, His heart was touched with compassion; first, because they were as sheep without a pastor . . . Undoubtedly their hearts are not touched with any pity or compassion at all over God's people, who, for their own private gain and commodity, thrust such pastors upon the Church, that when the Church hath them, it may justly be said that it hath no pastors. This is the plague, the poison, the bane of all religion: it threateneth to ruin Christianity. The other cause that moved Christ to compassion was, that the people who had tarried long with Him were hungry, and in the wilderness could

---

[1] Jewel: *Works*, Vol. II, pp. 837f., 861f.
[2] Sandys: *Works*, p. 246.

get no meat. By this we learn of our master Christ to bear pitiful hearts towards our needy, naked, and hungry brethren . . . The last thing which I propose to note in the person of our Saviour is, that He did not only conceive an inward pity and therewith content Himself; but His compassion broke out and declared itself in works of mercy. He sent them not away, as the manner is, laden with words and empty alms: He fed them largely, and gave them till every man had enough."[1]

Preaching a farewell sermon at St. Paul's Cross on the occasion of his translation from the bishopric of London to the archbishopric of York, Sandys was able to give the following testimony to those he was leaving: "My conscience beareth me record, I have endeavoured to tread in the same steps [as the apostle]. And in doctrine, which is the chiefest point, I dare affirm even the same which the holy apostle doth: I have delivered no other unto you than that which I have received of the Lord.[2] And this testimony of conscience that I have dealt sincerely in the house of God, as touching doctrine, hath been my great relief and comfort in all the stormy troubles which by the mighty assistance of almighty God I have waded through. Concerning diligence in the execution of mine office, although I have had a ready will, yet my weak body being not answerable to my desire, as all flesh herein is faulty, so for my part I must plead guilty. One debt and duty with St. Paul I protest I have truly paid you; for with a tender affection I have loved you . . . In using correction I have sought reformation, and not revenge; to punish hath been a punishment to myself: I never did it but with great grief; I have always laboured rather by persuasion to reclaim transgressors than by correction . . . My life and conversation amongst you I leave wholly to your secret judgments. I cannot say (for who can?) that my heart is clear. If 'in many things we offend all',[3] how can any man say he is no sinner, except he say also that God is a liar? Howbeit, this the God of my righteousness knoweth, that wittingly and willingly I have wronged no man."[4]

In accordance with their high estimate of the ministerial office, the Reformers wished the Christian minister to be treated with the respect due to his calling—not, however, with an excess of adulation any more than with contempt. "If the preacher be too much

---

[1] Sandys: *Works*, pp. 343ff.  [2] I Cor. 11:23.
[3] Jas. 3:2.  [4] Sandys: *Works*, pp. 418f.

honoured, then is God dishonoured," says Jewel: "if he be despised and nothing set by, then is Christ Himself despised and not regarded . . . We are," adds Jewel, "but God's servants, God's messengers, appointed to lead and guide you. Thus therefore ought every man to esteem the preachers of God's Gospel, as messengers, as servants, as ministers of Christ; thus ought every man to think and judge of them."[1]

VOCATION TO THE MINISTRY

It follows that none should be admitted to this dignified office except such as are truly called to it. This calling or vocation has a double aspect: primarily, it must be the inward calling of God; and, secondarily, there should be the outward calling of the congregation. Thus, in his *Visitation Book* of 1551, Bishop Hooper declares that "it is not lawful for any manner of person, of his own private authority, to take upon him to preach the Word of God or to minister His sacraments openly, unless the same be lawfully called or sent"; and that "those do we think only lawfully called or sent who are called or sent of God, whose calling and sending ought to be known either by manifest tokens and signs out of heaven, or else by such men unto whom appertaineth (by office) to appoint and send forth ministers into the Lord's vineyard and Church."[2] In his *Apology of the Church of England* Bishop Jewel refutes the charge of ministerial disorderliness which had maliciously been alleged against the Church of England in the following words: "We say that the minister ought lawfully, duly, and orderly to be preferred to that office of the Church of God, and that no man hath power to wrest himself into the holy ministry at his own pleasure and list. Wherefore these persons do us the greater wrong who have nothing so common in their mouth as that we do nothing orderly and comely, but all things troublesomely and without order, and that we allow every man to be a priest, to be a teacher, and to be an interpreter of the Scriptures."[3] Article XXIII, *Of ministering in the Congregation*, is also quite specific: "It is not lawful for any man to take upon him the office of public preaching or ministering the sacraments in the congregation before he be lawfully called and sent to execute the same. And those we ought to judge lawfully called and sent which be chosen and called to

---

[1] Jewel: *Works*, Vol. II, pp. 1047f.    [2] Hooper: *Works*, Vol. II, p. 123.
[3] Jewel: *Works*, Vol. III, p. 60.

this work by men who have public authority given unto them in the congregation to call and send ministers into the Lord's vineyard."

This, in turn, places a solemn responsibility on those who, as patrons, hold the right of nomination to particular livings when they fall vacant. Referring to the doom pronounced against unfaithful pastors in Ezek. 34:1f.—"Woe to the shepherds of Israel, who feed themselves, and not My flock! ye have eaten the fat and been clothed with the wool; but ye have not strengthened the weak, nor healed the sick, nor brought home the stray, nor sought the lost; but ye have ruled over them with harshness"—Pilkington observes: "He that either cannot or will not do these things, seeking his own ease and wealth, and not bringing the people to God, is a thief and murderer. Also, the patron of a benefice, or bishop, who admit any such as cannot do these duties to have cure of souls, are partakers of his wickedness . . . He that places an unworthy or unable minister wittingly in a benefice consents to the evil which he doeth, because he might stop him from it if he would."[1] And Sandys speaks as follows: "When bad men are placed in great rooms, when the base are exalted and lifted up into places of authority, then the bounds of wickedness are enlarged, and sin, going on without controlment, gathereth strength. Christ therefore required careful choice of ministers in His Church: His desire is to have them faithful and wise. Paul would place none but such as were well testified to be blameless in life and apt to teach with wholesome doctrine. The admitters of ministers are too lavish in our days: they have little regard or care whom they take: St. Paul's lesson, 'Lay not hands on any man rashly',[2] is forgotten. The preferrers unto livings are no less faulty: they choose of the worst; they respect no ability but of the purse. What numbers there are placed this day in the church, as Jason and Menelaus were placed by Antiochus in the priest's office, not for learning, but for money; not for desert, but for reward! It goeth full hardly with the Church of God when Balaam is the bishop, Judas the patron, and Magus the minister. This merchandise will make the house of God a den of thieves. No one thing this day is more necessary to be reformed in the Church of God."[3] Indeed, Sandys affirms on another occasion that, so far from being a matter of human preferment or a

---

[1] Pilkington: *Works*, p. 36.       [2] Tim. 5:22.
[3] Sandys: *Works*, pp. 120ff.

mercenary transaction, "the making of bishops, the bestowing of benefices, the presenting, instituting, and inducting of pastors, the placing of teachers, guides, and overseers in the Church, is and should be accounted the very work of the Holy Ghost."[1]

The important qualification is made by Hooper that the ministry consists not in its title but in its function. We know the ministry, he says, "not by the name alone, but by the work and administration in it, to the edifying of the Church and Body of Christ by the faithful administration of God's Word and His sacraments, according unto the commandment of Christ; from the which if any minister cease, he leaveth to be a minister, and should not be taken for such one".[2]

### THE PAPACY AND APOSTOLIC SUCCESSION

The authoritarian pretensions of the Pope were rejected by the Reformers with one mind and voice. For the Pope to claim to be the bishop of Rome was one thing, but that he had any right to set himself up as supreme pontiff and vicar of Christ on earth with absolute powers of jurisdiction over the universal Church was firmly denied. If indeed he was a bishop, then it was needful for him to answer to the demands made of all bishops and spiritual ministers in the New Testament, and not to lay claim to powers and prerogatives which find no justification in Scripture or in the early Church. "According to the judgment of the Nicene Council," writes Bishop Jewel in his *Apology of the Church of England*, "we say that the bishop of Rome hath no more jurisdiction over the Church of God than the rest of the patriarchs, either of Alexandria or Antioch, have. And as for the bishop of Rome, who now calleth all matters before himself alone, except he do his duty as he ought to do, except he administer the sacraments, except he instruct the people, except he warn them and teach them, we say that he ought not of right once to be called a bishop, or so much as an elder. For a bishop, as saith Augustine, 'is a name of labour and not of honour', because he would have that man understand himself to be no bishop who will seek to have preeminence and not to profit others. And that neither the pope, nor any other wordly creature, can no more be head of the whole Church, or a bishop over all, than he can be the bridegroom, the light, the salvation, and life of the Church: for these privileges and names belong only to Christ, and

---

[1] Sandys: *Works*, p. 241.     [2] Hooper: *Works*, Vol. II, p. 123.

be properly and only fit for Him alone."[1] Christ, moreover, "is ever present to assist His Church and needeth not any man to supply His room as His only heir to all His substance"; and, in any case, "there can be no one mortal creature who is able to comprehend in his mind the universal Church, that is to wit, all the parts of the world, much less able to put them in order and to govern them rightly and duly."[2]

Furthermore, the magnificent grandeur of the papacy is incompatible with the precepts of Christ. "Christ forbiddeth His disciples, and that oft," writes Tyndale in his *Obedience of A Christian Man*, ". . . not only to climb above lords, kings, and emperors in worldy rule, but also to exalt themselves one above another in the kingdom of God: but in vain, for the pope would not hear it, though He had commanded it ten thousand times. God's Word should rule only, and not bishops' decrees or the pope's pleasure. That ought they to preach purely and spiritually, and to fashion their lives after, and with all example of godly living and longsuffering to draw all to Christ."[3] And Hooper argues that, "seeing that Christ doth govern His Church always by His Holy Spirit and bindeth all the ministers thereof unto the sole Word of God, what abomination is this that any bishop of Rome, Jerusalem, Antioch, or elsewhere should claim to be Christ's vicar in the earth, and take upon him to make any laws in the Church of God to bind the conscience of man, beside the Word of God."[4]

Regarding the claim made by the papists that their bishops are the successors of the Apostles, and particularly of Peter whom they maintain was the first bishop of Rome, the Reformers were accustomed to point out that the Apostles' commission was essentially unsettled and itinerant in character, whereas the bishop was assigned the oversight of a limited locality, involving by comparison a settled and geographically restricted ministry, so that in terms of office alone it was incongruous to equate apostleship with episcopacy. "Paul," says Jewel commenting on II Thess. 2:5, "was not tied to any one city or island or country. He had the authority to preach to all cities and countries, to all lands and islands, from the east to the west. So did Christ appoint His

---

[1] Jewel: *Works*, Vol. III, p. 60.      [2] Jewel: *Ibid.*, p. 59.
[3] Tyndale: *Works*, Vol. I, p. 207.
[4] Hooper: *A Declaration of Christ and His Office*, 1547, in *Works*, Vol. I, p. 22.

apostles: 'Go ye into all the world and preach the Gospel unto every creature'.[1] They were not sent to Jerusalem, nor to Samaria, nor to Rome only, but into all the world. The whole world was their diocese and their province . . . Therefore if any of the apostles should have stayed in one only place and have gone no further, he had offended and done otherwise than Christ commanded. Here we see how foully they are deceived who say Peter was bishop of Rome, and did sit there five and twenty years."[2]

But far more important was the contention of the Reformers that the true succession of the apostles lay in the faithful handing down of their teaching. A ministry which preserved and passed on the apostolic doctrine and manner of life was indeed genuinely an apostolic ministry. This Rome had failed to do, and so the claim to have maintained an unbroken line from the apostles was spiritually worthless. What really mattered was the succession of the Word, not a succession of persons. Thus we find Bishop Hooper writing in 1550: "As concerning the ministers of the Church, I believe that the Church is bound to no sort of people or any ordinary succession of bishops, cardinals, or such like, but unto the only Word of God. Although there be diversity of gifts and knowledge among men: some know more, and some know less; and if he that knoweth least teach Christ after the Holy Scriptures, he is to be accepted; and he that knoweth most, and teacheth Christ contrary or any other ways than the Holy Scriptures teach, is to be refused . . . But thus I conclude of the ministers, of what degree or dignity soever they be, they be no better than records and testimonies, ministers and servants of God's Word and God's sacraments; unto the which they should neither add, diminish nor change anything. And for their true service and diligence in this part they should not be only reverenced of the people, but also honoured by the magistrates as the servants of God. And I believe that as many souls as perish by their negligence or contempt of God's Word shall be required at their hands."[3] So, too, Bishop Jewel, in his *Defence of the Apology*, retorts to his opponent Harding: "Succession, you say, is the chief way for any Christian man to avoid antichrist. I grant you, if you mean the succession of doctrine!"[4]

---

[1] Mk. 16:15.     [2] Jewel: *Works*, Vol. II, p. 508.

[3] Hooper: *A Godly Confession and Protestation of the Christian Faith*, in *Works*, Vol. II, pp. 90f.

[4] Jewel: *Works*, Vol. III, p. 348.

Previously, in the *Apology*, John Jewel had written as follows: "For whereas some use to make so great a vaunt that the pope is only Peter's successor, as though thereby he carried the Holy Ghost in his bosom and cannot err, this is but a matter of nothing and a very trifling tale. God's grace is promised to a good mind and to one that feareth God, not unto sees and successions ... Yet notwithstanding, because we will grant somewhat to succession, tell us, hath the pope alone succeeded Peter? and wherein, I pray you? In what religion? in what office? in what piece of his life hath he succeeded him? What one thing (tell me) had Peter ever like unto the pope, or the pope like unto Peter? Except peradventure they will say thus: that Peter, when he was at Rome, never taught the Gospel, never fed the flock, took away the keys of the kingdom of heaven, hid the treasures of his Lord, sat him down only in his castle in St. John Lateran, and pointed out with his finger all the places of purgatory and kinds of punishments, committing some poor souls to be tormented and other some again suddenly releasing thence at his own pleasure, taking money for so doing; or that he gave order to say private masses in every corner; or that he mumbled up the holy service with a low voice and in an unknown language; or that he hanged up the sacrament in every temple and on every altar and carried the same about before him, whithersoever he went, upon an ambling jennet, with lights and bells; or that he consecrated with his holy breath oil, wax, wool, bells, chalices, churches, and altars; or that he sold jubilees, graces, liberties, advowsons, preventions, first fruits, palls, the wearing of palls, bulls, indulgences, and pardons; or that he called himself by the name of the head of the Church, the highest bishop, bishop of bishops, alone most holy; or that by usurping he took upon himself the right and authority over other folks' churches; or that he exempted himself from the power of any civil government; or that he maintained wars, set princes together at variance; or that he, sitting in his chair, with his triple crown full of labels, with sumptuous and Persian-like gorgeousness, with his royal sceptre, with his diadem of gold, and glittering with stones, was carried about, not upon palfrey, but upon the shoulders of noblemen. These things, no doubt, Peter did at Rome in times past, and left them in charge to his successors, as you would say, from hand to hand; for these things be nowadays done at Rome by the popes, and be so done as though nothing else ought to be done.

"Or contrariwise," continues Jewel, "peradventure they had rather say thus: that the pope doth now all the same things which we know Peter did many a day ago; that is, that he runneth up and down into every country to preach the Gospel, not only openly abroad, but also privately from house to house; that he is diligent and applieth that business in season and out of season, in due time and out of due time; that he doth the part of an evangelist; . . . that he doth not feed his own self but his flock; that he doth not entangle himself with the worldly cares of this life; that he doth not use a sovereignty over the Lord's people; that he seeketh not to have other men minister to him, but himself rather to minister unto others; that he taketh all bishops as his fellows and equals . . . Unless therefore the popes do the like nowadays as Peter did the things aforesaid, there is no cause at all why they should glory so of Peter's name and of his succession."[1]

To the stipulation of Cardinal Bellarmine that "that is to be held and deemed undoubtedly apostolical which is esteemed as such in those churches wherein there is an unbroken succession of bishops from the apostles", Whitaker offers the following rejoinder: "I answer, in the first place, that the succession even of that [Roman Catholic] church is not entire and uninterrupted, as is plain from Platina and others. For Platina[2] and other historians testify that that see hath been vacant ten, yea, twenty times over, not merely for a day or a week or a month, but for one, two, or three years; furthermore that there were frequent schisms, and sometimes two or three popes in existence together. . . . Secondly, though we should concede the succession of that church to have been unbroken and entire, yet that succession would be a matter of no weight; because we regard not the external succession of places or persons, but the internal one of faith and doctrine."[3]

As for the claim that the papists, by virtue of their succession, were the only true *catholics*, Whitaker defined the term "catholics" as designating "those who profess sound, solid, and pure doctrine".[4] And Jewel, in a sermon on Lk. 11:15, made this protestation: "If we be heretics that teach this doctrine, what are the

[1] Jewel: *Works*, Vol. III, pp. 103f.

[2] Bartolomeo Platina (1421–1481) was the author of *Liber de vita Christi ac de vitis summorum pontificum omnium* which was published in Venice in 1479. Pope Sixtus IV appointed him librarian of the Vatican in 1475.

[3] Whitaker: *Disputation on Holy Scripture*, p. 510.

[4] Whitaker: *Ibid.*, p. 668.

ancient fathers, the doctors, the apostles, that have taught the same? If they were catholics, and have been evermore so taken, writing as they did, how is it that only we are not catholics, writing and saying as they did? They shall judge on our side against you . . . For I call heaven and earth to witness, and speak it before God and His holy angels, and before the consciences of all them that speak against us, that, touching the very substance of religion, we teach nothing this day but that what hath been taught before by Christ Himself, set abroad by His apostles, continued by the primitive Church, and maintained by the old and ancient doctors."[1]

At his Thirteenth Examination, preceding his martyrdom in 1555, we find John Philpot, Archdeacon of Winchester, engaged in the following exchange with the Archbishop of York (Nicholas Heath):

"*York*: How answer you this argument: 'Rome hath known succession of bishops, which your church hath not. Ergo, that is the catholic church, and yours is not, because there is no such succession can be proved in your church'.

*Philpot*: I deny, my lord, that succession of bishops is an infallible point to know the church by; for there may be a succession of bishops known in a place, and yet there be no church as at Antioch and Jerusalem, and in other places where the apostles abode as well as at Rome. But if you put to the succession of bishops succession of doctrine withal (as St. Augustine doth), I will grant it to be a good proof for the catholic church; but a local succession is nothing available."[2]

Early on, it is true—in 1535—Archbishop Cranmer expressed a desire in a letter to Thomas Cromwell that he and his fellow bishops might be called "apostles of Jesus Christ", but with the sole intention that they should divest themselves of the high-sounding titles that had accumulated over the centuries and get back to the simplicity and humility implicit in the New Testament conception of the ministry. "I pray God never to be merciful to me at the general judgment," he says, "if I perceive in my heart that I set more by any title, name, or style that I write than I do by the paring of an apple, farther than it shall be to

---

[1] Jewel: *Works*, Vol. II, pp. 1029f.
[2] Philpot, *Works*, p. 139.

the setting forth of God's Word and will. Even at the beginning first of Christ's profession Diotrephes desired *gerere primatum in ecclesia*, as saith St. John in his last epistle; and since he hath had more successors than all the apostles had, of whom have come all these glorious titles, styles, and pomp into the Church. But I would that I and all my brethren the bishops would leave all our styles and write the style of our offices, calling ourselves *apostolos Jesu Christi*: so that we took not upon us the name vainly, but were so even indeed; so that we might order our diocese in such sort that neither paper, parchment, lead, nor wax, but the very Christian conversation of the people might be the letters and seals of our offices, as the Corinthians were unto Paul, to whom he said: *Literae nostrae et signa apostolatus nostri vos estis.*[1]

BINDING AND LOOSING (THE POWER OF THE KEYS)

Part and parcel of the Roman Catholic concept of the ministry is the assignation to the priest of an arbitrary power to bind and loose the souls of men, to admit them to or shut them out from the kingdom of heaven, by his granting or withholding of absolution. This power of the keys, again associated with the pope as Peter's successor (cf. Mt. 16:19), is supposedly distributed to those priests who own allegiance to the papal supremacy. The Reformers did not deny that Christ had committed the function of binding and loosing to His ministers, but they rejected the abuse of this function in the Roman Church which led people to imagine that all that was necessary for the forgiveness of their sins was the utterance of the formula of absolution by a priest. This power of the keys was restored by the Reformers to its proper context, namely, the Word of the Gospel, which the minister of Christ is authorized to proclaim—a word that speaks forgiveness to all that receive it with repentance and faith, but condemnation to them that refuse it.

As this was a question which affected the very heart of the Gospel, the Reformers gave particular care to its explication. We may, for example, hear Bishop Latimer preaching: "There be peradventure some of you who will say, 'The priest can absolve me and forgive me my sins'. Sir, I tell thee, the priest or minister, call him what you will, he hath power given unto him from our Saviour to

[1] Cranmer: *Works*, Vol. II, p. 305; see II Cor. 3:2 and I Cor. 9:2.

absolve in such wise as he is commanded by Him . . . A godly
minister, who is instructed in the Word of God, can and may
absolve in open preaching; not in his own authority, but in the
name of God: for God saith, *Ego sum qui deleo iniquitates*: 'I am
He that cleanseth thy sins.' But I may absolve you as an officer of
Christ in the open pulpit in this wise: 'As many as confess their sins
unto God, acknowledging themselves to be sinners, and believe
that our Saviour, through His passion, hath taken away their sins,
and have an earnest purpose to leave sin; as many, I say, as be
so affectioned,' *Ego absolvo vos*: 'I, as an officer of Christ, as His
treasurer, absolve you in His name.' This is the absolution that I
can make by God's Word. Again, as many as will stand in defence
of their wickednesses, will not acknowledge them, and so have
no faith in our Saviour to be saved by Him through His merit, to
them I say, *Ego ligo vos*: 'I bind you.' And I doubt not but they
shall be bound in heaven; for they be children of the devil as long
as they be in such unbelief and purpose to sin. Here you see how
and in what wise a preacher may absolve or bind."[1]

The power of the keys entrusted by Christ to His ministers is a
power of declaration as His ambassadors, not of domination.
"Understand therefore," writes William Tyndale, "that to bind
and to loose is to preach the law of God and the Gospel or promises,
as thou mayest see in the third chapter of the second epistle to the
Corinthians, where Paul calleth the ministration of the law the
ministration of death and damnation, and the preaching of the
promises the ministering of the Spirit and of righteousness. And
so to expound it all the old doctors." He draws attention to the
observation of Jerome that the binding and loosing of the Christian
dispensation is parallel in significance to the authority which the
priest of the old law had to declare lepers clean or unclean. "The
priest there," continues Tyndale, "made no man a leper, neither
cleansed any man; and the priest judged only, by Moses' law,
who was clean and who was unclean, when they were brought
unto him. So here we have the law of God to judge what is sin and
what is not, and who is bound and who is not. Moreover, if any
man have sinned, yet if he repent and believe the promise, we are
sure by God's Word that he is loosed and forgiven in Christ . . .
Christ's authority, which He gave to His disciples, was to preach
the law and to bring sinners to repentance, and then to preach

---

[1] Latimer: *Works*, Vol. I, pp. 423f.

unto them the promises which the Father had made unto all men for His sake."[1]

Thomas Becon explains that it is by a metaphor that Christ calls the preaching of His Word a key: "As a key hath two properties, one to shut, another to open, so hath the Word of God. It openeth to the faithful the treasure of the gifts of God, grace, mercy, favour, remission of sins, quietness of conscience, and everlasting life; but to the unfaithful it shutteth all His treasures and suffereth them to receive none of them all so long as they persist and remain in the incredulity and unfaithfulness. These keys are given to so many as, being truly called unto the office of ministration, preach the Word of God. They loosen, that is to say, they preach to the faithful remission of sins by Christ. They also bind, that is, they declare to the unfaithful damnation. But he that preacheth not the Word of God can neither bind nor loose, though he challenge never so great dignity, authority, and power."[2]

Similarly, in his *Apology*, Jewel asserts "that Christ hath given to His ministers power to bind, to loose, to open, to shut, and that the office of loosing consisteth in this point, that the minister should either offer by the preaching of the Gospel the merits of Christ and full pardon to such as have lowly and contrite hearts and do unfeignedly repent them, pronouncing unto the same a sure and undoubted forgiveness of their sins and hope of everlasting salvation; or else that the minister, when any have offended their brothers' minds with a great offence and with a notable and open fault, whereby they have, as it were, banished and made themselves strangers from the common fellowship and from the body of Christ, then, after perfect amendment of such persons, doth reconcile them and bring them home again, and restore them to the company and unity of the faithful." And he declares further that "the minister doth execute the authority of binding and shutting as often as he shutteth up the gate of the kingdom of heaven against the unbelieving and stubborn persons, denouncing unto them God's vengeance and everlasting punishment; or else when he doth quite shut them out from the bosom of the Church by open excommunication." In support of his understanding of the keys he cites Chrysostom who says that they are the knowledge of the Scriptures, Tertullian who says that they

---

[1] Tyndale: *The Obedience of a Christian Man*, in *Works*, Vol. I, pp. 296ff.      [2] Becon: *Works*, Vol. II, p. 566.

are the interpretation of the law, and Eusebius who says that they are the Word of God.[1]

This doctrine of the keys leaves no room for the institution of the secret confessional which was, and is, so important a factor in the ministry of the unreformed church, since the power of binding and loosing is essentially one of evangelical proclamation. The pastoral office does, of course, involve private dealings with individuals who are troubled because of their sins or doubts. As the first of the exhortations in the communion service advises, the man whose conscience is not quieted by the public declaration of God's terms of forgiveness in Christ should go to his own pastor, "or to some other discreet and learned minister of God's Word, and open his grief'—not that he may hear a priestly absolution, but that "by the ministry of God's holy Word he may receive the benefit of absolution". Accordingly, Jewel observes that "Christ's disciples did receive this authority, not that they should hear private confessions of the people and listen to their whisperings, as the common massing priests do everywhere nowadays, and do it as though in that one point lay all the virtue and use of the keys; but to the end they should go, they should teach, they should publish abroad the Gospel, and be unto the believing a sweet savour of life unto life, and unto the unbelieving and unfaithful a savour of death unto death.[2] . . . Seeing then," he concludes, "the key, whereby the way and entry to the kingdom of God is opened unto us, is the Word of the Gospel and the expounding of the law and Scriptures, we say plainly, where the same Word is not, there is not the key. And seeing one manner of Word is given to all, and one only key belongeth to all, we say there is but one only power of all ministers as concerning opening and shutting."[3]

The quintessence of this teaching is enshrined in the absolution pronounced by the minister at Morning and Evening Prayer after the general confession of the people. In this absolution it is affirmed that God "hath given power and commandment to His ministers to declare and pronounce to His people, being penitent, the absolution and remission of their sins", and the people are assured that "He pardoneth all them that truly repent and unfeignedly believe His holy Gospel". From this it is perfectly plain that the absolution is announced only to those who are penitent, and that it

---

[1] Jewel: *Works*, Vol. III, pp. 6of.  [2] See II Cor. 2:16.
[3] Jewel: *Works*, Vol. III, p. 61.

is God, not the minister, who pardons the repentant believer of the Gospel. Further, we are exhorted to "beseech Him to grant us true repentance and His Holy Spirit, that those things may please Him which we do at this present, and that the rest of our life here-after may be pure and holy, so that at the last we may come to His eternal joy"—from which it is clear that even repentance itself, as well as the ability to live in a manner that will bring glory to God, is beyond the competence of sinful man and must be sought from God, through the inner and powerful operation of the Holy Spirit.

The importance of an energetic evangelical ministry is effectively urged by Jewel in a sermon on Mt. 9:37 ("The harvest truly is plenteous, but the labourers are few"). "But the labourers are few," he says lamenting the deficient state of the ministry in his day. "I say not, there be but few cardinals, few bishops, few priests that should be preachers, few archdeacons, few chancellors, few deans, few prebendaries, few vicars, few parish priests, few monks, few friars; for the number of these is almost infinite . . . But, alas, the number of the labourers is very small . . . The labourers are but few; but the destroyers and wasters are exceeding many; yea, such as should be the harvest-men most of all destroy the corn . . . The Christians in old time, when they lived under tyrants, and were daily put to most shameful death, and were hated and despised of all the world, yet never lacked ministers to instruct them. It is therefore most lamentable that Christians, living under a Christian prince, in the peace and liberty of the Gospel, should lack learned ministers to teach them and instruct them in the Word of God: this is the greatest plague that God doth send upon any people. Contrariwise, the greatest blessing which any people can receive at God's hands is to have prophets and preachers by whom they may be instructed . . . But when God taketh away His ministers who should preach peace, and open unto the people the will of God, and make known His judgments, it is a token that God is highly displeased with His people . . . In such a state as the flock is in which hath no shepherd, or the ship which is tossed by the tempests amid the surges and rocks of the sea, and hath no skilful pilot to guide it, or the young sucking child that hath no nurse to feed it, even in such state are your souls if you have not the ministry of God's Word abiding with you. You are children; the preacher is your nurse: you are a ship in danger of many wrecks through the boisterous tempests of this world; the preacher is your pilot to guide you safely towards the haven of rest: you are the flock; the preacher leadeth you from dangerous places to feed upon the wholesome pasture of God's holy Word. Whosoever they be that rejoice not in the increase of God's harvest, He forsaketh them and leaveth them comfortless, and giveth them few or no labourers . . . Labourers they must be, and not loiterers.[1] . . . Therefore, if they be pastors, let them feed the flock; if they be doctors, let them teach the people; if they be watchmen, let them stand upon their watch; if they be messengers, let them do their errand. This is the way to build up the Church of Christ."[2] And this passage well sums up the Reformed concept of the Christian ministry.

[1] An echo, this, from Latimer's sermon of the plough.
[2] Jewel: *Works*, Vol. II, pp. 1019ff.

# VI
# THE SACRAMENTS

Thus doth God make known His secret purpose to His Church:
first he declareth His mercy by His Word; then He sealeth it and
assureth it by His sacraments. In the Word we have His promises: in the sacraments we see them.

*John Jewel*

# THE SACRAMENTS

A sacrament is defined in the Catechism of the Church of England as "an outward and visible sign of an inward and spiritual grace given unto us, ordained by Christ Himself, as a means whereby we receive the same, and a pledge to assure us thereof". In brief, it is a sign, a means, and a pledge.

## THE SACRAMENTS AS SIGNS

A sacrament is *a sign*: that is, it is not intended as a mere formal ceremony or frivolous spectacle, for a sign is necessarily *significant*, filled with meaning. Thus the outward symbols of the Christian sacraments point meaningfully beyond themselves to a deep spiritual reality. This in turn requires that there should be a certain similitude, a symbolical appropriateness, of the sign to the reality which it signifies—but not an identity, else it would not be a sign, but the reality itself. In this connection the Reformers were fond of quoting Augustine's saying that "if sacraments had not some point of real resemblance to the things of which they are the sacraments, they would not be sacraments at all";[1] and Archbishop Whitgift speaks of "the similitude which sacraments have with the things whereof they be sacraments".[2] Bishop Jewel explains that "when in baptism our bodies are washed with water we are taught that our souls are washed in the blood of Christ", and that "the outward washing or sprinkling represents the sprinkling and washing which is wrought within us: the water signifies the blood of Christ"[3]; while John Bradford describes the similitude in the Holy Communion in the following way: "In the Lord's supper this similitude is, first, in nourishing, that, as bread nourisheth the body, so Christ's body broken feedeth the soul; secondly, in bringing together many into one, that, as in the sacrament many grains of corn are made 'one bread', many grapes are made one liquor and wine, so the multitude which worthily receiveth the sacrament are made 'one body' with Christ and His Church; last

[1] Augustine: Epistle XCVIII, to Boniface; Ridley: *Works*, p. 61; Cranmer: *Works*, Vol. I, p. 124.
[2] Whitgift: *Works*, Vol. III, p. 383.   [3] Jewel: *Works*, Vol. II, p. 1101.

of all, in one unlikely likeness or similitude, that, as bread eaten turneth into our nature, so we rightly eating the sacrament by faith turn into the nature of Christ."[1]

The significance of the sign resides, however, not only in its symbolical appropriateness, but even more so in the words or doctrine with which its institution is associated. In emphasizing the importance of a sacrament as a *visible word* the Reformers were following Augustine, who had written: "The word is added to the element and there results the sacrament, as if itself also a kind of visible word."[2] So William Tyndale observes that "the sacrament doth much more print lively the faith, and make it sink down in the heart, than do bare words only: as a man is more sure of what he heareth, seeth, feeleth, smelleth, and tasteth than what he heareth only";[3] and Bishop Hooper speaks of the holy communion as "a visible word that preacheth peace between God and man, exhorteth to mutual love and godly life, teacheth to condemn the world for the hope of the life to come".[4] And in his *Apology* Bishop Jewel writes: "We allow the sacraments of the Church, that is to say, certain holy signs and ceremonies which Christ would we should use, that by them He might set before our eyes the mysteries of our salvation, and might more strongly confirm our faith which we have in His blood, and might seal His grace in our hearts. And these sacraments, together with Tertullian, Origen, Ambrose, Augustine, Jerome, Chrysostom, Basil, Dionysius, and other catholic fathers, do we call figures, signs, marks or badges, prints, copies, forms, seals, signets, similitudes, patterns, representations, remembrances, and memories. And we make no doubt, together with the same doctors, to say that these be certain visible words, seals of righteousness, tokens of grace."[5]

This word which, audible in preaching, becomes visible in the sacrament is essentially the word of the Gospel. It is the word of Christ, or about Christ, who Himself is the Incarnate Word of God. The authority of a Christian sacrament is the authority of Christ Himself, who by adding His word to the element transformed it into a sacrament. Therefore those only are properly

---

[1] Bradford: *Works*, Vol. I, p. 88.

[2] Augustine: Tract. LXXX, 3, on the Gospel of John.

[3] Tyndale: *A Brief Declaration of the Sacraments*, in *Works*, Vol. I, p. 360.

[4] Hooper: *Works*, Vol. II, p. 90.          [5] Jewel: *Works*, Vol. III, p. 62.

Christian sacraments which are sacraments *of the Gospel*, instituted or commanded by Christ Himself, or, as Article XXV puts it, "ordained of Christ our Lord in the Gospel". Again, Article XIX speaks of the sacraments beng "duly administered according to Christ's ordinance" as a mark of the visible Church of Christ.

The number of the sacraments is by this definition limited to two, namely, baptism and the holy communion, and this delimitation is in harmony with the mind of the Church since the earliest centuries. Of course, by broadening the definition it is possible to increase the number of the sacraments, even to the extent of viewing the entire universe as full of sacramental significance. The number of seven sacraments on which the Roman Church insists can claim no greater antiquity than the twelfth century. In this connection the comment of Lancelot Andrewes is to the point: "For more than a thousand years the number of seven sacraments was never heard of. How, then, can the belief in seven sacraments be catholic, which means, always believed?"[1] Bradford insists, accordingly, that "there are two sacraments in Christ's Church: one of initiation, that is, wherewith we be enrolled, as it were, into the household and family of God, which sacrament we call baptism; the other wherewith we be conserved, fed, kept, and nourished to continue in the same family, which is called the Lord's supper, or the body and blood of our Saviour Jesus Christ, broken for our sins and shed for our transgressions."[2] Similarly, Archbishop Sandys affirms that "His sacraments are two in number, instituted by Christ to be received of Christians: by the one, which is baptism, we are received and incorporated into the Church of Christ; by the other, which is the eucharist or Lord's supper, we are nourished and fed unto life everlasting."[3] "We acknowledge there be two sacraments," writes Jewel in the *Apology*, "which, we judge, properly ought to be called by this name, that is to say, baptism and the sacrament of thanksgiving. For thus many we see were delivered and sanctified by Christ, and well allowed of the old fathers."[4] And in his *Treatise of the Sacraments*, after quoting from Ambrose and Augustine, he says: "Thus Augustine and Ambrose, unto whom I might also join other ancient fathers, reckon but two sacraments. Let no man then be offended

[1] Andrewes: quoted by W. H. Griffith Thomas, *Principles of Theology* (London, 1930), p. 354.    [2] Bradford: *Works*, Vol. I, p. 82.
[3] Sandys: *Works*, p. 87.    [4] Jewel: *Works*, Vol. III, p. 62.

with us for so doing: we do no new thing, but restore the ordinance of Christ, and keep the example of the holy fathers." Baptism and the Lord's supper are "properly and truly called the sacraments of the Church because in them the element is joined to the Word, and they take their ordinance of Christ, and be visible signs of invisible grace".[1]

THE SACRAMENTS AS MEANS

A Christian sacrament is also *a means*. In other words, the sacraments of the Gospel, in their capacity as signs, are not *bare* signs. They are, as Article XXV declares, "*effectual* signs of grace and God's will towards us, by the which He doth work invisibly in us". But their efficacy is not automatic (*ex opere operato*); for the external sign by itself is impotent to produce any spiritual effect. Water cannot cleanse, nor bread and wine nourish, the soul. The efficacy of a sacrament is indissolubly linked to the word of promise of which it is the sign—not, however, to the word as a mere pronouncement of a formula of consecration, but to the word as a proclamation of the Gospel to those who receive the sacrament. That is to say, the sacraments, to be effective, must be addressed, word-wise, to men and women as to intelligent, responsible, and needy persons of whom it is required that they should inwardly believe the word thus proclaimed to them. Augustine had demanded long since, in passages with which the Reformers were well familiar: "Whence has water so great an efficacy as in touching the body to cleanse the soul, save by the operation of the Word; and that *not because it is uttered, but because it is believed*?" and, with reference to Christ's discourse concerning "the meat which endures unto eternal life" (Jn. 6:27): "To what purpose do you make ready teeth and stomach? Believe, and you have eaten already." Or again, he explains that to eat of the bread that comes down from heaven (Jn. 6:50f.) "belongs to the virtue of the sacrament, not to the visible sacrament"; it is the eating of the man "who eats inwardly, not outwardly, who eats in his heart, not who presses with his teeth".[2]

"I believe . . . the holy sacraments . . . to be the signs of the reconciliation and great atonement made between God and us through Jesus Christ," writes Hooper. "They are seals of the Lord's promises, and are outward and visible pledges and gages

---

[1] Jewel: *Works*, Vol. II, p. 1103.
[2] Augustine: Tract. LXXX, XXV, and XXVI, on the Gospel of John.

of the inward faith, and are in number only twain, that is to say, baptism and the holy supper of the Lord. The which two are not void and empty signs, but full; that is to say, they are not only signs whereby something is signified, but also they are such signs as do exhibit and give the thing that they do signify indeed."[1] And Jewel asserts of the doctrine of the Church of England: "We affirm that Christ doth truly and presently give His own self in His sacraments: in baptism, that we may put Him on; and in His supper, that we my eat Him by faith and spirit, and may have everlasting life by His cross and blood . . . For, although we do not touch the body of Christ with teeth and mouth, yet we hold Him fast, and eat Him by faith, by understanding, and by the spirit."[2] The sacraments, therefore, "are not bare signs: it were blasphemy so to say. The grace of God doth always work with His sacraments; but we are taught not to seek that grace in the sign, but to assure ourselves, by receiving the sign, that it is given by the thing signified."[3]

The effect of the sacraments, then, cannot be dissociated from the manner in which they are received. They are means of divine grace only to the heart which gratefully believes the promises of which they are the signs. To quote Article XXV again: "In such only as worthily receive the same they have a wholesome effect or operation." Cranmer defines "the true effect of the sacraments" as follows: "As the washing outwardly in water is not a vain token, but teacheth such a washing as God worketh inwardly in them that duly receive the same, so likewise is not the bread a vain token, but showeth and teacheth to the godly receiver what God worketh in him by His almighty power secretly and invisibly. And therefore as the bread is outwardly eaten indeed in the Lord's supper, so is the very body of Christ inwardly by faith eaten of all them that come thereto in such sort as they ought to do, which eating nourisheth them unto everlasting life."[4] Again, when rebutting the misrepresentation of his teaching, he states: "Although the sacramental tokens be only significations and figures, yet doth Almighty God effectually work, in them that duly receive His sacraments, those divine and celestial operations which He hath promised and by the sacraments be signified. For else they were vain and unfruitful sacraments, as well to the godly as to the

---

[1] Hooper: *Works*, Vol. II, p. 45.　　[2] Jewel: *Works*, Vol. II, p. 64.
[3] Jewel: *Works*, Vol. II, p. 1102.　　[4] Cranmer: *Works*, Vol. I, p. 17.

ungodly. And therefore I never said of the whole supper that it is but a signification or a bare memory of Christ's death; but I teach that it is a spiritual refreshing wherein our souls be fed and nourished with Christ's very flesh and blood to eternal life."[1] Richard Hooker also is quite emphatic concerning the manner of the efficacy of the sacraments as a means of grace when he says that the benefit received through them is received "from God Himself the Author of the sacraments, and not from any other natural or supernatural quality in them", and that "they contain *in themselves* no vital force or efficacy, they are not physical but *moral instruments* of salvation, duties of service and worship, which unless we perform as the Author of grace requireth, they are unprofitable. For," he pointedly adds, "all receive not the grace of God who receive the sacraments of His grace."[2]

It is necessary to affirm, moreover, that the Christian sacraments are not without effect even when received unworthily; but in that case it is the opposite effect which they mediate: they then become, not means of grace, but means of judgment. Hence the assertion of Article XXV that "they that receive them unworthily purchase to themselves damnation, as Saint Paul saith";[3] and similarly Article XXIX says of the holy communion that "the wicked, and such as be void of a lively faith, although they do carnally and visibly press with their teeth (as Saint Augustine saith) the sacrament of the body and blood of Christ, yet in no wise are they partakers of Christ; but rather, to their condemnation do eat and drink the sign of so great a thing". The third of the longer exhortations in the communion service also echoes the Pauline admonition regarding the great danger of receiving the sacrament unworthily: "For then we are guilty of the body and blood of Christ our Saviour; we eat and drink our own damnation, not considering the Lord's body; we kindle God's wrath against us; we provoke Him to plague us with divers diseases and sundry kinds of death. Judge therefore yourselves, brethren, that ye be not judged of the Lord; repent you truly of your sins past; have a lively and steadfast faith in Christ our Saviour; amend your lives, and be in perfect charity with all men; so shall ye be meet partakers of those holy mysteries."

[1] Cranmer: *Works*, Vol. I, p. 148.
[2] Hooker: *Laws of Ecclesiastical Polity*, V, lvii, 4.
[3] An allusion to I Cor. 11:29.

THE SACRAMENTS AS PLEDGES AND SEALS

It was far from the Reformers, however, to imagine that the grace of God could in any way be created by the faith of man. God's grace is God's initiative on behalf of man who is helpless because of sin. Divine grace precedes all. Faith is man's response of gratitude and appropriation to the grace that is freely offered in Christ. It embraces, with humility and wonder, the saving promises of the Gospel. Human unbelief cannot nullify the reality of the work of Christ. The Word of God, which is visible in the sacraments, is prior both to those sacraments and to that faith of which their participation is an expression. Hence the Reformers were accustomed to speak of a sacrament not only as a sign and a means of grace, but also as *a pledge* of God's faithfulness and as *a seal* affixed as it were to His Word. A pledge, like an engagement ring, is a visible token and guarantee that the promise made is true and will be fulfilled. Likewise a seal attached to a document is simply a visible assurance of the authenticity of that document: it adds nothing to the text of the document. So sacraments are seals added to the Word of the Gospel, without, however, adding anything to the Word itself. And as a seal by itself, or affixed to a wordless sheet of paper, is void of all value and significance, so too the sacraments, if divorced from the Word of God, degenerate into empty superstitions. "Christ hath ordained them," writes Jewel, "that by them He might set before our eyes the mysteries of our salvation, and might more strongly confirm the faith which we have in His blood, and might seal His grace in our hearts. As princes' seals confirm and warrant their deeds and charters, so do the sacraments witness unto our conscience that God's promises are true and shall continue for ever. Thus doth God make known His secret purpose to His Church: first he declareth His mercy by His Word; then He sealeth it and assureth it by His sacraments. In the Word we have His promises: in the sacraments we see them."[1]

As pledges and seals, the sacraments are intended to be assurances to our faith and aids to our infirmity. "God's gift, without sealing, is sure," says Sandys; "as He Himself is all one, without changing: yet, to bear with our infirmity, and to make us more secure of His promise, to His writing and Word He added these outward signs and seals, to establish our faith and to certify us that

[1] Jewel: *Works*, Vol. II, p. 1099.

His promise is most certain." Again, he describes the sacraments as "pledges and assurances of remission of sins and salvation, purchased by the death of Christ", and as "God's seals added unto His most certain promises for the confirmation of our weak faith, weak by reason of the infirmity of our flesh".[1] The sacraments "have their peculiar and proper promises", writes Hooper of the ordinances of both Old and New Testaments, "unto the which they hang annexed, as a seal unto the writing, and therefore be called, after St. Paul, confirmations or seals of God's promises.[2] They have peculiar elements, by the which they signify the heavenly mysteries that sacramentally they contain, and be the thing indeed. They are called sacraments, that is to say, visible signs of invisible grace; they have their proper ceremonies that testify unto us the obsignation and confirmation of God's heavenly gifts."[3]

Bradford rejoices in the sacrament of holy communion in the following words: "Truly, O Christ, Thou art the food of the soul: and therefore our heavenly Father giveth Thee unto us that we being refreshed in communicating of Thee might be received into immortality. Now because this mystery is of itself incomprehensible, Thou dost exhibit and give unto us a figure and image hereof in visible signs: yea, as though Thou paidest down present earnest, Thou makest us so certain hereof as if with our eyes we saw it. And this is the end wherefor Thou didst institute this Thy supper and banquet, namely, that it might confirm us, as of Thy body once so offered for us that we may feed on it, and in feeding feel in us the efficacy and strength of Thy alone sacrifice; so of Thy blood once so shed for us that it is unto us a continual potion and drink . . . for the covenant which Thou once hast stricken with us in Thy blood Thou dost as it were renew the same as concerning the confirmation of our faith so often as Thou reach unto us this holy cup to drink of. O wonderful consolation which cometh to the godly by reason of this sacrament!"[4]

And Cranmer praises the worth of the sacraments in the following way: "Our Saviour Christ hath not only set forth these things most plainly in His holy Word, that we may hear them with our ears, but He hath also ordained one visible sacrament of spiritual regeneration in water, and another visible sacrament of spiritual nourishment in bread and wine, to the intent that as much as

[1] Sandys: *Works*, pp. 303f., 87.   [2] The allusion is to Rom. 4:11.
[3] Hooper: *Works*, Vol. II, p. 88.   [4] Bradford: *Works*, Vol. I, pp. 260f.

is possible for man we may see Christ with our eyes, smell Him at our nose, taste Him with our mouths, grope [that is, grasp] Him with our hands, and perceive Him with all our senses. For as the Word of God preached putteth Christ into our ears, so likewise these elements of water, bread, and wine, joined to God's Word, do after a sacramental manner put Christ into our eyes, mouths, hands, and all our senses. And for this cause Christ ordained baptism in water, that as surely as we see, feel, and touch water with our bodies, and be washed with water, so assuredly ought we to believe, when we be baptized, that Christ is verily present with us, and that by Him we be newly born again spiritually, and washed from our sins, and grafted in the stock of Christ's own body, and be apparelled, clothed, and harnessed with Him, in such wise that as the devil hath no power against Christ so hath he none against us, so long as we remain grafted in that stock, and clothed with that apparel, and harnessed with that armour. So that the washing in water of baptism is, as it were, showing of Christ before our eyes, and a sensible touching, feeling, and groping of Him, to the confirmation of the inward faith which we have of Him. And in like manner Christ ordained the sacrament of His body and blood in bread and wine, to preach unto us that, as our bodies be fed, nourished, and preserved with meat and drink, so as touching our spiritual life towards God we be fed, nourished, and preserved by the body and blood of our Saviour Christ; and also that He is such a preservation unto us that neither the devils of hell, nor eternal death, nor sin can be able to prevail against us so long as by true and constant faith we be fed and nourished with that meat and drink . . . Thus our Saviour Christ, knowing us to be in this world, as it were, but babes and weaklings in faith, hath ordained sensible signs and tokens whereby to allure and draw us to more strength and more constant faith in Him."[1]

In his *Catechism* Thomas Becon propounds seven purposes for which the sacraments were instituted:

"First, that they should be unto us testimonies, pledges, signs, or seals of God's grace, favour, and mercy, to teach us that God is merciful unto us, and will forgive us our sins, justify and save us for Christ's sake, and that all the benefits of Christ doth belong and are freely given unto us of God the Father, if with faith we come and receive those holy mysteries . . .

[1] Cranmer: *Works*, Vol. I, pp. 41f.

7*

"Secondly, that they should be certain tokens and marks whereby the Church of Christ may be discerned from the synagogue of antichrist . . .

"Thirdly, that they should be signs, tokens, and marks of our confession, in the which we outwardly profess what we inwardly think and believe . . .

"Fourthly, that they should be as sinews and bonds to link and knit together the congregation of God publicly and openly, whereby they may be known to be of one company, and of one spirit, of one faith, and of one doctrine and profession. . .

"Fifthly, that they should be unto us memorials, to put us in remembrance what mutual benevolence, what love, and hearty friendship one to another ought to reign among us. For seeing we all are partakers of the same mysteries, baptized with one baptism, and eat together of one bread, and drink together of one cup, by this means protesting openly that we are members one of another's body, whereof Jesus Christ is the Head; who seeth not how far all enmity, debate, strife, malice, envy, and all displeasure ought to be from us? . . .

"Sixthly, that they should be testimonials unto us, to testify and witness how nigh Christ joins Himself unto us, that He giveth Himself whole unto us, and that He will dwell in us and endow us with all His benefits and riches, so that whatsoever is Christ's the same is ours. . .

"Seventhly, that they should be unto us a singular consolation and an exceeding great comfort in all our troubles, perils, dangers, and adversities, while in receiving them we behold and consider the merciful good will of God toward us, with this persuasion, that that God, who hath instituted these sacraments, delivered them unto us as pledges of His most hearty good will toward us, and hath also commanded us to use them for our comfort, will not leave us succourless, but in His time will deliver us from all those miseries and bring us into the haven of quietness . . ."[1]

THE SACRAMENTS OF THE OLD TESTAMENT

Baptism and holy communion as sacraments of the New Testament answer to circumcision and the passover as sacraments of the Old Testament. "God," says Hooker, "hath annexed them for ever unto the New Testament, as other rites were before with the

[1] Becon: *Works*, Vol. II, pp. 199ff.

Old."[1] Hooper explains that "in the law of Moses was circumcision and the paschal lamb; and in their places we have baptism
and the supper of the Lord, diverse in external elements and
ceremonies, but one in effect, mystery, and the thing itself; saving
that their sacraments showed the graces of God to be given unto
men in Christ to come, and ours declare the graces of God to be
given in Christ that is already come: so that the sacraments be not
changed, but rather the elements of the sacraments".[2]

The passover is explained by Tyndale as "a very prophecy of
the passion of Christ, describing the very manner and passion of
His death and the effect and virtue thereof also; in whose stead is
the sacrament of the body and blood of Christ come, as baptism
in the room or stead of circumcision".[3] But although with the
coming of Christ the outward and visible signs were changed, yet
there is no essential discontinuity; for the grace of God is the same
in both Testaments and Christ is the one Mediator and Redeemer
through the entire duration of human history. Thus Article VII
states that "the Old Testament is not contrary to the New: for both
in the Old and New Testament everlasting life is offered to mankind by Christ, who is the only Mediator between God and man,
being both God and man".

Contrasting the believers of the former dispensation with those
of the Christian era, Cranmer writes: "Only this difference was
between them and us, that our redemption by Christ's death and
passion was then only promised, and now it is performed and past.
And as their sacraments were figures of His death to come, so be
ours figures of the same now past and gone. And yet it was all but
one Christ to them and us, who gave life, comfort, and strength
to them by His death to come, and giveth the same to us by His
death passed. And He was in their sacraments spiritually and
effectually present, and for so much truly and really present, that
is to say, in deed, before He was born, no less than He is now in
our sacraments present after His death and ascension into heaven.
But as for carnal presence, He was to them not yet come; and to us
He is come, and gone again unto His Father, from whom he
came."[4] So, again, Cranmer asserts that the Old Testament
"fathers and prophets did eat Christ's body and drink His blood in
promise of redemption to be wrought, and we eat and drink the

[1] Hooker: *Op. cit.*, V, lvii, 2.    [2] Hooper: *Works*, Vol. II, p. 88.
[3] Tyndale: *Works*, Vol. I, p. 354.    [4] Cranmer: *Works*, Vol. I, p. 60.

same flesh and blood in confirmation of our faith in the redemption already wrought."[1] Roger Hutchinson speaks of the abiding relevance of both old and new covenants (or testaments) in the following manner: "In the time of the old testament, before Christ's incarnation, such as in all their ceremonies had an eye to the Seed promised, and believed in Christ to come, were of the new testament, under grace, and Christians . . . And such, again, as at these days do not believe, but live after the flesh, are yet under the old testament, under the law, under the stroke of the axe, which is put to the root of all evil trees. For both testaments were effectual from the beginning of the world, the one in virtuous and godly men, the other upon the unvirtuous and ungodly."[2]

THE SYMBOLISM OF BAPTISM

The spiritual reality to which the symbol of baptism points is twofold. Firstly, it symbolizes the washing away of sin by the blood of Christ. The water applied in baptism is the outward and visible sign of the inward "washing of regeneration and renewing of the Holy Spirit" (Tit. 3:5). Secondly, it is symbolical of death, burial, and resurrection by identification of the believer with Christ—in His death and burial, implying the crucifixion with Him of the old rebellious nature; and in His resurrection from the dead, implying the newness of life and service in which the Christian is to walk. Those who have been baptized should reckon themselves to be dead indeed unto sin, but alive unto God in Christ Jesus (Rom. 6:11); or, as the baptismal service of the Book of Common Prayer puts it: "Baptism doth represent unto us our profession, which is to follow the example of our Saviour Christ and to be made like unto Him; that, as He died and rose again for us, so should we who are baptized die from sin and rise again unto righteousness, continually mortifying all our evil and corrupt affections, and daily proceeding in all virtue and godliness of living."

The sacrament of baptism, then is a visible word which speaks of cleansing from defilement, death to sin, and resurrection to newness of life in Christ. It is, in short, the sacrament of regeneration. Jewel draws attention to its inner reality when he describes it as "our regeneration or new birth, whereby we are born anew in Christ and are made the sons of God and heirs of the kingdom of

[1] Cranmer: *Works*, Vol. I, p. 75.          [2] Hutchinson: *Works*, pp. 326f.

heaven", and "the sacrament of the remission of sins and of that washing which we have in the blood of Christ". But he is careful to give this warning: "Not the water, but the blood of Christ, reconcileth us unto God, strengtheneth our conscience, and worketh our redemption. We must seek salvation in Christ alone and not in any outward thing."[1] And Becon stresses that the baptism of the Holy Spirit is so necessary "that without it the baptism of water profiteth nothing".[2]

To the same purpose is the assertion of the Catechism that "repentance, whereby they forsake sin, and faith, whereby they steadfastly believe the promises of God made to them in that sacrament", are required of those that receive baptism. "Our baptism," says Bishop Latimer, "is not only ordained for that cause, to know a Christian from a Turk or heathen, but it hath a further signification: it signifieth that we must wash away the old Adam, forsake and set aside all carnal lusts and desires, and put on Christ, receive Him with a pure heart, and study to live and go forward in all goodness, according unto His will and commandment."[3]

## THE BAPTISM OF INFANTS

In view of these considerations, the question arises as to the permissibility of the practice of infant baptism which was retained by the Reformers. On what scriptural grounds could this sacrament be administered to little children who as yet were incapable of the response of repentance, faith, and obedience? Jewel offers the following justification of the practice: "For this cause are infants baptized, because they are born in sin and cannot become spiritual but by this new birth of water and the Spirit. They are the heirs of the promise: the covenant of God's favour is made unto them. God said to Abraham: 'I will establish My covenant between Me and thee and thy seed after thee in their generations for an everlasting covenant, to be God unto thee and to thy seed after thee.'[4] Therefore saith the apostle: 'If the root be holy, so are the branches.' And again: 'The unbelieving husband is sanctified by the wife; and the unbelieving wife is sanctified by the husband: else were your children unclean; but now are they holy.'[5] When the disciples rebuked those that brought little children to Christ that He might

---

[1] Jewel: *Works*, Vol. II, pp. 1104, 1106.
[2] Becon: *Works*, Vol. II, p. 203.    [3] Latimer: *Works*, Vol. II, p. 133.
[4] Gen. 17:7.    [5] Rom. 11:16, I Cor. 7:14.

touch them, He said: 'Suffer little children to come unto Me and
forbid them not, for of such is the kingdom of God.' And again:
'Their angels always behold the face of My Father who is in
heaven.' "[1]

The administration of the corresponding sacrament of circumcision to infant children under the terms of the Abrahamic covenant
was seen to be of particular relevance. "As God took the seed of
Abraham to be partakers of the covenant which He gave to
Abraham, so He appointed that every man-child of eight days old
should be circumcised," continues Jewel. "And 'Abraham circumcised his son Isaac when he was eight days old, as God had
commanded him'.[2] May we think that the promise of God hath an
end, so that it reacheth not to our children? Or might the children
of the Jews receive the sign of the covenant, and may not the children
of the Christians? Whatsoever was promised to Abraham, the
same is also performed unto us. We enjoy the same blessings and
free privilege of God's favour. St. Paul to the Galatians saith:
'Know ye that they which are of faith are the children of Abraham'.
Again: 'If ye be Christ's, then are ye Abraham's seed and heirs by
promise'.[3] Now is the sign of the covenant also changed, and baptism is instead of circumcision, as St. Paul declareth, and calleth
them circumcised who are baptized: 'in whom', meaning Christ,
'also ye are circumcised with circumcision made without hands, by
putting off the sinful body of the flesh, through the circumcision
of Christ, in that you are buried with Him through baptism'.[4] Our
Saviour giveth charge to His apostles to 'baptize all nations in the
name of the Father and of the Son and of the Holy Ghost'.[5] The
apostles baptized not only such as professed their belief, but whole
households. 'The keeper of the prison was baptized with all that
belonged unto him'.[6] So was Crispus, the chief ruler of the synagogue, and his household, and the household of Stephanas.[7]

"Infants are a part of the Church of God," concludes Jewel;
"they are the sheep of Christ and belong to His flock: why should
they not bear the mark of Christ? They have the promise of salvation: why should they not receive the seal whereby it is confirmed
unto them? They are of the fellowship of the faithful: Augustine
saith: *Ubi ponis parvulos non baptizatos? profecto in numero creden-*

---

[1] Mk. 10:14, Mt. 18:10.          [2] Gen. 21:4.          [3] Gal. 3:7, 29.
[4] Col. 2:11f.                     [5] Mt. 28:19.          [6] Acts 16:33.
[7] Acts 18:8, I Cor. 1:16.

*tium*: 'Where place you young children who are not yet baptized? Verily in the number of them that believe'. Why then should not they be partakers of the sacrament together with the faithful?"[1]

In answer to the question: What if infants die before they receive the sacrament of baptism? Becon writes: "God's promise of salvation unto them is not for default of the sacrament minished or made vain and of no effect. For the Spirit is not so bound to the water that He cannot work His office where the water wanteth, or that He must of necessity always be there where the water is sprinkled. Simon Magus had the sacramental water, but he had not the Holy Ghost, being indeed an hypocrite and filthy dissembler. In the chronicle of the apostles' Acts we read that while Peter preached the Holy Ghost came upon them that heard him, yea, and that before they were baptized; by reason whereof Peter burst out into these words and said: 'Can any man forbid water that these should not be baptized who have received the Holy Ghost as well as we?'[2] True Christians, whether they be old or young, are not saved because outwardly they be washed with the sacramental water, but because they be God's children by election through Christ . . . Notwithstanding, the sacrament of baptism ought not therefore to be neglected, but with all reverence to be embraced both of old and young. For he that despiseth the sacrament despiseth not the sacrament only, but the author of the sacrament, who is Christ Jesus the Lord."[3]

A child when he has grown to years of responsibility may indeed repudiate the grace of which the sacrament administered to him in infancy is a symbol and pledge. In the pre-Christian age great numbers of Jews who, in accordance with the divine command, had received the outward seal of circumcision showed themselves, by the rebellion of unbelief, to be altogether uncircumcised in heart. In a word, they possessed the sign, but not the reality to which it pointed. And this is equally the case with baptism. That the want of the sacrament does not exclude from salvation is shown by Christ's promise to the penitent thief, who died without being baptized. On the other hand, that participation in the sacrament does not guarantee salvation is shown, as Becon has reminded us (not to mention the many other Reformers who do the same), by the example of Simon Magus, who received it unworthily and to his

[1] Jewel: *Works*, Vol. II, pp. 1104f.　　[2] Acts 8:9ff., 18ff., 10:44ff.
[3] Becon: *Works*, Vol. III, p. 617.

condemnation. In the rite of confirmation the opportunity is afforded to those who have been baptized in childhood, so that (in the words of the Prayer Book service) "they may themselves, with their own mouth and consent, openly before the Church, ratify and confirm" the promises made at their baptism.

But the fact that some may choose to repudiate the reality to which their baptism points by no means implies that the ceremony of baptism is a vain formality. It has already been observed that the sacraments are always effective as means, either of grace to those who receive them rightly, which is the main purpose of their institution, or of condemnation to those who abuse them. For every believer, his baptism, though an event of the past, should constantly be before him as a witness and reminder of the grace and truth of which it is eloquent. This is one reason why baptism should ordinarily be *publicly* administered, "when the most number of people come together"—so that (as the Prayer Book rubric says) "in the baptism of infants every man present may be put in remembrance of his own profession made to God in his baptism". Circumcision, declares Latimer, "was a certain sure, infallible, and effectual token of God's good will towards them to whom it was given: for as many as did believe the coven-ant of God, it did ascertain them of the good will of God towards them, that they should be delivered out of all their troubles and adversities, and that they should be sure of the help of God . . . So let us ever consider, in what trouble and calamity soever we be, let us remember that we be baptized, that God hath promised to help us, to deliver us from all our sins and wickedness, to be our God."[1] But for those who treat their baptism in an irrespon-sible or superstitious manner Latimer has the sternest of admoni-tions: "I heard of late," he says, "that there be some wicked persons, despisers of God and His benefits, who say, 'It is no matter whatsoever we do; we be baptized: we cannot be damned; for all those that be baptized and called Christians shall be saved'. This is a false and wicked opinion; and I assure you that such who bear the name of Christians and be baptized, but follow not God's commandments, that such fellows, I say, be worse than the Turks and heathen: for the Turks and heathen have made no promise unto Christ to serve Him. These fellows have made promise in baptism to keep Christ's rule, which thing

[1] Latimer: *Works*, Vol. II, pp. 133ff.

they do not; and therefore they be worse than the Turks: for they break their promise made before God and the whole congregation.'[1]

Baptism, properly received, brings one into the closest relationship with the cross of Christ, not merely as the place of cleansing from sin, but also as the sign under which the Christian must willingly fight and suffer. The recipient is signed with the sign of the cross "in token that hereafter he shall not be ashamed to confess the faith of Christ crucified and manfully to fight under His banner". "O that we considered often and in deed what we have professed in baptism!" writes Bradford from prison to "certain godly men". "Then the cross and we should be well acquainted together; for we are 'baptized into Christ's death'."[2] And he wrote in similar vein to others during those days when he was awaiting a martyr's death. To Richard Hopkins, sheriff of Coventry: "You have professed in baptism to fight under the standard of your Captain Christ: and will you now, for peril's sake, leave your Lord? You made a solemn vow that you would forsake the world: and will you be forsworn, and run to embrace it now? . . . Think therefore the cross, if it come for confession of Christ, no strange thing to God's children; but rather take it as the Lord's medicine, by the which He helpeth our infirmities and setteth forth His glory. Our sins have deserved cross upon cross. Now if God give us His cross, to suffer for His truth and confessing Him, as He doth by it bury our sins, so doth He glorify us, making us like to Christ here, that we may be like unto Him elsewhere: for 'if we be partakers of the affliction, we shall be partakers of the consolation'; if we be like in ignomiy, we shall be like in glory."[3] To lovers of the Gospel: "Remember your profession, how that in baptism you made a solemn vow to renounce the devil, the world, etc. You promised to fight under Christ's standard . . . Go to, then, pay your vow to the Lord; fight like men and valiant men under Christ's standard 'take up your cross' and follow your Master, as your brethren M. Hooper, Rogers, Taylor, and Saunders have done, and as now your brethren M. Cranmer, Latimer, Ridley, Ferrar, Bradford, Hawkes, etc. be ready to do. The ice is broken before you; therefore be not afraid, but be content to die for the Lord. You have no cause to waver or doubt of the doctrine thus declared by the blood

---

[1] Latimer: *Works*, Vol. I, p. 346.    [2] Bradford: *Works*, Vol. I, p. 384.
[3] Bradford: *Ibid.*, pp. 396ff. See II Cor. 1:7, II Tim. 2:12.

of the pastors."[1] And to the brethren throughout the realm of England: "But with what face can we look for this, that are so fearful, unwilling, and backward to leave that which, will we, nill we, we must leave; and that so shortly, as we know not the time when? Where is our renouncing and forsaking of the world and the flesh which we solemnly took upon us in baptism? Ah, shameless cowards that we be, who will not follow the trace of so many, fathers, patriarchs, kings, priests, prophets, apostles, evangelists and saints of God, yea, even of the very Son of God!"[2]

THE SYMBOLISM OF HOLY COMMUNIOM

The inner reality to which the sacrament of holy communion points is that of spiritual nourishment and growth. The Reformers were unanimous in their insistence that the eating and receiving of Christ in the sacrament was not in any sense physical but spiritual, not with the mouth but in the heart of him who believes the promise of which the sacrament is a visible word—thus the bread is administered with the words: "Take and eat this in remembrance that Christ died for thee, and feed on Him in thy heart by faith with thanksgiving." Accordingly, also, the presence of Christ is a spiritual presence within the heart of every believing recipient; and, being inward and spiritual, it is incomparably more real than a mere outward or physical presence. "Christ is present," says Cranmer, "whensoever the Church prayeth unto Him and is gathered together in His name. And the bread and wine be made unto us the body and blood of Christ (as it is in the Book of Common Prayer), but not by changing the substance of bread and wine into the substance of Christ's natural body and blood, but that in the godly using of them they be unto the receivers Christ's body and blood . . . And Christ Himself to some is a stone to stumble at, to some is a raising from death, not by conversion of substances, but by good or evil use: that thing which to the godly is salvation, to the ungodly is damnation. So is the water in baptism and the bread and wine in the Lord's supper to the worthy receivers Christ Himself and eternal life, and to the unworthy receivers everlasting death and damnation, not by conversion of one

---

[1] Bradford: *Works*, Vol. I, p. 410. This was evidently written some time between 9 February 1555, when Hooper and Taylor suffered martyrdom, and 30 March of the same year, when Bishop Ferrar was burnt.

[2] Bradford: *Ibid.*, pp. 417f.

substance into another, but by godly or ungodly use thereof. And therefore in the book of the holy communion we do not pray absolutely that the bread and wine may be made the body and blood of Christ, but that unto us in that holy mystery they may be so; that is to say, that we may so worthily receive the same that we may be partakers of Christ's body and blood, and that therewith in spirit and truth we may be spiritually nourished."[1]

"I teach," says Cranmer, "that no man can eat Christ's flesh and drink His blood but spiritually, which forasmuch as evil men do not, although they eat the sacramental bread until their bellies be full and drink the wine until they be drunken, yet they eat neither Christ's flesh nor drink His blood, neither in the sacrament nor without the sacrament, because they cannot be eaten and drunken but by spirit and faith, whereof ungodly men be destitute, being nothing but world and flesh. This therefore is the sum of my teaching in this fourth book, that in the true ministration of the sacrament Christ is present spiritually, and so spiritually eaten of them that be godly and spiritual. And as for the ungodly and carnal they may eat the bread and drink the wine, but with Christ Himself they have no communion or company; and therefore they neither eat His flesh nor drink His blood, which whosoever eateth hath (as Christ saith Himself) life by Him, as Christ hath life by His Father."[2] Again: "Every good and faithful Christian man feeleth in himself how he feedeth of Christ, eating His flesh and drinking of His blood. For he putteth the whole hope and trust of his redemption and salvation in that only sacrifice which Christ made upon the cross, having His body there broken and His blood there shed for the remission of his sins. And this great benefit of Christ the faithful man earnestly considereth in his mind, cheweth it and digesteth it with the stomach of his heart, spiritually receiving Christ wholly into him, and giving again himself wholly unto Christ ... For as Christ is a spiritual meat, so is He spiritually eaten and digested with the spiritual part of us, and giveth us spiritual and eternal life, and is not eaten, swallowed, and digested with our teeth, tongues, throats, and bellies."[3]

Latimer also preaches to the same effect. "Our Saviour, the Bridegroom," he says, "offereth Himself at His last supper which

---

[1] Cranmer: *Works*, Vol. I, p. 79.
[2] Cranmer: *Ibid.*, p. 203. See Jn. 6:54, 57.
[3] Cranmer: *Ibid.*, pp. 207f.

He had with His disciples, His body to be eaten and His blood to be drunk. And to the intent that it should be done to our great comfort, and then again to take away all cruelty, irksomeness, and horribleness, He showeth unto us how we shall eat Him, in what manner and form, namely, spiritually, to our great comfort: so that whosoever eateth the mystical bread and drinketh the mystical wine worthily, according to the ordinance of Christ, he receiveth surely the very body and blood of Christ spiritually, as it shall be most comfortable unto his soul. He eateth with the mouth of his soul and digesteth with the stomach of his soul the body of Christ. And to be short: whosoever believeth in Christ, putteth his hope, trust, and confidence in Him, he eateth and drinketh Him: for the spiritual eating is the right eating to everlasting life."[1] And Bradford writes: "We teach these benefits to be had by the worthy receiving of the sacrament, namely, that we abide in Christ and Christ in us; again, that we attain by it to a celestial life, or a life with God; moreover, that by faith and in spirit we receive not only Christ's body and blood but also whole Christ, God and man. Besides these we grant that by the worthy receiving of this sacrament we receive remission of our sins and confirmation of the new testament. Last of all, by worthy receiving we get by faith an increase of incorporation with Christ and amongst ourselves who be His members: than which things what more can be desired?"[2]

Two further quotations from Cranmer will serve to sum up this doctrine, which was so crucial an issue between the theologians of Rome and the theologians of the Reformation. Firstly, concerning "the whole effect and strength of this sacrament" Cranmer writes: "This spiritual meat of Christ's body and blood is not received in the mouth and digested in the stomach (as corporal meats and drinks commonly be), but is received with a pure heart and sincere faith. And the true eating and drinking of the said body and blood of Christ is with a constant and lively faith to believe that Christ gave His body and shed His blood on the cross for us, and that He doth so join and incorporate Himself to us that He is our Head and we His members, and flesh of His flesh and bone of His bones, having Him dwelling in us, and we in Him. And herein standeth the whole effect and strength of this sacrament. And this faith God worketh inwardly in our hearts by His Holy Spirit, and confirmeth the same outwardly to our ears by hearing of His Word,

[1] Latimer: *Works*, Vol. I, pp. 458f.    [2] Bradford: *Works*, Vol. I, p. 99.

and to our other senses by eating and drinking of the sacramental bread and wine in His holy supper."[1] And, secondly, concerning "the true understanding of the true presence" he declares: "My doctrine is that the very body of Christ, which was born of the virgin Mary and suffered for our sins, giving us life by His death, the same Jesus, as concerning His corporal presence, is taken from us and sitteth at the right hand of His Father; and yet He is by faith spiritually present with us, and is our spiritual food and nourishment, and sitteth in the midst of all them that be gathered together in His name. And this feeding is a spiritual feeding and an heavenly feeding, far passing all corporal and carnal feeding; and therefore there is a true presence and a true feeding indeed, and not 'in a figure only or not at all', as you most untruly report my saying to be.[2] This is the true understanding of the true presence, receiving, and feeding upon the body and blood of our Saviour Christ."[3]

The sacrament of holy communion is one means, but not the only means, whereby the Christian is enabled to feed upon Christ. "The spiritual eating of His flesh and drinking of His blood by faith," says Cranmer, "by digesting His death in our minds as our only price, ransom, and redemption from eternal damnation, is the cause wherefor Christ said that if we eat not His flesh and drink not His blood we have not life in us, and if we eat His flesh and drink his blood we have everlasting life. And if Christ had never ordained the sacrament yet should we have eaten His flesh and drunken His blood, and have had thereby everlasting life, as all the faithful did before the sacrament was ordained, and do daily when they receive not the sacrament. And so did the holy men that wandered in the wilderness and in all their lifetime very seldom received the sacrament; and many holy martyrs, either exiled or kept in prison, did daily feed of the food of Christ's body and drank daily the blood that sprang out of His side, or else they could not have had everlasting life, as Christ Himself said in the gospel of St. John, and yet they were not suffered with other Christian people to have the use of the sacrament." It follows that "the mystery of eating Christ's flesh and drinking His blood extendeth further than the supper: for none feed nor be nourished by Him

[1] Cranmer: *Works*, Vol. I, p. 43.

[2] The reference is to what Gardiner has written concerning his doctrine of the reality of Christ's presence.　　　[3] Cranmer: *Ibid.*, p. 185.

but that be lively members of His body; and so long and no longer
feed they of Him than they be His true members and receive life
from Him".[1]

Accordingly, Cranmer distinguishes "three manner of eatings:
one spiritual only, another spiritual and sacramental both together,
and the third sacramental only". "There is," he explains, "a
spiritual eating only, when Christ by a true faith is eaten without
the sacrament; also there is another eating both spiritual and
sacramental, when the visible sacrament is eaten with the mouth
and Christ Himself is eaten with a true faith; and the third eating
is sacramentally only, when the sacrament is eaten and not Christ
Himself. So that in the first is Christ eaten without the sacrament;
in the second He is eaten with the sacrament; and in the third the
sacrament is eaten without Him, and therefore is called sacramental
eating only, because only the sacrament is eaten and not Christ
Himself. After the first two manner of ways godly men do eat,
who feed and live by Christ; the third manner of ways the wicked
do eat; and therefore, as St. Augustine saith, 'they neither eat
Christ's flesh nor drink His blood, although every day they eat the
sacrament thereof, to the condemnation of their presumption'."[2]

A SACRAMENT OF UNITY

The holy communion is significant, further, as a sacrament of
unity. It is an expression of Christian oneness, or communion—of
the oneness and communion of Christians with Christ and, consequently, with each other, as those who are *in Christ*. This oneness is symbolized by the one loaf and the one cup of which all who
are present partake. "The cup of blessing which we bless, is it not a
communion of the blood of Christ?" asks the Apostle. "The bread
which we break, is it not a communion of the body of Christ? seeing
that we, who are many, are one bread, one body: for we all partake
of the one loaf" (I Cor. 10:16f.). It is a particular purpose of this
holy banquet, says Becon, "that it should be a sign and a token of
the unity and concord, of the hearty good will and singular friendship, and of the perfect agreement in doctrine and religion that
ought to be among them that profess Christ".[3] So, too, Cranmer
writes that "Christ ordained the sacrament to move and stir all men

[1] Cranmer: *Works*, Vol. I, pp. 25, 204.
[2] Cranmer: *Ibid.*, p. 205; cf. p. 71. The reference is to Augustine:
Tract. XXVI, on the Gospel of John.          [3] Becon: *Works*, Vol. II, p. 231.

to friendship, love, and concord, and to put away all hatred,
variance, and discord, and to testify a brotherly and unfeigned love
between all them that be the members of Christ: but the devil, the
enemy of Christ and all His members, hath so craftily juggled
herein that of nothing riseth so much contention as of this holy
sacrament. God grant," he exclaims, "that, all contention set
aside, both the parties may come to this holy communion with
such a lively faith in Christ and such an unfeigned love to all
Christ's members, that as they carnally eat with their mouths the
sacramental bread, and drink the wine, so spiritually they may eat
and drink the very flesh and blood of Christ who is in heaven and
sitteth on the right hand of His Father; and that finally by His
means they may enjoy with Him the glory and kingdom of heaven.
Amen!"[1]

Cranmer explains that, "as the bread and wine which we do eat
be turned into our flesh and blood and be made our very flesh and
our very blood, and so be joined and mixed with our flesh and
blood that they be made one whole body together, even so be all
faithful Christians spiritually turned into the body of Christ, and
so be joined unto Christ, and also together among themselves, that
they do make but one mystical body of Christ, as St. Paul saith:
'We be one bread and one body, as many as be partakers of one
bread and one cup'. And," he continues, "as one loaf is given
among many men, so that every one is partaker of the same loaf,
and likewise one cup of wine is distributed unto many persons,
whereof every one is partaker, even so our Saviour Christ (whose
flesh and blood be represented by the mystical bread and wine in
the Lord's supper) doth give Himself unto all His true members,
spiritually to feed them, nourish them, and to give them continual
life by Him. And as the branches of a tree or members of a body,
if they be dead or cut off, they neither live nor receive any nourishment or sustenance of the body or tree, so likewise ungodly and
wicked people, who be cut off from Christ's mystical body or be
dead members of the same, do not spiritually feed upon Christ's
body and blood, nor have any life, strength, or sustentation thereby
. . . Whereas nothing in this life is more acceptable before God or
more pleasant unto man than Christian people to live together
quietly in love and peace, unity and concord, this sacrament doth
most aptly and effectuously move us thereunto. For when we be

[1] Cranmer: *Works*, Vol. I, p. 30.

made all partakers of this one table what ought we to think but that we be all members of one spiritual body, whereof Christ is the Head; that we be joined together in one Christ, as a great number of grains of corn be joined together in one loaf? Surely they have very hard and stony hearts who with these things be not moved; and more cruel and unreasonable be they than brute beasts that cannot be persuaded to be good to their Christian brethren and neighbours for whom Christ suffered death, when in this sacrament they be put in remembrance that the Son of God bestowed His life for His enemies. For we see by daily experience that eating and drinking together maketh friends and continueth friendship: much more then ought the table of Christ to move us so to do . . . Wherefore whose heart soever this holy sacrament, communion, and supper of Christ will not kindle with love unto his neighbours and cause him to put out of his heart all envy, hatred, and malice, and to grave in the same all amity, friendship, and concord, he deceiveth himself if he think that he hath the Spirit of Christ dwelling within him."[1]

The sacrament of holy communion, moreover, is both commemorative and anticipatory. Not only does it look back to the salvation-event of the past, but it also looks forward to the consummation of that salvation in the future. It is commemorative in accordance with Christ's command: "Do this in remembrance of Me." As the third of the longer exhortations in the communion service explains, this sacrament was ordained by Christ "to the end that we should always remember the exceeding great love of our Master and only Saviour, Jesus Christ, thus dying for us, and the innumerable benefits which by His precious blood-shedding He hath obtained to us". And it is anticipatory in accordance with Paul's declaration: "As often as ye eat this bread and drink this cup ye proclaim the Lord's death till He come" (I Cor. 11:26). This is echoed in the Prayer Book service when, in the prayer of consecration, the reminder is given that Christ instituted this sacrament as "a perpetual memory of that His precious death, *until His coming again*". The holy communion is indeed a bridge between the two comings of Christ.[2] In the intervening period between the ascension and the return of Christ the purpose of this sacrament is not,

---

[1] Cranmer: *Works*, Vol. I, pp. 42f.

[2] How well does Bengel say, "*Hoc mysterium duo tempora extrema conjungit*", commenting on I Cor. 11:26 (*Gnomon Novi Testamenti*).

as it were, to draw Him down from heaven, but rather to uplift the Christian to His heavenly presence, so that (in the words of the collect of Ascension Day) the worshipper may "also in heart and mind thither ascend, and with Him continually dwell". This is the significance of the *Sursum corda*, that great moment in the communion service when, in response to the exhortation: "Lift up your hearts!" the people unitedly answer: "We lift them up unto the Lord!"

"The body of Christ, sitting above all heavens, is worshipped of us, being here beneath in earth," says Jewel in a sermon preached at St. Paul's Cross in 1560. "Therefore the priest at the communion, before he enter into the holy mysteries, giveth warning unto the people to mount up with their minds into heaven, and crieth unto them, *Sursum corda*, 'Lift up your hearts', according to the doctrine of St. Paul: *Si una surrexistis cum Christo, ea quae sursum sint quaerite, ubi Christus est sedens ad dextram Patris*: 'If ye be risen again with Christ, seek for those things that be above, where Christ is sitting at the right hand of His Father'. And again: *Nostra conversatio est in coelis, unde Salvatorem expectamus*: 'Our conversation or dwelling is in heaven, from whence we look for our Saviour' . . . Christ's body is in heaven: thither therefore must we direct our hearts; there must we feed; there must we refresh ourselves; and there must we worship it."[1] And Cranmer gives the following admonition: "All that love and believe Christ Himself, let them not think that Christ is corporally in the bread; but let them lift up their hearts unto heaven and worship Him sitting there at the right hand of His Father. Let them worship Him in themselves, whose temples they be, in whom He dwelleth and liveth spiritually; but in no wise let them worship Him as being corporally in the bread. For He is not in it, neither spiritually, as He is in man, nor corporally, as He is in heaven, but only sacramentally, as a thing may be said to be in the figure whereby it is signified."[2] In similar vein Hooper declares: "I believe that this receiving is not done carnally or bodily, but spiritually, through a true and lively faith; that is to say, the body and blood of Christ are not given to the mouth and belly for the nourishing of the body, but unto our faith for the nourishing of the spirit and inward man unto eternal life. And for that cause we have no need that Christ should come down from heaven to us, but that we should ascend

[1] Jewel: *Works*, Vol. I, p. 12.  [2] Cranmer: *Works*, Vol. I, p. 238.

unto Him, lifting up our hearts through a lively faith on high unto the right hand of the Father where Christ sitteth, from whence we wait for our redemption; and we must not seek for Christ in these bodily elements."[1]

## WHY TRANSUBSTANTIATION WAS REJECTED

It is doctrine such as this which explains the Reformers' rejection of the mass with its concomitant teaching of transubstantiation. "I acknowledge," Cranmer writes to Gardiner, "that not many years past I was in darkness concerning this matter, being brought up in scholastical and Romish doctrine, whereunto I gave too much credit. And therefore I grant that you have heard me stand and defend the untruth, which I then took for the truth; and so did I hear you at the same time. But praise be to the ever-living God who hath wiped away these Saulish scales from mine eyes! and I pray unto His divine Majesty with all my heart that He will likewise do once the same to you. Thy will be fulfilled, O Lord!"

Transubstantiation was firstly rejected as being contrary to the teaching of Christ: "That bread and wine remain after the words of consecration, and be eaten and drunken in the Lord's supper, is most manifest by the plain words of Christ Himself when He ministered the same supper to His disciples. For, as the evangelists write,'Christ took bread and brake it, and gave it to His disciples, and said: Take, eat, this is My body' . . . But the same is more plain and evident of the wine, that it remaineth and is drunken at the Lord's supper, as well by the words that go before as by the words that follow after the consecration. For before the words of consecration Christ took the cup of wine and gave it unto His disciples and said, 'Drink ye all of this'; and after the words of consecration followeth, 'They drank all of it' . . . Also, when the communion was ended, Christ said unto His apostles: 'Verily, I say unto you that I will drink no more henceforth of this fruit of the vine until that day that I shall drink it new with you in My Father's kingdom'. By these words it is clear that it was very wine that the apostles drank at that godly supper. For the blood of Christ is not the fruit of the vine, nor the accidents of wine, nor none other thing is the fruit of the vine but the very wine only."[2]

[1] Hooper: *Works*, Vol. II, pp. 48f.
[2] Cranmer: *Works*, Vol. I, pp. 241ff.

Secondly, transubstantiation was rejected as being contrary to reason. In this connection the following were among the arguments used by Cranmer: "We see also," he says, "that the wine, though it be consecrated, yet it will turn to vinegar, and the bread will mould, which then be nothing else but sour wine and mouldy bread, which could not wax sour nor mouldy if there were no bread nor wine there at all . . . The sacramental bread and wine also will nourish, which nourishment naturally cometh of the substance of meats and drinks, and not of the accidents . . . And most of all, it is against the nature of accidents to be in nothing. For the definition of accidents is to be in some substance, so that if they be they must needs be in something; and if they be in nothing, then they be not."[1]

Thirdly, it was contrary to the evidence of the senses: "The papistical doctrine is also against all our outward senses, called our five wits. For our eyes say they see there bread and wine; our noses smell bread and wine; our mouths taste and our hands feel bread and wine. And although the articles of our faith be above all our outward senses, so that we believe things which we can neither see, feel, hear, smell, nor taste; yet they be not contrary to our senses, at the least so contrary, that in such things which we from time to time do see, smell, feel, hear, and taste we shall not trust our senses, but believe clean contrary. Christ never made any such article of our faith. Our faith teacheth us to believe things that we see not, but it doth not bid us that we shall not believe what we see daily with our eyes, and hear with our ears, and grope with our hands. For, although our senses cannot reach so far as our faith doth, yet so far as the compass of our senses doth usually reach our faith is not contrary to the same, but rather our senses do confirm our faith. . . For if we once admit this doctrine, that no credit is to be given to our senses, we open a large field and give a great occasion unto an innumerable rabblement of most heinous heresies."[2]

Fourthly, it is shown with characteristic thoroughness that transubstantiation is contrary to "the faith and doctrine of the old authors of Christ's Church".[3]

Cranmer's condemnation did not extend to all members of the Roman Catholic Church indiscriminately, but to those who were responsible for teaching and disseminating a doctrine which he

[1] Cranmer: *Works*, Vol. I, p. 250.     [2] Cranmer: *Ibid.*, pp. 255f.
[3] Cranmer: *Ibid.*, pp. 263ff.

considered to be so destructive of the Gospel. "I charge none with the name of papists but that be well worthy thereof," he says. "For I charge not the hearers but the teachers, not the learners but the inventors of the untrue doctrine of transubstantiation; not the king's faithful subjects, but the pope's darlings whose faith and belief hangeth of his only mouth. And I call it their doctrine not only because they teach it, but because they made it and were the first finders of it."[1]

The Reformers' uncompromising repudiation of the sacrifice of the mass was the consequence of their conviction that it was dishonouring to Christ and incompatible with the New Testament doctrine of salvation. Accordingly, they felt bound to denounce the sacerdotalism of the mass in the strongest terms. So Cranmer writes: "The greatest blasphemy and injury that can be against Christ, and yet universally used through the popish kingdom, is this, that the priests make their mass a sacrifice propitiatory, to remit the sins as well of themselves as of others, both quick and dead, to whom they list to apply the same. Thus under pretence of holiness the papistical priests have taken upon them to be Christ's successors, and to make such an oblation and sacrifice as never creature made but Christ alone, neither He made the same any more times than once, and that was by His death upon the cross . . . And that sacrifice was of such force that it was no need to renew it every year, as the bishops did of the old testament, whose sacrifices were many times offered, and yet were of no great effect or profit because they were sinners themselves that offered them, and offered not their own blood, but the blood of brute beasts; but Christ's sacrifice once offered was sufficient for evermore . . . It is an abominable blasphemy to give that office or dignity to a priest which pertaineth only to Christ, or to affirm that the Church hath need of any such sacrifice: as who should say that Christ's sacrifice were not sufficient for the remission of our sins, or else that His sacrifice should hang upon the sacrifice of a priest . . . The papists, to excuse themselves, do say that they make no new sacrifice, nor none other sacrifice than Christ made . . . And here they run headlong into the foulest and most heinous error that ever was imagined. For if they make every day the same oblation and sacrifice for sin that Christ Himself made, and the oblation that He made was His death and the effusion of His most precious blood upon the cross,

[1] Cranmer: *Works*, Vol. I, p. 240.

for our redemption and price of our sins, then followeth it of necessity that they every day slay Christ and shed His blood."[1]

This was a crucial issue between Rome and the Reformers. It was for their refusal to acknowledge and accept the doctrine of the mass that the majority of the martyrs of the Reformation were put to death. The situation was subsequently summed up by Bishop Jewel, when he stated: "The mass and God's Word cannot dwell in one house together, the one is so contrary to the other."[2] Thus we find John Bradford writing from prison: "The chief thing which I am condemned for as an heretic is because I deny the sacrament of the altar, which is not Christ's supper, but a plain perverting of it (being used as the papists now use it to be a real, natural, and corporal presence of Christ's body and blood under the forms and accidents of bread and wine), that is, because I deny transubstantiation, which is the darling of the devil and daughter and heir to antichrist's religion, whereby the mass is maintained, Christ's supper perverted, His sacrifice and cross imperfited, His priesthood destroyed, the ministry taken away, repentance repelled, and all true godliness abandoned. In the supper of our Lord or sacrament of Christ's body and blood I confess and believe that there is a true and very presence of whole Christ, God and man, to the faith of the receiver (but not of the stander-by or looker-on), as there is a very true presence of bread and wine in the senses of him that is partaker thereof. This faith, this doctrine, which consenteth with the Word of God and with the true testimony of Christ's Church, which the popish church doth persecute, will I not forsake: and therefore am I condemned as an heretic, and shall be burned."[3]

In speaking of the consecration of the elements, then, the Reformers did not imply that any change was effected in the water or in the bread and wine themselves. The only change is in the use to which they are put. Cranmer explains the Reformed doctrine of consecration in the following terms: "Consecration is the separation of anything from a profane and worldly use unto a spiritual and godly use. And therefore when usual and common water is taken from other uses and put to the use of baptism in the name of

---

[1] Cranmer: *Works*, Vol. I, pp. 345ff.  [2] Jewel: *Works*, Vol. II, p. 874.
[3] Bradford: *Farewell to Lancashire and Cheshire*, in *Works*, Vol. I, p. 450; cf. also *Farewell to the City of London*, pp. 435f., and *Farewell to the Town of Walden*, p. 456.

the Father and of the Son and of the Holy Ghost, then it may rightly be called consecrated water, that is to say, water put to an holy use. Even so, when common bread and wine be taken and severed from other bread and wine to the use of the holy communion, that portion of bread and wine, although it be of the same substance that the other is from the which it is severed, yet it is now called consecrated or holy bread and holy wine. Not that the bread and wine have or can have any holiness in them, but that they be used to an holy work and represent holy and godly things."[1]

ALTAR OR TABLE?

In conformity with their eucharistic doctrine the Reformers not only removed the term *altar* from the Prayer Book, speaking instead of the table or the Lord's table or the holy table, but also took steps, supported by royal injunctions, to secure the substitution of tables for altars in the churches of the land. Thus in 1550 Ridley, then Bishop of London, received the following instruction from the king in parliament: "Where it is come to our knowledge that, being the altars within the more part of the churches of this realm already upon good and godly considerations taken down, there do yet remain altars standing in divers other churches, by occasion whereof much variance and contention ariseth among sundry of our subjects, which, if good foresight were not had, might perchance engender great hurt and inconvenience; we let you wit that, minding to have all occasion of contention taken away, which many times groweth by those and such like diversities, and considering that, amongst other things belonging to our royal office and cure, we do account the greatest to be to maintain the common quiet of our realm, we have thought good by the advice of our council to require you, and nevertheless specially to charge and command you, for the avoiding of all matters of further contention and strife about the standing or taking away of the said altars, to give substantial order throughout all your diocese that with all diligence all the altars in every church or chapel, as well in places exempted as not exempted, within your said diocese, be taken down and in the stead of them a table be set up in some convenient part of the chancel, within every such church or chapel to serve for the ministration of the blessed communion . . . Given,

[1] Cranmer: *Works*, Vol. I, p. 177.

under our signet, at our place of Westminster, the 24th day of November, the fourth year of our reign."[1]

In was doubtless in consequence of the receipt of this same decree that Bishop Hooper included the following (number XLIII) in a group of articles which he issued to his diocese of Gloucester: "Whereas in divers places some use the Lord's board after the form of a table and some of an altar, whereby dissention is perceived to arise among the unlearned; therefore, wishing a godly unity to be observed in all our diocese, and for that the form of a table may more move and turn the simple from the old super-stitious opinions of the popish mass and to the right use of the Lord's supper, we exhort you to erect and set up the Lord's board after the form of an honest table, decently covered, in such place as shall be thought most meet, so that the ministers and communicants may be seen, heard, and understood of all the people there being present; and that ye do take down and abolish all the altars or tables. Further, that the minister in the use of the communion and prayers thereof turn his face towards the people."[2] An explanation of the reasons for preferring a table to an altar was given by Bishop Ridley. "The form of a table," he wrote, in words which Hooper echoes in the quotation just given, "shall more move the simple from the superstitious opinions of the popish mass unto the right use of the Lord's supper. For the use of an altar is to make sacrifice upon it; the use of a table is to serve for men to eat upon. Now, when we come unto the Lord's board, what do we come for? to sacrifice Christ again and to crucify Him again? or to feed upon Him that was once crucified and offered up for us? If we come to feed upon Him, spiritually to eat His body and spiritually to drink His blood (which is the true use of the Lord's supper), then no man can deny but the form of a table is more meet for the Lord's board than the form of an altar . . . Christ did institute the sacrament of His body and blood at His last supper at a table, and not at an altar; as it appeareth manifestly by the three evangelists. And St. Paul calleth the coming to the holy communion the coming unto the Lord's supper. And also it is not read that any of the apostles or the primitive Church did ever use any altar in the ministration of holy communion. Wherefore, seeing the form of a table is more agreeable to Christ's institution and with the usage of the apostles

---

[1] Reproduced in Cranmer: *Works*, Vol. II, p. 524.
[2] Hooper: *Works*, Vol. II, p. 128.

and the primitive Church than the form of an altar, therefore the form of a table is rather to be used than the form of an altar in the administration of the holy communion."[1]

Finally, none can better sum up the doctrinal basis which lay behind the Reformers' position in this controversy concerning the true nature and purpose of the sacrament of holy communion than Archbishop Cranmer who was the leader of the Church of England in those reforming days. "That all men may the better understand this sacrifice of Christ, which He made for the great benefit of all men, it is necessary to know the distinction and diversity of sacrifices," he says. "One kind of sacrifice there is which is called a propitiatory or merciful sacrifice, that is to say, such a sacrifice as pacifieth God's wrath and indignation, and obtaineth mercy and forgiveness for all our sins, and is the ransom of our redemption from everlasting damnation. And although in the old testament there were certain sacrifices called by that name, yet in very deed there is but one sacrifice whereby our sins be pardoned and God's mercy and favour obtained, which is the death of the Son of God our Lord Jesu Christ; nor ever was any other sacrifice propitiatory at any other time, nor ever shall be. This is the honour and glory of this our High Priest, wherein He admitteth neither partner nor successor. For by His own oblation He satisfied His Father for all men's sins and reconciled mankind unto His grace and favour . . . Another kind of sacrifice there is which doth not reconcile us to God, but is made of them that be reconciled by Christ, to testify our duties unto God, and to show ourselves thankful unto Him. And therefore they be called sacrifices of laud, praise, and thanksgiving. The first kind of sacrifice Christ offered to God for us; the second kind we ourselves offer to God by Christ."[2]

[1] Ridley: *Works*, pp. 322f.        [2] Cranmer: *Works*, Vol. I, p. 346.

# VII

# CHURCH AND STATE

The marks whereby this [holy catholic or universal] Church is known unto me in this dark world . . . are these: the sincere preaching of God's Word, the due administration of the sacraments, charity, and faithful observing of ecclesiastical discipline according to the Word of God.

*Nicholas Ridley*


Among all the most noble and most famous deeds of kings and princes none is more godly, commendable, nor profitable to the commonwealth than to promote and set forth unto their subjects the pure and sincere religion of the eternal God, King of all kings and Lord of all lords.

*John Hooper*

# CHURCH AND STATE

## THE VISIBILITY AND INVISIBILITY OF THE CHURCH

Article XIX defines the visible Church of Christ as "a congregation of faithful men, [that is, men of faith, believers] in the which the pure Word of God is preached and the sacraments be duly ministered according to Christ's ordinance in all those things that of necessity are requisite to the same". This definition makes it plain that the Reformers affirmed the *visibility* of the Christian Church: hence the postulation of certain "marks" by which the true Church may be discerned. These marks, by which the true may be distinguished from the false, are the proclamation of the pure Word of God[1] and the due ministration of the sacraments as instituted by Christ.[2] Thus Bishop Hooper writes: "These two marks, the true preaching of God's Word and right use of the sacraments, declare what and where the true Church is. Unto the which Church I would all Christian men should associate themselves although there may happen to be some things desired in manners and discipline. For no church, as touching this part, can be absolutely perfect. But where the doctrine is sound, and no idolatry defended, that church is of God, as far as mortal man can judge. And where this doctrine and right use of sacraments be not, there is no church of Christ, though it seem never so holy."[3]

A third mark of differentiation of the true Church was also commonly propounded, namely, that of discipline. This, no doubt, is implicit in the terms of Article XIX when it speaks of Christ's Church as "a congregation of faithful men", which would indicate an assembly of persons whose profession of faith is not contradicted and invalidated by the indiscipline of their conduct either as individuals or in association with each other. Accordingly, in another of his writings, Hooper declares: "I believe that the Lord

[1] We have seen, in chapter IV, how the Reformers regarded preaching as the primary means of grace.

[2] The preceding chapter has shown how the ministry of the sacraments was regarded as an integral part of the ministry of the Word.

[3] Hooper; *Works*, Vol. II, p. 87.

God hath given us three principal signs and marks by which we may know this His Church, that is to say, the Word, the sacraments, and discipline. I call that only the Word which was revealed by the Holy Ghost unto the holy patriarchs, prophets and apostles of Jesus Christ; which Word is contained within the canonical books of the Old and New Testament; by which Word we are made clean, and thereby do receive the selfsame thing and as much as we do by the sacraments: that is to say, Jesus Christ by His Word, which is the word of faith, giveth and communicateth Himself unto us, as well as by the sacraments, albeit it be another manner and fashion.'[1]

Ridley, in fact, speaks of four marks of the true Church, adding charity to those already mentioned. "The holy catholic or universal Church," he says, "which is the communion of saints, the house of God, the spouse of Christ, the body of Christ, the pillar and stay of the truth: this Church I believe according to the creed; this Church I do reverence and honour in the Lord. But the rule of this Church is the Word of God, according to which rule we go forward unto life. 'And as many as walk according to this rule', I say with St. Paul, 'peace be upon them and upon Israel, which pertaineth unto God'.[2] The guide of this Church is the Holy Ghost. The marks whereby this Church is known unto me in this dark world, and in the midst of this crooked and froward generation, are these: the sincere preaching of God's Word, the due administration of the sacraments, charity, and faithful observing of ecclesiastical discipline according to the Word of God. And that church, or congregation, which is garnished with these marks, is in very deed that heavenly Jerusalem which consisteth of those that be born from above. This is the mother of us all: and, by God's grace, I will live and die the child of this Church."[3]

At the same time, however, the Reformers spoke of the *invisibility* of the Church. Following Christ's parables of the wheat and tares and of the good and bad fish, they taught that the visible Church, even when distinguished by these marks of authenticity, was a mixed company in which it was impossible for any man to make an infallible separation of the genuine members from the spurious (just as the apostles themselves had failed to discern the treachery of Judas Iscariot's heart). The members of the invisible

---

[1] Hooper: *Works*, Vol. II, p. 43.  [2] Gal. 6:16.
[3] Ridley: *Works*, pp. 122f.

Church are, indeed, members of the visible Church also, but exactly who they are is known only to God, in accordance with His hidden counsel of election. In the ultimate issue, it is the elect alone who constitute the Church of Christ, and their precise number and identity are known to God alone. It was in this ultimate sense that the Reformers spoke of an invisible Church. In his work *The Catholic Doctrine of the Church of England* Thomas Rogers explains the distinction between the visibility and the invisibility of the Church as follows: "A true saying is it, the Lord and He only knoweth who are His.[1] For to man the Church of Christ is partly invisible, and visible partly. The invisible are all the elect, who be or shall be either in heaven triumphing, or on earth fighting against the flesh, the world, and the devil. These as members of the Church are said to be invisible: not because the men be not seen, but for that their faith and conscience to Godward is not perfectly known unto us. The members of the visible Church are some of them for God, and some against God; all of them notwithstanding deemed parts of the Church and accounted faithful, so long as they make no manifest and open rebellion against the Gospel of Christ."[2] Again: "When we do say that the Church is visible, invisible, and that there is a Western, East, Greek, Latin, English church, we mean not that there be divers churches of Christ, but that one and the same Church is diversely taken and understood, and also hath many particular churches, as the sea many rivers and arms branching from it. For the visible Church is not many congregations, but one company of the faithful."[3]

So too Hooper asserts: " I believe and confess one only catholic and universal Church, which is an holy congregation and assembly of all faithful believers, who are chosen and predestinate unto everlasting life before the foundations of the world were laid: of whose number I count myself, and believe that I am, through the only grace and mercy of the Father and by the merits of my good Lord and Master Jesus Christ, and not by means of my good works and merits, which indeed are none. I believe that this Church is invisible to the eye of man and is only to God known, and that the same Church is not set, compassed, and limited within a certain place or bounds, but is scattered and spread abroad throughout all the world, but yet coupled together in heart, will, and spirit by

[1] II Tim. 2:19.      [2] Rogers: *Works*, pp. 164f.
[3] Rogers: *Ibid.*, pp. 167f.

the bond of faith and charity, having and altogether acknowledging
one only God, one only head and mediator Jesus Christ, one faith,
one law, one baptism, one spiritual table . . . This Church containeth in it all the righteous and chosen people, from the first
righteous man unto the last that shall be found righteous in the end
of the world: and therefore do I call it universal . . . I believe that
this Church is like unto the ark of Noah, within which is safety and
life, and without the same is but death, decay, and destruction.
For as Christ is and doth reign in His Church, even so Satan is and
doth reign in and through all that are out of that Church: the
which true Church is maintained and upholden by the Spirit of
Christ, is ruled and governed by His holy Word, and is nourished
and fed with His holy sacraments." [1]

Ridley points out that in Scripture the term "church" is used
in three senses. Firstly, it is used of "that Church which is His
body and of which Christ is the head", and which consists "only
of living stones and true Christians, not only outwardly in name
and title, but inwardly in heart and in truth". Secondly, it is used
of what Augustine called "the mingled Church", [2] which is com-
pounded of both genuine and false professors of the Christian
faith. And, thirdly, it is used of "the multitude of evil men" who
are in this mixed company and do constitute "the malignant
church and synagogue of Satan". In other words, the regenerate
and the unregenerate together form a commixture within the
comprehensive sphere of the visible Church. This fact is regarded
by Ridley as significant for the understanding of the fluctuations
in the history of the Church. "Of the universal Church, which is
mingled of good and bad, thus I think," he wrote to Latimer:
"Whensoever they who be chief in it, who rule and govern the
same, and to whom the rest of the whole mystical body of Christ
doth obey, are the lively members of Christ, and walk after the
guiding and ruling of His Word, and go before the flock towards
everlasting life, then undoubtedly councils gathered together of
such guides and pastors of the Christian flock do indeed represent
the universal Church; and, being so gathered in the name of
Christ, they have a promise of the gift and guiding of His Spirit
into all truth. But that any such council hath at any time allowed
the mass, such a one as ours was of late, in a strange tongue, and

[1] Hooper: *Works*, Vol. II, pp. 40ff.
[2] *Permixta Ecclesia*—Augustine: *De Doctrina Christiana*, III, 32.

stuffed with so many absurdities, errors, and superstitions,[1] that I utterly deny and I affirm it to be impossible. For like as there is no agreement between light and darkness, between Christ and Belial, so surely superstition and the sincere religion of Christ, will-worship and the pure worshipping of God, such as God requireth of His, that is, in spirit and truth, can never agree together. But ye will say, where so great a company is gathered together it is not credible but there be two or three gathered in the name of Christ. I answer, if there be one hundred good and two hundred bad, forasmuch as the decrees and ordinances are pronounced according to the greater number of the multitude of voices, what can the lesser number of voices avail? It is a known thing, and a common proverb, 'oftentimes the greater part overcometh the better'."[2]

In Nowell's Catechism the visible Church is defined as "nothing else but a certain multitude of men who, in what place soever they be, do profess the doctrine of Christ, pure and sincere, even the same which the evangelists and prophets have, in the everlasting monuments of Holy Scriptures, faithfully disclosed to memory, and who do truly call upon God the Father in the name of Christ, and moreover do use His mysteries, commonly called sacraments, with the same pureness and simplicity (as touching their substance) which the apostles of Christ used and have put in writing". While these are "the chief and the necessary marks of the visible Church, such as without which it cannot be indeed, nor rightly be called, the Church of Christ . . . yet also in the same Church, if it be well ordered, there shall be seen to be observed a certain order and manner of governance, and such a form of ecclesiastical discipline, that it shall not be free for any that abideth in that flock publicly to speak or do anything wickedly or in heinous sort without punishment, yea, and so that in that congregation of men all offences (so far as is possible) be avoided". In answer to the question: "Are not, then, all they that be in this visible Church of the number of the elect to everlasting life?" the answer is given: "Many, by hypocrisy and counterfeiting of godliness, do join themselves to this fellowship, who are nothing less than true members of the Church. But, forasmuch as wheresoever the Word of God is sincerely taught

[1] The reference is to the restoration of the Romish worship under Mary: both Ridley and Latimer were in prison when this was written.

[2] Ridley: *Works*, pp. 125f., 130.

and His sacraments rightly ministered there are ever some appointed to salvation by Christ, we count all that whole company to be the Church of God, seeing that Christ also promiseth that He Himself will be present with two or three that be gathered together in His name."[1]

THE RESTORATION OF THE APOSTOLIC RELIGION

Preaching on Rom. 13:12 ("The night is past and the day is at hand: let us cast away the works of darkness, and let us put on the armour of light"), with Elizabeth on the throne of England and the Reformation restored to the land, Jewel exhorted his hearers in the following terms: "Let us consider how mercifully God hath dealt with us. He hath restored unto us the light of His Gospel and hath taught us the secrets of His heavenly will. We hear Him talk with us familiarly in the Scriptures, as a father talketh with his child. Thereby He kindleth our faith and strengtheneth our hope; thereby our hearts receive joy and comfort. We have the holy ministration of the sacraments; we know the covenant of baptism; we know the covenant and mystery of the Lord's supper. We fall down together and confess our life before God; we pray together, and understand what we pray. This was the order of the primitive Church: this was the order of the apostles of Christ. If we compare this with the former, we shall soon see the difference between light and darkness . . . The sun is risen: the day is open: God hath made His kingdom wonderful among us. It is now time, now is it time that we should arise from sleep; for now is our salvation near. Now, it is in our mouth: we can speak of it: God grant it may be nearer us even in our hearts. The night is past: God grant it be past for ever; that we be never again thrown into the darkness of death; that the Word of life, the truth of Christ, be never again taken from us." And he concluded with this prayer: "And Thou, O most merciful Father, we beseech Thee for Thy mercy's sake, continue Thy grace and favour towards us: let the sun of Thy Gospel never go down out of our hearts; let Thy truth abide, and be established among us for ever. Help our unbelief, increase our faith, give us hearts to consider the time of our visitation; apparel us thoroughly with Christ, that He may live in us, and so Thy name may be glorified in us in the sight of all the world. Amen." In another sermon (on Ps. 67:3f.) he surveyed the situation in similar fashion:

[1] Nowell: *Catechism*, pp. 174ff.

"Therefore were we carried away," he says, "therefore were we led into error, therefore lost we the knowledge of God, because prophecy failed, because God's Word was not taught and preached unto us. But now it hath pleased God to reveal Himself unto us; now we know what is what; now can we discern light from darkness, good from bad; now we understand and know this, I say; now we have the Scriptures in our mother tongue, that every man may read and understand them—the same Scriptures that Christ hath sealed with His own blood . . . Now we are able to know our profession, now we are able to know our religion, to know God, to know Christ, to know our salvation. Now have we the use of the primitive Church, the communion under both kinds; now have we prayers in our known tongue, as in the apostles' time, as in the fathers' and doctors' times they were used . . . Therefore have we most just cause to say with the prophet David: *Laetentur et exultent populi*: 'Let the people rejoice and be glad'." Again, in a sermon on Lk. 10:23 ("Blessed are the eyes which see what ye see"), he says: "Now we know that Christ is our only Saviour, our Redeemer, and that 'His blood alone', as St. John saith, 'hath washed away our iniquities.' Now we know what we pray. Now we know wherefore and to what end the sacraments were left unto us; what our baptism meaneth. Now we have God's testament and His holy Word restored unto us . . . And therefore blessed are our eyes, and the eyes which see what we see."[1]

In this way the Reformed church was vindicated as having restored and appropriated to itself the primary marks of the true Church of Christ, namely, the authentic biblical ministration of both Word and sacraments. As for the mark of ecclesiastical discipline, Hooper affirms that it is "very commodious and profitable, yea, and very necessary to the catholic Church for the comfort of the good and for the punishment of the evil", and that it is "the ordinance of Christ in His Church, and in like manner the same was practised by the apostles in the primitive Church, and that because all should be done honestly and in good order, which is a thing honest and necessary for every congregation".[2] In a pastoral epistle to the Bishop of Chester dated 13 February 1583 Archbishop Sandys stresses this need for the exercise of discipline by those who hold positions of authority in the Church: "It is our

---

[1] Jewel: *Works*, Vol. II, pp. 1045f., 1058f., 1083.
[2] Hooper: *Works*, Vol. II, p. 51.

part," he says, "to cut off the fibres of superstition and the roots of idolatry with the sharp sickle of the divine Word; to sow also good corn by the propagation of the Gospel in the minds of men, to overthrow the citadels and towers of Jericho by the trumpet of the heavenly Spirit, but as far as in us lies to build the walls and sacred temple of Jerusalem; to shake down with the utmost vigour the cruelty and tyranny of antichrist, but to establish by diligent preaching the kingdom and dominion of the Son of God. For not only does the Lord seem to require this labour of us in feeding His flock, but He also demands that sin should not be permitted to burst the bonds of established laws and fly abroad with impunity. For the Lord would have lust to be repressed, wickedness to be checked, licentious manners to be restrained, and those things which have utterly fallen asunder to be bound up by severe laws and condign punishments."[1]

## EXCOMMUNICATION

Jewel speaks of excommunication as "a principal part of the discipline of the Church—a matter which many know not, which some do foully abuse and over lightly give forth, and which many regard not as they ought". He regards excommunication, when scripturally applied, as a necessary, though, drastic, measure, designed for the well-being of the Church and its members. "Let no man despise it," he warns: "it is the sword of God, the power of the Holy Ghost, the discipline of Christ: it is an ordinance which the Church hath received from above. By it the goats are divided from the lambs, the weed from the good corn, and the sons of God from the sons of Belial . . . If any therefore be excommunicate from the Church and removed from the fellowship of the Gospel and from the hope of the life to come, let him humble himself, and pray unto God that He will open his eyes and that he may see in what case he standeth. Let him lay forth his heart in the sight of God, and consider his fault, and behold his misery, and think thus with himself: 'I was sometimes the child of God and a member of His body; I was a branch of the vine which God hath planted, and a sheep of His pasture. But now, alas! I am divided from the pastures of life. I am fruitless and withered, and cut off from that blessed vine. I receive no moisture from that heavenly root; I am no more a member of the body of Christ. I am out of

[1] Sandys: *Works*, p. 440.

paradise and have no joy or pleasure; I am out of the temple, and cannot offer any sacrifice; I am fallen from that heavenly Jerusalem, from the city of God, from the fellowship of the saints, and cannot kneel down, nor lift up my hands, nor make my prayers. God will not hear me: I am none of His; I am as a heathen and a publican; I cannot think of those things which are on high above'! But why art thou cut off from thy brethren and banished out of the flock of Christ? Because of thine ungodliness and looseness of life. Because thou hast offended heaven and earth, and hast offended against the Church of God, and lived in fornication and adultery, and both thy body and thy mind are defiled; thou art unworthy to dwell in the house of God: His house is holy."

In response to the question: "By what authority is this done?" Jewel says: "Thou must not think that the judge or officer doth it. It is not the judgment of any mortal man. It is the judgment of the almighty and everlasting God. It is His hand that bringeth this to pass against thee. It is His word: it is His key. His hand is mighty; His work shall stand; His word is forcible; His key is the key of David: it openeth, and no man shutteth; it shutteth, and no man openeth. God is departed from thy heart: His Spirit will not dwell in a filthy soul; there is no agreement between God and Belial. Thy soul is void of grace and of the fear of God . . . Wreak not thyself upon thy neighbour that accused thee, nor upon the judge that pronounced sentence against thee. The sentence is none of his: this is not his work; he hath not judged thee. The hand of God is stretched forth to thy punishment: it is thine own life and wickedness which forceth judgment upon thee. The judge sitteth in the place of God, in the seat of justice: he cannot bless what God hath cursed . . . As for the judge and minister who giveth sentence against thee, he mourneth and lamenteth for thee. When he striketh thee, he striketh himself. We are all one flesh and one blood, and all together make one body, and are one another's members. Therefore, when he doth excommunicate thee from the brethren, he cutteth off an arm from his own body."[1]

In the course of his debate with Thomas Cartwright, Archbishop Whitgift makes a distinction between the visible and the invisible government of the Church. "There are two kinds of government in the Church," he says, "the one visible, the other invisible; the one spiritual, the other external. The invisible and spiritual

[1] Jewel: *Works*: Vol. II, pp. 942ff.

government of the Church is when God by His Spirit, gifts, and ministry of His Word doth govern it, by ruling in the hearts and consciences of men and directing them in all things necessary to everlasting life: this kind of government indeed is necessary to salvation, and it is in the Church of the elect only. The visible and external government is that which is executed by man, and consisteth of external discipline and visible ceremonies practised in that Church, and over that Church, that containeth in it both good and evil, which is usually called the visible Church of Christ, and compared by Christ to 'a field' wherein both 'good seeds' and 'tares were sown', and to 'a net that gathered of all kinds of fishes'."[1] Whitgift vigorously defends, moreover, the Reformed doctrine that the Christian ruler has an important part to play in the external government of the Church. "Indeed," he affirms, "the true spiritual government of the Church is the ruling of Christ by His Spirit in the hearts of the elect; neither do I deny but that admonition, exhortation, and excommunication pertain also the spiritual government of the Church, because they pertain to the inward man and use no corporal force or punishment; but I deny the whole government of the Church to consist herein, for I have proved before, and it cannot be denied but that God hath chiefly and principally committed the government of His Church to the Christian magistrate by the sword also, and by convenient laws and orders to govern the same by an external kind of government."[2]

It is noteworthy that Whitgift, in common with the other divines of the sixteenth century, though a defender of the episcopal form of government which the Church of England had retained, refuses to make episcopacy a mark of the true Church (not even when countering the insistent claims which Cartwright put forward for the presbyterian form of government). The Reformed view is summed up in Whitgift's affirmation that "there is no one certain kind of government in the Church which must of necessity be perpetually observed".[3] Or again: "That any one kind of government is so necessary that without it the Church cannot be saved, or that it may not be altered into some other kind thought to be more expedient, I utterly deny; and the reasons that move me so to do be these: The first is, because I find no one certain and perfect kind of government prescribed or commanded in the Scriptures

---

[1] Whitgift: *Works*, Vol. I, pp. 183f.
[2] Whitgift: *Works*, Vol. III, pp. 485f.    [3] Whitgift: *Ibid.*, p. 214.

to the Church of Christ; which no doubt should have been done, if it had been a matter necessary unto the salvation of the Church. Secondly, because the essential notes of the Church be these only: the true preaching of the Word of God and the right administration of the sacraments."[1] He acknowledges that "the substance and matter of government must indeed be taken out of the Word of God, and consisteth in these points, that the Word be truly taught, the sacraments rightly administered, virtue furthered, vice repressed, and the Church kept in quietness and order"; but he declares, once more, that "the offices in the Church, whereby this government is wrought, be not namely and particularly expressed in the Scriptures, but in some points left to the discretion and liberty of the Church, to be disposed according to the state of times, places, and persons."[2]

THE TWO SWORDS

The relationship between Church and state was a question that received careful discussion in the writings of the Reformers. The ecclesiastical sphere and the civil sphere were regarded as distinct, but none the less as interdependent and sharing in mutual responsibilities, since in a professedly Christian society both Church and state acknowledge and are subject to the supreme authority of Almighty God. The position was crystallized in the doctrine of the two swords. Thus Hooper declares: "I believe and receive in this Church two swords, that is to say, two powers: the one is ecclesiastical and spiritual, which lieth and consisteth in the only administration of the Word and of the sacraments, which beareth neither rod nor staff other than the tongue, neither doth use any other knife than the sword of the Spirit, which is the Word of God. Likewise I confess that all those that have this sword in their hands ought to be without blame as well in their living as in their doctrine; otherwise they ought to be deposed and others to be placed in their rooms, and to put and ordain others that are better in their places. The other power is temporal, that is to say, the magistrate, who hath authority over external and civil things, to render according to every man that which of right to him appertaineth. I believe that the magistrate is an ordinance of God set in His Church for the defence of the good and the godly, and to chasten and punish the wicked; and also to the magistrate must be

---

[1] Whitgift: *Works*, Vol. I, pp. 184f.     [2] Whitgift: *Ibid.*, p. 6.

given tribute, honour, and reverence and obedience in all things
that be not in any wise contrary to God's Word. And I do understand this not only of the faithful magistrate but also of the infidel
and wicked tyrant, unto whom we must obey as unto the Lord in
all things, so that [that is, provided that ] he command nothing
contrary to the Word of God: for then we ought rather to obey
God than man, after the examples of the apostles Peter and John."[1]

Hooper, further, states his belief that "to the magistrates it doth
appertain, not only to have regard unto the commonwealth, but
also unto ecclesiastical matters, to take away and to overthrow all
idolatry and false serving of God, to destroy the kingdom of antichrist and all false doctrine, to promote the glory of God and to
advance the kingdom of Christ, to cause the word of the Gospel
everywhere to be preached, and the same to maintain unto death
... To such a magistrate every person, of what estate, degree, or
condition soever he be, ought to be subject, and him in all honest
and reasonable things to obey, because he representeth the person
of a great Lord before whom every knee ought to bow. And the
same must not be forgotten in our prayers, to the end that the
Lord may vouchsafe to guide and direct all his ways, and that
under him we may live in godly peace and tranquillity."[2]

This position was derived from the explicit teaching of the New
Testament. Thus, commenting on the classic passage, Rom. 13:1f.,
Hooper says: "St. Paul pronounceth generally that every soul, that
is to say, every man, should be obedient unto the higher power: in a
kingdom and monarchy, where one is appointed to rule, all the
subjects of the same realm are bound to obey the one king appointed by God, of what condition, state, or degree soever they be;
as the king himself is bound to be obedient unto the law, and unto
God, where the laws be not contrary to the law of God and the law
of nature. And here is no exception to be made. No man in a kingdom is or ought to be privileged or exempt from the obedience of
the king, which is the higher power ... Christ and His apostles paid
tribute and other duties unto the higher powers of the earth. And
the powers that here St. Paul speaketh of be not only kings and
emperors, but all such as be appointed to any public office and
common regiment ... So Joseph obeyed Pharaoh; and Christ, our
Saviour, Pilate; St. Paul the emperors of Rome, Caligula and Nero.
And when St. Paul commandeth us to be obedient he meaneth

[1] See Acts 4:19, 5:29.          [2] Hooper: *Works*, Vol. II, pp. 53f.

not only we should speak reverently and honourably of the higher power, or make courtesy unto him, but to obey the laws set forth by the powers, except they command things against God's laws: then must we obey more God than men; and yet not to strive and fight with the magistrates, but suffer patiently death rather than to offend God: or else our obedience is nothing but hypocrisy and dissimulation . . . The laws of a magistrate be of two conditions and sorts: either they concern God, or man. If they concern or appertain to God, either they be according to the Word of God, or contrary to the Word of God. If they be according to the Word of God, of necessity and bondage, upon pain of damnation, they must be obeyed. If they be repugnant to the Word of God, they should not be obeyed. Yet rather should a man suffer death than to defend himself by force and violent resisting of the superior powers, as Christ, His apostles, and the prophets did. If the laws concern and appertain unto man and unto things civil, they must simply, without exception, be obeyed, except they repugn and be contrary to the law of nature: as Pharaoh's law and commandment was to the midwives, that they should have killed all the men-children that the women of Israelites brought forth."[1]

Church and state together form the solidarity of a Christian society, and every member, both as churchman and as citizen, has an important part to play in the harmonious functioning of the whole. "The walls of the city," says Pilkington, in his *Exposition upon Nehemiah*, "may well be compared to the magistrates, who both defend the people from their enemies and also govern the citizens within; as the walls keep out others from invading, so they keep in the inhabitants from straying abroad: and the gates of the city may well be compared unto the ministers, who open the door of life to all penitent persons by the comfortable preaching of mercy promised in Christ, and shut heaven's gates against all reprobate and impenitent sinners by terrible thundering of His vengeance threatened to such in His Word. The walls are destroyed and the gates burned when the rulers and ministers do not their duty, but care for other things . . . As the magistrate therefore both with word and sword must defend God's cause, His religion, temple, people, ministers, and doctrine, so must the preacher and those that be learned with their pain, prayer, preaching, and all other means that they can: yea, if our goods or lives were required

[1] Hooper: *Works*, Vol. II, pp. 101ff.

for the defence of it, no state of man ought to refuse it. For this end
are we born and live, to glorify our God and set forth His praise:
for this purpose are all things given us, and therefore must not be
spared, but spent and bestowed, when His glory requireth. The
faithful Christian man, moreover, is superior to the most illustrious prince, who also is under obligation to be obedient to God's
Word. Accordingly, Pilkington comments: "It is no rebellion
against princes to do that which God commandeth; for princes
themselves are bound, as well as other meaner degrees, to serve
the Lord God of heaven with all their might and main; and unto
the same God they must make account of their doings, as all others
must . . . It is more glorious to be called God's servants than to have
all the titles of honour and dignity that the world can give. He that
serveth the Lord truly is master of sin, hell, death, and the devil,
and by the assistance of God's Holy Spirit shall not be overcome
of them, but shall overcome and conquer them: which is greater
honour than any worldly prince can give."[1]

The mutual responsibility of all, whether small or great, is
summed up by Pilkington in his *Exposition upon Haggai*. "Let us
do all we can, therefore," he says, "and pray the Lord to further
our work; the rulers with the sword defend the good and punish
the evil; the preachers with the Word, the schoolmasters by their
teaching, the fathers by bringing up their children, the masters by
correction of their servants, the people in obeying their heads and
neighbourly love; and every one defend true religion to the uttermost of his power . . . Thus hath every man a part in building
God's house: but the greatest portion is left to every man, which
is his own conscience, to amend what he finds amiss in himself,
because every man knows himself best."[2]

"In this world God hath two swords; the one is a temporal
sword, the other a spiritual," declared Latimer in a sermon
preached before King Edward VI on 8 March 1549. "The temporal sword resteth in the hands of kings, magistrates, and rulers
under him; whereunto all subjects, as well the clergy as the laity,
be subject, and punishable for any offence contrary to the same
book. The spiritual sword is in the hands of ministers and preachers; whereunto all kings, magistrates, and rulers ought to be obedient . . . The king correcteth transgressors with the temporal
sword; yea, and the preacher also, if he be an offender. But the

---

[1] Pilkington: *Works*, pp. 348, 361, 364.    [2] Pilkington: *Ibid.*, p. 66.

preacher cannot correct the king, if he be a transgressor of God's Word, with the temporal sword; but he must correct and reprove him with the spiritual sword, fearing no man . . . Therefore let the preacher, teach, improve, amend, and instruct in righteousness with the spiritual sword, fearing no man, though death should ensue."[1]

The Reformers repudiated the medieval doctrine, held by the papal church, that the clergy could claim immunity from the civil laws and were not indictable before the secular courts. Thus, in his examination before James Brokes, Bishop of Gloucester, at Oxford, Cranmer affirmed: "The laws of this realm are that the king of England is the supreme and sole governor of all his countries and dominions, and that he holdeth his crown and sceptre of himself, by the ancient laws, customs, and descents of the kings of the realm, and of none other. The pope saith that all emperors and kings hold their crowns and regalities of him, and that he may depose them when he list: which is high treason for any man to affirm and think, being born within the king's dominions. The laws of England are that all bishops and priests, offending in cases of felony or treason, are to be judged and tried by the laws and customs of the realm. The pope's laws are that the secular power cannot judge the spiritual power, and that they are not under their jurisdiction: which robbeth the king of the one part of his people."[2] So also Tyndale writes, in his *Obedience of a Christian Man*: "No person, neither any degree, may be exempt from this ordinance of God; neither can the profession of monks and friars, or anything that the pope or bishops can lay for themselves, except them from the sword of the emperor or kings, if they break the laws. For it is written: 'Let every soul submit himself unto the authority of the higher powers.' Here is no man except; but all souls must obey. The higher powers are the temporal kings and princes, unto whom God hath given the sword to punish whosoever sinneth. God hath not given them swords to punish one and to let another go free and sin unpunished. Moreover, with what face durst the spiritualty, who ought to be the light and an example of good living unto all others, desire to sin unpunished, or to be exempted from tribute, toll, or custom, that they would not bear pain with their brethren to the maintenance of kings and officers, ordained of God to punish sin? 'There is no power but of

[1] Latimer: *Works*, Vol. I, pp. 85f.    [2] Cranmer: *Works*, Vol. II, p. 222.

God.' By power understand the authority of kings and princes. 'The powers that be are ordained of God; whosoever therefore resisteth the power resisteth God': yea, though he be pope, bishop, monk, or friar. 'They that resist shall receive unto themselves damnation.' Why? For God's Word is against them, which will have all men under the power of the temporal sword: for 'rulers are not to be feared for good works, but for evil'. Hereby seest thou that they that resist the powers, or seek to be exempt from their authority, have evil consciences, and seek liberty to sin unpunished, and to be free from bearing pain with their brethren. 'Wilt thou be without fear of the power? So do well, and thou shalt have laud of the same,' that is to say, of the ruler. With good living ought the spiritualty to rid themselves from the fear of the temporal sword, and not with craft, and with blinding the kings, and bringing the vengeance of God upon them, and in purchasing licence to sin unpunished."[1]

THE NECESSITY FOR CIVIL GOVERNMENT

Cranmer's statement *De Rebus Civilibus*, which is number twelve in "a book containing divers articles" probably intended as heads of agreement for the conference of English and German theologians held in London in 1538, sets forth clearly the necessity for civil government to which all persons should be subject without respect of persons. "The unhappy condition of mortal men, corrupted by sin," it reads, "rushes headlong into iniquity and viciousness unless it is restrained by healthy authority, nor can there be such a thing as public welfare apart from just government and obedience. For this reason our most benevolent God ordained kings, princes, and governors, to whom He gave authority not only for procuring that the people should live in accordance with the precepts of the divine law, but also of controlling and ruling the same people by other laws acceptable to the state and by just jurisdiction. God, moreover, has appointed these persons as His ministers on earth for the welfare of society, and as the leaders and rulers of His people, and He has made all other persons, without distinction, subject to them. For this reason there is much precise information about them in the Scriptures. Firstly, they are to be instructed in the heavenly precepts unto wisdom and virtue, so that they may know whose ministers they are and may rightly and

[1] Tyndale: *Works*, Vol. I, pp. 178f. Quotations from Rom. 13:1ff.

beneficently exercise the judgment and authority entrusted to them by God. Thus it is said: 'Be instructed, you who judge the earth; serve the Lord in fear'. Secondly, He requires, and gives them authority for this purpose, that they should provide and formally establish (to the utmost of their ability) beneficial and just laws for the good of the state, by means of which not only will equity, justice, and tranquillity be maintained, but also reverence toward God will be promoted, and especially that they should make it their care to ensure the observance of the law of God and the Christian religion—as Augustine plainly teaches, when he says: 'Kings, as regards their kingly office, serve God in accordance with their divine commission if in their kingdoms they command what is good and forbid what is evil, with respect not only to society in general but also to divine religion'.[1] . . . Since, therefore, it is necessary that the people should acknowledge and reverence, as an ordinance of God, the authority of princes as supremely needful for the state and society, in the Scriptures God everywhere enjoins that all persons, whatever their status or condition, should give prompt and faithful obedience to their princes, and not merely through fear of bodily punishment, but because this is God's will; as Peter urges: 'Submit yourselves to every ordinance of man for the Lord's sake, whether it be to the king, as supreme, or unto governors, as unto them that are sent by the will of God'.[2] And Paul speaks as follows: 'Put them in mind to be subject to principalities and powers, to obey magistrates, to be ready to every good work, to speak evil of no man'.[3]

"These things being so," Cranmer concludes, "not only is it lawful for Christian princes and governors to possess kingdoms and territories, and to enjoy public dignities and offices which are directed towards the promotion and provision of public security, but also, when in the performance of such duties they have respect to the honour of God and relate their own dignity and power to His glory, they are truly pleasing to God and deserving of His favour and grace . . . It is right, therefore, that Christians in all places, each according to his status and condition, should, in accordance with the laws of God, the decrees of princes, and the honourable customs of separate regions, submit to and perform such duties and offices as are needful to this mortal life and by

---

[1] The allusion seems to be to Augustine: *Epist.* clxxxv, 19, *ad Bonifacium.*     [2] I Pet. 2:13ff.     [3] Tit. 3:1.

which it is adorned and preserved: namely, that they should earn their livelihood by honest trades, do business, enter into contracts, possess property, demand what is theirs by right, serve as soldiers, engage in lawful marriage, perform what they have sworn to do, and such like. And as all these things are by divine sanction permitted to Christians in all places, according to the condition and status of each, so when godly subjects offer prompt and due obedience to their princes and governors because of the fear of God, and zealously perform such other things as their office and the well-being of the state demand, they please God greatly and do good works for which God promises and faithfully bestows immense rewards."[1]

The high conception which the Reformers held of the dignity of the office of magistrates is well brought out in a sermon preached by Bishop Jewel on Rom. 12:16-18. "In the Scriptures," he says, "the magistrates are called shepherds, for that they ought so to guide the people committed to their charge as the shepherd doth his flock. Therefore they are called also captains, for that they ought to have such respect to God's people as the good captain hath regard to his soldiers. Therefore likewise are they called heads, for that, like as the head governeth the whole body, so should they rule and govern the people, as members of their body. Therefore in like are they called fathers, for that the people are so in subjection unto them as the child is in obedience unto his father. But chiefly it is required . . . in such as are magistrates that they themselves know God, that they themselves, I say, above all other men, have perfect knowledge of God and His laws, so that the people by that mean may follow him, and they all together may follow God."[2] "We must pray to God to give us good princes and rulers", exhorts Archbishop Sandys when preaching at York in celebration of the twentieth year of Elizabeth's accession to the throne: "under a good prince we ought to lead a good life; a good prince should procure peace, piety, and honesty to the people; a good people should live peaceably, godly, and honestly under their prince."[3]

Indeed, there should be a reciprocity of responsibility between ruler and people: "Now as magistrates and rulers should by good government procure peace, promote religion, and preserve

---

[1] Cranmer: *Works*, Vol. II, pp. 478ff. [The translation is mine. P.E.H.]
[2] Jewel: *Works*, Vol. II, pp. 1095f.     [3] Sandys: *Works*, p. 76.

honesty among men, so our apostle requireth at the people's hands
that they under government lead a peaceable, quiet, and honest
life. There is a double peace, the one outward, the other inward:
peace with men and peace with God. With God there is no peace
but in Christ. Through faith in Him we have peace with God, and
not otherwise. He hath peace with God whose sins are remitted:
for 'blessed are they whose iniquities are pardoned'.[1] But our sins
are remitted only in the blood of Christ Jesus: 'His blood doth
purge us from all sin'.[2] Christ therefore is our only peacemaker
with God." As for peace with men, that is best achieved in a well
ordered God-honouring society. But "we may not for peace' sake
flatter men in their sin; for that is to be partaker of evil. We must
have peace with all, if it may be, and so far as in us lieth, ever
preferring a good conscience and a Christian mind. For it may not
be, which may not be honestly. Follow thse things that belong
unto peace, but unto godly peace."[3] Again, in a sermon preached
before the queen: "The prince is as the head, without whose discreet and wise government the laws would cease and, the people
being not ruled by order of laws, ruin and confusion would soon
follow: each contending and striving against other, the end would
be the utter subversion of all. The ministers of the Word are as the
eyes to watch, and not to wink or sleep, and as the mouth to speak,
and not be dumb: for then they perform not their allotted function.
They are placed as watchmen over the Church, for the good and
godly direction therof; to take heed both to themselves and to all
the flock whereof the Holy Ghost hath made them overseers; to
feed the Church of God, which He hath purchased with His own
blood; to warn the people of the enemy ever at hand, always ready
to assault; to teach and instruct the people of God in the way of
their salvation, to tell them of their sins, to cry unto them, and not
to cease.[4] The judges are as ears, who should sit in open places to
hear the causes and complaints of the people, opening the one ear
to the plaintiff, and reserving the other to the defendant's answer.
The nobility are as the shoulders and arms to bear the burden of
the commonwealth, to hold up the head, and defend the body with
might and force, with wise counsel and good advice. Men of lower
degrees are set as inferior parts in the body, painfully to travail for
the necessary sustentation both of themselves and others. All these

[1] Ps. 32:1, Rom. 4:7.  [2] I Jn. 1:7.
[3] Sandys: *Works*, pp. 85f.  [4] Cf. Acts 20:28ff.

members are so necessary that none can want without the ruin of the whole. For every one hath need of other, and by the help of the other is maintained."[1]

## CO-OPERATION BETWEEN CHURCH AND STATE

The commonwealth envisaged by the Reformers, then, was one in which there was the closest co-operation and interrelationship between Church and state. The function of rulers is to govern the citizenry and to wield the civil sword, but they should do so with a view to promoting true religion and the cause of the Gospel. "The greatest blessing which God giveth to any people," says Jewel, "is a godly prince to rule over them. The greatest misery that can fall upon any people is to have a godly prince taken from them. For by a godly prince He doth so rule the people as if God Himself were with them in visible appearance. The prince walketh in the ways of the Lord; the nobles follow the steps of the prince; and the people fashion themselves to the example of the nobles. The face of a godly prince shineth as the sunbeams and bringeth joy and comfort to his subjects."[2] And Hooper starts a sermon preached before king and council during Lent 1550 with these words: "Among all other most noble and most famous deeds of kings and princes none is more godly, commendable, nor profitable to the commonwealth than to promote and set forth unto their subjects the pure and sincere religion of the eternal God, King of all kings and Lord of all Lords."[3]

When writing of the duty of kings in his *Obedience of a Christian Man* Tyndale admonishes: "Let kings, if they had rather be Christian in deed than so to be called, give themselves altogether to the wealth of their realms after the example of Christ, remembering that the people are God's, and not theirs; yea, are Christ's inheritance and possession, bought with His blood. The most despised person in his realm is the king's brother, and fellow-member with him, and equal with him in the kingdom of God and of Christ. Let him therefore not think himself too good to do them service, neither seek any other thing in them than a father seeketh in his children, yea, than Christ sought in us."[4] Jewel illustrates the theme by reference to figures of history: "As David, Hezekiah, and Justinian did, so should every good and godly officer do: he

[1] Sandys: *Works*, pp. 99f.　　　　[2] Jewel: *Works*, Vol. IV, p. 1153.
[3] Hooper: *Works*, Vol. I, p. 435.　　[4] Tyndale: *Works*, Vol. I, p. 202.

must not give himself unto sleep, nor his eyelids unto rest, before he hath provided a temple for the God of Jacob; he must not go home unto his own house before he hath purged God's Church; he must have as great respect to the salvation of God's flock as he hath regard to the safeguard of his own soul; he must remember that his chair is God's chair, that his sword is God's sword."[1]

There were indeed certain personages in whom the offices of prophet and prince were combined, and this was seen as a proof of the deep harmony that ideally should exist in any commonwealth between the ecclesiastical and the civil powers. "Samuel was both a prophet and a prince, a minister and a magistrate: so was Melchizedek, Moses, David, Christ," says Sandys in a sermon preached before parliament at Westminster. ". . . The matching of these two offices doth teach what agreement, love, and liking should be between these two officers. They are God's two hands to build up withal the decayed walls of Jerusalem. If the one hand set forward and the other put backward, God's work will be ill wrought. The wisdom of God matched Moses and Aaron, two brethren, the one the minister, the other the magistrate, that, knit together in brotherly love, they might labour together with both hands for the furtherance of God's building. When the Word and the sword do join, then is the people well ruled, and then is God well served." Sandys urges that "the first point of kingly service unto God is to purge and cleanse His Church", and then that "the next point of princely service done to God is to nurse the Church with wholesome food till we all grow up to a perfect man in Christ Jesus. That this food may be ministered," he continues, "that this Word may be preached everywhere to God's people, good princes and such as are in authority must take special care. For this is truly to serve and fear God. It is not enough that princes and magistrates embrace the Gospel, that they feed upon the food of salvation themselves; but they, as heads and pastors, must see this bread broken and delivered to the people."[2]

In particular, the youthful Josiah was regarded as the ideal prototype of the reforming monarch, and the boy-king Edward was joyfully acclaimed by the Reformers as the Josiah of their day. On the occasion of his coronation, which took place on 20 February 1547, Archbishop Cranmer addressed him in the following terms: "The solemn rites of coronation have their ends and

---

[1] Jewel: *Works*, Vol. II, p. 1096.    [2] Sandys: *Works*, pp. 36f., 42, 44.

utility, yet neither direct force nor necessity: they be good admonitions to put kings in mind of their duty to God, but no increasement of their dignity. For they be God's anointed, not in respect of the oil which the bishop useth, but in consideration of their power which is ordained, of the sword which is authorized, of their persons which are elected by God, and endued with the gifts of His Spirit for the better ruling and guiding of His people . . . Your majesty is God's vice-gerent and Christ's vicar within your own dominions, and to see, with your predecessor Josiah, God truly worshipped and idolatry destroyed, the tyranny of the bishops of Rome banished from your subjects and images removed. These acts be signs of a second Josiah, who reformed the Church of God in his days. You are to reward virtue, to revenge sin, to justify the innocent, to relieve the poor, to procure peace, to repress violence, and to execute justice throughout your realms. For precedents, on those kings who performed not these things the old law shows how the Lord revenged His quarrel; and on those kings who fulfilled these things, He poured forth His blessings in abundance. For example, it is written of Josiah in the book of the Kings thus: 'Like unto him there was no king before him that turned to the Lord with all his heart, according to all the law of Moses, neither after him arose there any like him.'[1] This was to that prince a perpetual fame of dignity, to remain to the end of days."[2]

The seemingly exaggerated terms in which the Reformers were accustomed to speak of the monarch and his office must be understood against the background both of their doctrine of the monarchy and of the history of their times. Their doctrine was essentially simple: that Scripture regards the prince or magistrate who wields the secular sword as a minister of God, and enjoins that all persons, clerical as well as lay, should submit to his authority, though always with the provision that nothing be commanded which is plainly repugnant to the law and Word of God. Historically, their attitude was a repudiation of the claim of the pope, a foreigner, to exercise jurisdiction over the realm of England. In describing the circumstances of his appointment as Archbishop of Canterbury, which took place in 1532, Cranmer explains how he told the king, Henry VIII, that he neither would nor could accept the office at the pope's hand, seeing that the king "was only the supreme governor of this church of England, as well in causes ecclesiastical

<hr>

[1] II Kings 23:25.      [2] Cranmer: *Works*, Vol. II, pp. 126f.

as temporal, and that the full right and donation of all manner of bishoprics and benefices, as well as of any other temporal dignities and promotions, appertained to his grace, and not to any other foreign authority, whatsoever it was: and therefore if he (Cranmer) might serve God in that vocation, him, and his country, seeing it was his pleasure so to have it, he would accept it and receive it of his majesty, and of none other stranger who had no authority within this realm, neither in any such gift nor in any other thing."[1]

So, too, after Mary's accession to the throne and the outlawing of the Reformation, Cranmer, a prisoner on trial for his life, declared before the tribunal which had been set up to try him: "It is not the loss of my promotions that grieveth me. The greatest grief I have at this time is, and one of the greatest that ever I had in all my life, to see the king and queen's majesties, by their proctors, here to become my accusers, and that in their own realm and country, before a foreign power. If I have transgressed the laws of the land, their majesties have sufficient authority and power, both from God and by the ordinance of this realm, to punish me; whereunto I both have and at all times shall be content to submit myself. Alas! what hath the pope to do in England? whose jurisdiction is so far different from the jurisdiction of this realm that it is impossible to be true to the one and true to the other. The laws also are so diverse that whosoever sweareth to both must needs incur perjury to the one. Which as oft as I remember, even for the love that I bear to her grace, I cannot but be heartily sorry to think upon it, how that her highness, the day of her coronation, at which time she took a solemn oath to observe all the laws and liberties of this realm of England, at the same time also took an oath to the bishop of Rome and promised to maintain that see. The state of England being so repugnant to the supremacy of the pope, it was impossible but she must be forsworn in the one. Wherein if her grace had been faithfully advertized by her council, then surely she would never have done it."[2]

## THE ROYAL SUPREMACY

It was against this background of doctrine and history, then, that the Reformers formulated their designation of the monarch as "Head of the Church"; but it was a designation to which exception was taken by the papists, who taught the supremacy of the pope as

[1] Cranmer: *Works*, Vol. II, p. 223.    [2] Cranmer: *Ibid.*, p. 221.

Peter's successor, and, later in the century, by the puritans, who misconstrued the expression as an invasion of the sovereign rights of Christ as alone the supreme Head of the Church. There was, it should go without saying, no suggestion of any kind of usurpation of the divine prerogatives by a human creature. Such an idea would have been unthinkable to the Reformers with their strong doctrine of the absolute sovereignty of Almighty God. The sovereignty of kings was no more than temporal, within the framework of a particular community of men, and it was always a subsidiary authority, subject and answerable to the supreme authority of God and His Word. This is clearly shown in the epistle prefixed by Hooper to his *Godly Confession and Protestation of the Christian Faith*, dated 20 December 1550, which is addressed "to the most virtuous and mighty Prince Edward the Sixth, our most redoubted Sovereign Lord, King of England, France, and Ireland, defender of the faith, and in earth, next and immediately under God, the supreme head of the churches of England and Ireland . . ."[1]

At his second examination before the Lord Chancellor (Stephen Gardiner, Bishop of Winchester), on 29 January 1555, Bradford had the following exchange with his accuser: " 'Is it not against God's Word', quoth my Lord Chancellor, 'that a man should take a king to be supreme head of the Church in his realm?' 'No', quoth Bradford, '. . . it is not against God's Word, but with it, being taken in such sense as it may be well taken; that is, attributing to the king's power the sovereignty in all his dominions'. 'I pray you', quoth the Lord Chancellor, 'where find you that?' 'I find it in many places', quoth Bradford, 'but specially in the thirteenth to the Romans, where St. Paul writeth, every soul to be obedient to the superior power: but what power? *Quae gladium gestat*, the power verily which beareth the sword; which is not the spiritual, but the temporal power: as Chrysostom full well noteth', quoth Bradford, 'upon the same place, which your honour knoweth better than I. He (Chrysostom I mean) there plainly showeth that bishops, prophets, and apostles owe obedience to the temporal magistrates'."

Cranmer's trial at Oxford took place in September of the same year. Like Bradford and others who had been condemned before him, he denied the papal supremacy: "I will never consent to the bishop of Rome; for then should I give myself to the devil: for I

[1] Hooper: *Works*, Vol. II, p. 65.

have made an oath to the king, and I must obey the king by God's
laws. By the Scripture the king is chief, and no foreign person in
his own realm above him. There is no subject but to a king. I am a
subject, I owe my fidelity to the crown. The pope is contrary to the
crown. I cannot obey both." Shortly after this, the following
exchange took place between him and his interrogator, Dr. Martin,
one of Queen Mary's commissioners:

"*Martin*: Now, sir, . . . you denied that the pope's holiness was
supreme head of the Church of Christ.
"*Cranmer*: I did so.
"*Martin*: Who say you then is supreme head?
"*Cranmer*: Christ.
"*Martin*: But whom hath Christ left here in earth His vicar and
head of His Church?
"*Cranmer*: Nobody.
"*Martin*: Ah! why told you not King Henry this when you made
him supreme head? and now nobody is. This is treason against
his own person, as you then made him.
"*Cranmer*: I mean not but every king in his own realm and domin-
ion is supreme head, and so was he supreme head of the church
of Christ in England."

Following further interrogation and a careful explanation of his
position by Cranmer, the matter was broached again: "After this,
Doctor Martin demanded of him who was supreme head of the
church of England. 'Marry', quoth my Lord of Canterbury,
'Christ is the head of this member, as He is of the whole body of the
universal Church'. 'Why', quoth Doctor Martin, 'you made King
Henry the Eighth supreme head of the church'. 'Yea', said the
archbishop, 'of all the people of England, as well ecclesiastical as
temporal'. 'And not of the Church?' said Martin. 'No', said he,
'for Christ is only head of His Church, and of the faith and religion
of the same. The king is head and governor of his people, who are
the visible church'. 'What!' quoth Martin, 'you never durst tell the
king so'. 'Yes, that I durst', quoth he, 'and did, in the publication
of his style, wherein he was named supreme head of the church;
there was never other thing meant'."[1]

Under Elizabeth the same doctrine was consistently taught.
Thus, in his *Apology of the Church of England*, Jewel declares:

[1] Cranmer: *Works*, Vol. II, pp. 213, 219, 224.

"We believe that there is one Church of God, . . . and that this
Church is the kingdom, the body, and the spouse of Christ, and
that Christ alone is the prince of this kingdom; that Christ alone is
the head of this body, and that Christ alone is the bridegroom of
this spouse . . . We say that there neither is nor can be any one
man who may have the sole superiority of this universal state; for
that Christ is ever present to assist His Church, and needeth not any
man to supply His room as His only heir to all His substance."[1]
In 1569, when the pope sent a bull to England announcing the
"damnation and excommunication" of Elizabeth and her ad-
herents, Jewel delivered a spirited rejoinder, subsequently published under the title *A View of a Seditious Bull sent into England
from Pius Quintus, Bishop of Rome*. The pope's interference is
denounced as "a matter of great blasphemy against God, . . . for it
deposeth the queen's majesty (whom God long preserve!) from
her royal seat and teareth the crown from her head: it dischargeth
all us her natural subjects from all due obedience." Of Christ,
Jewel affirms categorically that "God hath appointed Him over
all things to be the head of the Church".

To the charge that Elizabeth had usurped the place of the
supreme head Jewel retorts: "This is untrue . . . Where is she ever
called the supreme head? Peruse the acts of parliament, the records,
the rolls, and the writs of chancery or exchequer which pass in her
grace's name: where is she ever called the supreme head of the
Church? No, no, brethren, she refuseth it, she would not have it,
nor be so called. Why then doth Christ's vicar blaze and spread
abroad so gross untruth? Why should he say Queen Elizabeth
maketh herself the head of the Church? Nay, yet more: *Monstrose
praecipuam ejus auctoritatem atque jurisdictionem usurpans*: 'Taking
upon her monstrously the chief authority and jurisdiction of the
same'. Here I might well say: *O monstrum hominis!* 'O monster in
the likeness of man!' He imagineth that her majesty preacheth in
the pulpits, that she administereth the sacraments, that she sitteth
in the consistories and heareth all spiritual causes. Which if she do,
she doth more than the pope doth. It were monstrous to see the
pope in a pulpit! And it is monstrous to see antichrist sit in the
temple of God, to see a bishop girded with both swords, to see a
priest take upon him the rule of heaven and earth, the 'servant of
servants' advanced above all the princes of the world, and to set

[1] Jewel: *Works*, Vol. III, p. 59.

his foot upon their necks, a wretched man to claim authority over the angels of God, and a sinful creature to suffer himself to be called by the name of God. This is a misshapen wonder and a monster in nature. Let the pope therefore look upon himself and know what supreme authority, and over whom, he taketh it upon him monstrously. Queen Elizabeth doth not anything 'monstrously'. She preacheth not, she ministereth not the sacraments, she doth neither excommunicate nor absolve from excommunication, she sitteth not to give sentence in spiritual causes, she challengeth not the dispensation of the keys of the kingdom of heaven. She doth nothing but which she may lawfully do, nothing but whereunto the Lord God hath given her especial warrant. Her majesty is supreme governor over her subjects. The bishops within her realm are subjects to her. She governeth: they yield obedience. When occasion is offered to dispose of anything specially appertaining to the service of God, or to judge of any controversy arising in spiritual causes, she commendeth and giveth to her learned divines the due consideration thereof . . . To be short, Queen Elizabeth doth as did Moses, Joshua, David, Solomon, Josiah, Jehoshaphat, as Constantine, Valentinian, Gratian, Theodosius, Arcadius, Honorius, and other godly emperors have done."[1]

Later in the century, William Fulke, when reminded by his adversary Gregory Martin that Calvin had disapproved the assignation of the title "supreme head of the Church" to any monarch, responded: "For the name of 'supreme head', in that sense which Calvin and other abroad did mislike it, it was never allowed nor by authority granted to the kings, Henry and Edward but in the same sense it is now granted to Queen Elizabeth, whom we acknowledge to have the same authority in causes ecclesiastical which her father and brother, kings before her, had and exercised to God's glory. But as Stephen Gardiner understood that title in conference with Bucer at Ratisbon we do utterly abhor it, and so did all godly men always, that a king should have absolute power to do in religion what he will."[2] Again, in reply to the objection of Nicholas Sanders that "the Scripture never calleth any king head of the Church", Fulke says: "Neither do we call any king head of the Church, but only Christ; but in every particular church the Scripture alloweth the king to be the chief magistrate, not only in

[1] Jewel: *Works*, Vol. IV, pp. 1133, 1139, 1144f.
[2] Fulke: *Works*, Vol. I, pp. 488f.

governing the commonwealth, but also in making godly laws for the furtherance of religion, having all sorts of men, as well ecclesiastical as civil, subject unto him, to be governed by him, and punished also, not only for civil offences, but also for heresy and neglect of their duties in matters pertaining to the religion of God." And he explained further that "the king's supremacy is perfectly distinct from any power the apostles had: for, although he have authority over ecclesiastical persons and in causes ecclesiastical, according to God's Word, yet is he no ecclesiastical officer but a civil magistrate, having chief authority in all causes, not absolute to do what he will, but only what God commandeth him, namely, to provide by laws that God may be truly worshipped and all offences against His religion may be punished."[1]

With reference to the "puritan" or "presbyterian" complaints, Archbishop Whitgift explained the Anglican position in the following way: "Christ is 'the only Head of the Church', if by the head you understand that which giveth the body life, sense, and motion; for Christ only by His Spirit doth give life and nutriment to His body; He only doth pour spiritual blessings into it and doth inwardly direct and govern it. Likewise He only is the head of the whole Church; for that title cannot agree to any other. But, if by the head you understand an external ruler and governor of any particular nation or church (in which signification head is usually taken), then I do not perceive why the magistrate may not as well be called the head of the church, that is, the chief governor of it in the external policy, as he is called the head of the people and of the commonwealth. And, as it is no absurdity to say that the civil magistrate is head of the commonwealth, next and immediately under God (for it is most true), so is it none to say that, under God also, he is head of the church, that is, chief governor, as I have before said." As for the pope's supremacy, it is usurped, affirms Whitgift, "both because it taketh from magistrates that which is due unto them, and also usurpeth the authority of Christ in remitting and retaining sins, in making laws contrary to God's laws which he saith be necessary to salvation, and in challenging authority over the whole Church of Christ and an hundred such like presumptions."[2]

The matter is summed up in the words of Article XXXVII, which declares: "The King's Majesty hath the chief power in this

[1] Fulke: *Works*, Vol. II, pp. 261f.    [2] Whitgift: *Works*, Vol. II, p. 85.

realm of England and other his dominions, unto whom the chief government of all estates of this realm, whether they be ecclesiastical or civil, in all causes doth appertain, and is not, nor ought to be, subject to any foreign jurisdiction. Where we attribute to the King's Majesty the chief government, by which titles we understand the minds of some slanderous folks to be offended, we give not to our princes the ministering either of God's Word or of the sacraments, the which thing the injunctions also lately set forth by Elizabeth our queen do most plainly testify; but that only prerogative which we see to have been given always to all godly princes in Holy Scriptures by God Himself; that is, that they should rule all estates and degrees committed to their charge by God, whether they be ecclesiastical or temporal, and restrain with the civil sword the stubborn and evil-doers."

UNITY AND SCHISM

The unity of the Church was inevitably a question to which the Reformers had to give attention, especially in view of the fact that they had separated themselves from the Church of Rome, in which they had been brought up. Were they in fact, as their critics charged them with being, guilty of the sin of schism? Or had the point been reached at which separation was not only permissible but imperative? The great criterion in their judgment was that of truth: under no circumstances might unity be pursued or purchased at the expense of truth, since unity, if it is unity in error or in unconcern for the truth, is not Christian unity. The principle is pointedly stated by Latimer in a sermon preached in 1552: "St. Paul to the Corinthians saith, *Sitis unanimes*, 'Be of one mind'; but he addeth, *secundum Jesum Christum*, 'according to Jesus Christ': that is, according to God's holy Word; else it were better war than peace. We ought never to regard unity so much that we would, or should, forsake God's Word for her sake . . . Therefore let us set by unity; let us be given to love and charity; but so that it may stand with godliness. For peace ought not to be redeemed *jactura veritatis*, with the loss of the truth, that we should seek peace so much that we should lose the truth of God's Word."[1] It was precisely this principle which caused Latimer and his fellow Reformers to choose to suffer death rather than be united and at peace with the errors of the papal religion.

[1] Latimer: *Works*, Vol. I, p. 487.

What was deplorable, then, was not that there was a break in unity in the sixteenth century—for the Reformation was radically a reaffirmation of unity in truth—but that by setting its face against the reform of its unscriptural teachings and practices the Church of Rome made such a break inevitable. It was not that the Reformers esteemed unity lightly; far from it. "Of a truth unity and concord doth best become religion," admits Jewel; "yet is not unity the sure and certain mark whereby to know the Church of God. For there was the greatest consent that might be amongst them that worshipped the golden calf and among them who with one voice jointly cried against our Saviour Jesu Christ, 'Crucify Him!' " As both the New Testament and the history of the early centuries show, it is a mark of the true Church to stand apart from and to refuse to have fellowship with those who persist in false teaching which is destructive of the Gospel. The accusation against the Reformers that they "have gone away from the unity of the catholic Church" is, says |Jewel, "not only a matter of malice", but is all the worse because, "though it be most untrue, yet hath it some show and appearance of truth". "We have indeed put ourselves apart," he explains, "not as heretics are wont, from the Church of Christ, but, as all good men ought to do, from the infection of naughty persons and hypocrites." Indeed, Jewel (together with the other Reformers) was insistent that their teaching and churchmanship restored the pattern laid down by Christ Himself and His apostles and followed in the early centuries. He protests that "when they (sc. our adversaries) leave nothing unspoken that may never so falsely and maliciously be spoken against us, yet this one thing they are never able truly to say, that we have swerved either from the Word of God, or from the apostles of Christ, or from the primitive Church. Surely we have ever judged the primitive Church of Christ's time, of the apostles, and of the holy fathers to be the catholic Church.

The Reformers, in fact, faced with the refusal of the papal church to be reformed, had to make a choice: either to consort with, and thereby appear to consent to, the unscriptural company in which they had grown up; or, the more difficult and costly course, to separate themselves for the sake of the truth. They were at the dividing of the ways. As Jewel points out: "It is doubtless an odious matter for one to leave the fellowship whereunto he hath been accustomed . . . Neither had we departed therefrom but of very necessity and much against our wills."[1]

If an onus of proof rested on the Reformers—an onus which they certainly did not shirk!—to demonstrate that their doctrines and practices were compatible with those of original Christianity, the onus rested no less firmly on the papists, not merely to disprove this, but also to show that, on the contrary, the religion they professed was fontal. "These men's part," argues Jewel again, "had been, first to have clearly and truly proved that the Romish church is the true and right-instructed Church of God, and that the same, as they do order it at this day, doth agree with the primitive Church of Christ, of the apostles, and of the holy fathers, which we doubt not but was indeed the true catholic Church. For our parts," he continues, "if we could have judged ignorance, error, superstition, idolatry, men's inventions, and the same commonly disagreeing with the Holy Scriptures, either pleased God, or to be sufficient for the obtaining everlasting salvation; or if we could ascertain (= convince) ourselves that the Word of God was written but for a time only, and afterward again ought to be abrogated and put away; or else that the saying and commandments of God ought to be subject to man's will, that whatsoever God saith and commandeth, except the bishop of Rome willeth and commandeth the same, it must be taken as void and unspoken: if we could have brought ourselves to believe these things, we grant there had been no cause at all why we should have left these men's company." As for the action the Reformers had taken, "to depart from that church whose errors were proved and made manifest to the world, which church also had already evidently departed from God's Word; and yet not to depart so much from itself as from the errors thereof; and not to do this dishonestly or wickedly, but quietly and soberly—we have done nothing herein against the doctrine either of Christ or of His apostles".[2]

It is important, then, not to consider *that* the Reformers separated themselves, but to consider *what* they separated themselves from. Jewel's cogent polemic reaches its greatest force when he insists that he and his colleagues had forsaken the church as it was then, in their day, not the Church as it was originally, in the earliest days. "It is true we have departed from them (sc. the papists),"

[1] Jewel: *Works*, Vol. III, pp. 69, 76f.      [2] Jewel: *Ibid.*, pp 78f.

9

he says, "and for so doing we both give thanks to almighty God and greatly rejoice on our own behalf. But yet for all this, from the primitive Church, from the apostles, and from Christ we have not departed. True it is, we were brought up with these men in darkness and in the lack of knowledge of God . . . Wherefore, though our departing were a trouble to them, yet ought they to consider withal how just cause we had of our departure . . . If we be schismatics because we have left them, by what name shall they be called themselves, who have forsaken the Greeks, from whom they first received their faith, forsaken the primitive Church, forsaken Christ Himself, and the apostles, even as children should forsake their parents? . . . We truly have renounced that church wherein we could neither have the Word of God sincerely taught, nor the sacraments rightly administered, nor the name of God duly called upon . . . Let them compare our churches and theirs together, and they shall see that themselves have most shamefully gone from the apostles, and we most justly have gone from them."[1]

Similarly, Archbishop Sandys emphasizes that the only true unity is unity in the truth. "We must consider which is true unity," he says in a sermon on Phil. 2:2f. "For every agreement is not that concord whereunto we are in this place exhorted. Lucifer with other angels consented together; Eve and Adam and the serpent were all of one mind; so were the builders of the tower of Babel; so were they of Sodom, *a puero usque ad senem*, 'from the child to the man of grey hairs'; so were Dathan and Abiram, with their accomplices; so were the worshippers of the golden calf; so were the sacrificers in Dan and Bethel; so were Pilate and Herod; so were the Jews that cried with one voice, 'Let him be crucified!'; and so are they who have joined themselves in holy league with no other intent than those wicked confederates had of whom the prophet saith, 'They assembled themselves together against the Lord and against His Christ'. But it is unity of the Spirit, unity in the truth, unity in Christ and in His Gospel, whereunto our apostle here exhorteth us . . . Unity must be in verity: 'Thy Word is verity'; in this we must agree . . . For unity in religion not grounded upon Christ and His Gospel is not concord but conspiracy. And here we have always to praise our God that in public doctrine touching the substance of religion we all agree in one truth; we all build upon one foundation, Christ Jesus slain and

[1] Jewel: *Works*, Vol. III, pp. 91f.

offered up for our full redemption according to the doctrine of the Scriptures."[1] Again, when preaching on II Cor. 13:11, Sandys says: "The bond of unity is verity; neither can they be truly one who are not one in truth. And therefore, although an angel should come from heaven with all show of learning and all appearance of unspotted and undefiled purity, teaching things contrary to that one truth which you have received, reach him no hand, salute him not in token of consent: unity with him is enmity with God. But if all be builded upon the settled foundation of God's truth, if all be members of one body, servants to one master, soldiers fighting under one banner, children of one and the same father, then is the name of unity and peace amiable."[2]

REFORMED ECUMENICITY

While in England the Reformation led to doctrinal harmony, that is, to a notable realization of unity in the truth, on the Continent a prolonged dispute arose over sacramental doctrine between certain Germans on the one hand and the French and Swiss evangelicals on the other. This was a development which alarmed Archbishop Cranmer for one, and the concern of the Reformers for the establishment of scriptural unity and unanimity on this and all other important matters is strikingly manifested in the correspondence that passed between Thomas Cranmer and the leading Continental Reformers. Indeed, as early as 1537 we find Cranmer writing to the Swiss scholar Joachim Vadian concerning the eucharistic controversy: "It cannot be told how greatly this so bloody controversy has impeded the full course of the Gospel both throughout the whole Christian world and especially among ourselves," he admonishes. "It brings very great danger to yourselves and occasions to all others a stumbling-block greater than I can express. Wherefore, if you will listen to me, I exhort and advise you, yea, I beg, beseech, and implore and adjure you in the bowels of Jesus Christ to agree and unite in a Christian concord, to exert your whole strength in establishing it, and at length to afford to the churches the peace of God which passeth all understanding, so that we may, with united strength, extend as widely as possible one sound, pure, evangelical doctrine, conformable to the discipline of the primitive Church. We should easily convert even the Turks

[1] Sandys: *Works*, pp. 94f.     [2] Sandys: *Ibid.*, p. 429.

to the obedience of our Gospel, if only we could agree among ourselves and unite together in some holy confederacy."[1]

This ecumenical project of a representative conference or synod of Reformed leaders from different countries, who together would forge a consensus of doctrine and thus lead the way to united action and advance, continued over the years to play a large part in the strategic thinking and planning of Archbishop Cranmer. He foresaw the great source of strength to the Reformed cause that close collaboration and interchange of thought would bring. To this end, as well as for the strengthening of the situation in his own land, he sent invitations to a number of Continental scholars to visit England and work with him and his colleagues. Among those who responded and made the journey were Martin Bucer and Peter Martyr, both of whom were to make important contributions to the movement of reform in England.

Thus on 4 July 1548 Cranmer writes as follows to the Polish scholar John à Lasco: "We are desirous of setting forth in our churches the true doctrine of God, and have no wish to adapt it to all tastes or to deal in ambiguities, but, laying aside all carnal considerations, to transmit to posterity a true and explicit form of doctrine agreeable to the rule of the sacred writings, so that there may not only be set forth among all nations an illustrious testimony respecting our doctrine, delivered by the grave authority of learned and godly men, but that all posterity may have a pattern to imitate. For the purpose of carrying this important design into execution we have thought it necessary to have the assistance of learned men who, having compared their opinions together with us, may do away with all doctrinal controversies and build up an entire system of true doctrine. We have therefore invited both yourself and some other learned men; and as they have come over to us without any reluctance, so that we scarcely have to regret the absence of any of them, with the exception of yourself and Melanchthon, we earnestly request you both to come yourself and, if possible, to bring Melanchthon along with you."[2] A Lasco did in fact come to England and served as pastor of the "foreigners' church" in London between the years 1550 and 1553. But Cranmer's hope of bringing Melanchthon across the Channel was never realized.

To Martin Bucer in Strasbourg Cranmer writes on 20 October 1548, at a time when fierce persecution was raging in France: "To

[1] *Original Letters*, p. 14.    [2] *Original Letters*, p. 17.

you, my Bucer, our kingdom will be a most safe harbour, in which, by the blessing of God, the seeds of true doctrine have happily begun to be sown. Come over therefore to us, and become a labourer with us in the harvest of the Lord. You will not be of less benefit to the universal Church of God while you are with us than if you retain your former position. In addition to this you will be better able to heal the wounds of your distressed country in your absence than you are now able to do in person."[1]

A few months later, on 10 February 1549, Cranmer despatches a letter to the German theologian Philip Melanchthon, in which he says: "I pray God to direct us and to gather unto Himself a perpetual church among us, not only out of our countrymen, but also from among those of foreign nations, as according to His infinite mercy He has already begun to do. For many pious and learned men have come over to us, some from Italy, some from Germany, and we are daily expecting more. If you will consent to increase and adorn this society of the Church with your presence, I know not by what means you will be able more efficiently to set forth the glory of God. I am aware that you have often desired that wise and godly men should take counsel together and, having compared their opinions, send forth under the sanction of their authority some work that should embrace the chief subjects of ecclesiastical doctrine and transmit the truth uncorrupted to posterity. This object we are anxiously endeavouring to accomplish to the utmost of our power."[2]

On 20 March 1552 Cranmer reassures the Swiss Reformer Henry Bullinger that there is no intention of sending delegates from the Church of England to the Council of Trent and explains his better plan for the convening of a congress of Reformed theologians. "You write to me upon two subjects," he says, "one of a public, the other of a private nature. With respect to that which is public, namely, that I should advise the king's majesty not to send any delegate to the Council of Trent, there was no need of any advice of mine to dissuade him from a measure which never came into his mind. But I considered it better, forasmuch as our adversaries are now holding their councils at Trent to confirm their errors, to recommend his majesty to grant his assistance that in England, or elsewhere, there might be convoked a synod of the most learned and excellent persons, in which provision might be made for the

---

[1] *Original Letters*, p. 20.  [2] *Original Letters*, pp. 21f.

purity of ecclesiastical doctrine, and especially for an agreement upon the sacramental controversy. To this plan (as considering it most useful to the Christian commonwealth) I perceived that the mind of his majesty was very favourably disposed. We must not therefore suffer ourselves to be wanting to the Church of God in a matter of such importance. I have written upon the subject to masters Philip (Melanchthon) and Calvin, and I pray you to devise the means by which this synod may be assembled with the greatest convenience, either in England or elsewhere."[1]

The same day Cranmer writes to John Calvin in Geneva in similar vein: "As nothing tends more injuriously to the separation of the churches than heresies and disputes respecting the doctrines of religion, so nothing tends more effectually to unite the churches of God, and more powerfully to defend the fold of Christ, than the pure teaching of the Gospel and harmony of doctrine. For this reason I have often wished, and still continue to do so, that learned and godly men who are eminent for erudition and judgment might meet together in some place of safety, where, by taking counsel together and comparing their respective opinions, they might handle all the heads of ecclesiastical doctrine and hand down to posterity, under the weight of their authority, some work not only upon the subjects themselves but also upon the forms of expressing them. Our adversaries are now holding their councils at Trent for the establishment of their errors; and shall we neglect to call together a godly synod for the refutation of error and for restoring and pro-pagating the truth? They are, as I am informed, making decrees respecting the worship of the host (artolatry): therefore we ought to leave no stone unturned, not only that we may guard others against this idolatry, but also that we may ourselves come to an agreement upon the doctrine of this sacrament. It cannot escape your prudence how exceedingly the Church of God has been injured by dissentions and varieties of opinion respecting this sacrament of unity; and though they are now in some measure removed, yet I could wish for an agreement in this doctrine, not only as regards the subject itself, but also with respect to the words and forms of expression."[2]

Calvin replied during the following month expressing his un-qualified approval of such a project. "You truly and wisely judge," he says to Cranmer, "that in the present disturbed state

[1] *Original Letters*, p. 23.          [2] *Original Letters*, pp. 24f.

of the Church no more suitable remedy can be adopted than the assembling together of godly and discreet men, well disciplined in the school of Christ, who shall openly profess their agreement in the doctrines of religion . . . I know . . . that your care is not confined to England alone, but that you are at the same time regardful of the world at large. Then not only is the generous disposition of your most serene king to be admired, but also his rare piety in honouring with his favour the godly design of holding an assembly of this kind, and in offering a place of meeting within his realm. And I wish it could be effected that grave and learned men from the principal churches might meet together at a place appointed and, after diligent consideration of each article of the faith, hand down to posterity a definite form of doctrine according to their united opinion . . . As far as I am concerned, if I can be of any service, I shall not shrink from crossing ten seas, if need be, for that object. If rendering a helping hand to the kingdom of England were the only point at issue, that of itself would be a sufficient motive to me. But now, when the object sought after is an agreement of learned men, gravely considered and well framed according to the standard of Scripture, by which churches that would otherwise be far separated from each other may be made to unite, I do not consider it right for me to shrink from any labours or difficulties."[1]

Finally, we may quote from Cranmer's letter to Melanchthon of 27 March 1552 on the same project: "We read in the Acts of the Apostles that when a dispute had arisen . . . the apostles and elders came together to consider of this matter, and, having compared their opinions, delivered the judgment of their council in a written epistle. This example I wish we ourselves could imitate, in whose churches the doctrine of the Gospel has been restored and purified. But although all controversies cannot be removed in this world (because the party which is hostile to the truth will not assent to the judgment of the Church), it is nevertheless to be desired that the members of the true Church should agree among themselves upon the chief heads of ecclesiastical doctrine. But it cannot escape your notice how greatly religious dissentions, especially in the matter of the Lord's supper, have rent the churches asunder . . . And it is truly grievous that the sacrament of unity is made by the malice of the devil food for disagreement and (as it were) the apple

[1] *Original Letters*, pp. 711ff.

of contention. I could wish, therefore, that those who excel others in erudition and judgment should be assembled together, after the example of the apostles, and declare their judgment as well respecting other subjects of dispute as likewise respecting this controversy, and attest their agreement by some published document. But you will perhaps say, 'And I also have often expressed the same wish; but this matter cannot be effected without the aid of princes'. I have therefore consulted with the king's majesty, who places his kingdom of England at your disposal, and most graciously promises not only a place of security and quiet but also his aid and assistance towards these godly endeavours. I have written likewise to masters Calvin and Bullinger and exhorted them not to be wanting in a work so necessary and so useful to the commonwealth of Christendom."[1]

This grand project never came to fulfilment, however; for Edward VI died, Mary ascended the throne, and Cranmer and the other leaders of the English Reformation were imprisoned and put to death. Yet Cranmer, with his ecumenical vision, achieved much for the cause of church unity, both by his success in bringing outstanding foreign theologians to England for periods of varying duration and also by the pains he took to maintain contact through the exchange of letters with the leading Reformers of the Continental countries. Today, in our ecumenically minded age, this correspondence (not to speak of the voluminous correspondence which passed between English and Continental churchmen, and the open and cordial relations that prevailed between them, under Elizabeth and her successors on the throne of England) may profitably remind us of the proper methods, objectives, and boundaries of ecclesiastical reunion, as well as of the importance of Christian unity in the truth.

[1] *Original Letters*, pp. 25f.

# INDEX

# INDEX

(*Note*: The names of the early fathers and the passages of Scripture cited in the preceding pages are not included here, since, compared with the copiousness with which both Scripture and the fathers are quoted in the writings of the English Reformers, the listing of the few references which it has been felt sufficient to give in this volume could well convey a misleading impression. The reader is respectfully referred to the footnotes in this connection.)